A TIME TO BETRAY

The Astonishing Double Life of a CIA Agent
inside the Revolutionary Guards of Iran

REZA KAHLILI

THRESHOLD EDITIONS

New York   London   Toronto   Sydney

Threshold Editions
A Division of Simon & Schuster, Inc.
1230 Avenue of the Americas
New York, NY 10020

First Threshold Editions hardcover edition April 2010

THRESHOLD EDITIONS and colophon are trademarks of
Simon & Schuster, Inc.

For information about special discounts for bulk purchases, please
contact Simon & Schuster Special Sales at 1-866-506-1949 or
business@simonandschuster.com.

The Simon & Schuster Speakers Bureau can bring authors to your
live event. For more information or to book an event contact the
Simon & Schuster Speakers Bureau at 1-866-248-3049 or visit our
website at www.simonspeakers.com.

Designed by Renata Di Biase

Manufactured in the United States of America

10 9 8 7 6 5 4 3 2 1

ISBN 978-1-4391-8903-0
ISBN 978-1-4391-8967-2 (ebook)

I dedicate this book to the young people of my country, to those who have lost their lives but not the battle, and to those who are still fighting with their fists raised in the air. I raise my fist with you to demand a free Iran. Our country deserves so much better.

CONTENTS

DISCLAIMER

This is a true story of my life as a CIA agent in the Revolutionary Guards of Iran; however, every effort has been made to protect my identity (Reza Kahlili is not my real name), my family, and my associates. To do so, it was necessary to change all the names (except for the officials of the Islamic Republic of Iran) and alter certain events, chronology, circumstances, and places to avoid the retaliation decreed by the Islamic rulers of Iran for all those who challenge their authority.

A TIME TO BETRAY

TRUTH OR LIES

"I WAS FOLLOWED," I said.

CIA agent Steve Clark uncrossed his legs. He leaned forward, his expression stiffening. "Followed?"

I tried not to let my voice reflect my nervousness. "Yes. I thought I might be imagining it, but I took a few diversions and the tail was still there. It took me an hour to lose him."

Agent Clark leveled his blue eyes at me. "Wally, I want you to be completely aware of the consequences if things go wrong. The United States government will deny any relationship to you. There won't be a navy fleet coming to your rescue. I'm sorry to be so blunt, but you must understand this. Do I make myself clear?"

I swallowed hard and said, "Yes. I understand." It was difficult to miss Agent Clark's message: I was disposable.

It was 1981. The revolutionary Islamic government had been in power in Iran for more than two years. In that time, it had ensnared my country and my people in its brutal grip. I had seen friends executed in cold blood, their last look carved in my memory forever. But now, I was as far away from that government as I had been since the revolution, in a safe house high above California's Malibu.

With my CIA contact.

Making plans to return to my homeland as a spy.

The world's most powerful intelligence agency had given me the code name Wally. I never thought to ask them why they chose it. It was hard to believe that I looked like a Wally in their eyes, but maybe that was why they gave the name to me. The assignment they asked me to undertake would have been dangerous for any Iranian. But I was not just any Iranian. I was a member of the dreaded Sepah-e-Pasdaran, the Ayatollah Khomeini's Revolutionary Guards.

Now that Agent Clark knew I understood that I was ultimately on my own, he moved forward. "We've arranged for you to be trained in Europe. We chose London since you mentioned your in-laws live there. This should not arouse any suspicion. In London, you'll meet the people who will be your contacts from here on out. These are good people, Wally."

He handed me a slip of paper with a phone number to call my new contact in London, a woman named Carol. "Under no circumstances should you use a private phone. Always make your calls from public phones."

I stared at the number for a long time, trying to keep my feelings in check. I was terrified at the thought of where my return to Iran would lead me. The Revolutionary Guards looked everywhere for spies. No one was above suspicion. And they were likely to be especially wary of me when I got back. I hadn't just traveled out of the country; I'd gone to the United States, a sworn enemy. They knew I'd gone to college in America and I'd given them a good reason for my being there now, but they would certainly question me when I returned. How would I hold up to their scrutiny?

If they caught me, I knew what would happen. I had seen what they did to spies and to those who opposed the government. The Guards drugged them, raped their wives and children in front of them, and gouged out their eyeballs, all in an effort to get them to talk. I thought of my wife, Somaya, and shuddered.

As they did every day, the visions came to me of what I had witnessed in the infamous Evin Prison, where the government kept political detainees. They'd paraded teenage girls in front of me as they led them to their deaths. These girls were barely out of their childhood, barely old enough to think for themselves, much less form thoughts against the state. They knew nothing about the machinations of politics. They were innocent in every sense of the word and certainly innocent of the trumped-up charges that led to their imprisonment. Yet they suffered fates too brutal for even the most vicious criminal. None of these girls would ever know the joys of romantic love. None of them would ever hold her own baby in her arms. Their few remaining moments of life had been filled with a level of abuse few can imagine.

"Wally?"

Agent Clark startled me out of my thoughts. I realized he had been watching me as I stared off into space. "Yes?"

"There is one other thing, and I don't want you to take it personally. It's just part of the procedure we have to go through." He cleared his throat. "You'll have to undergo a lie-detector test."

I didn't protest. This made sense, of course. Agent Clark might have been comfortable with me and confident about my motives, but if I were a professional spy on behalf of the Revolutionary Guards, they would have trained me to behave exactly as I had in the CIA's presence. The lie-detector test was insurance.

Agent Clark arranged for the test to take place in the Hacienda Hotel in El Segundo, just south of Los Angeles International Airport. I entered through the restaurant, as instructed, and walked to the back hall. This led to a bank of elevators. From there I headed to room 407, taking the stairway instead of the elevator to make sure no one was following me. At the room, I used the key Agent Clark had given me. He was already there.

The agent administering the test arrived shortly thereafter, carrying an oversized briefcase. He didn't offer his name, only nodding instead. I noticed that he'd tied the knot on his thin tie too tight.

Though I wasn't hiding anything from the CIA, I began to feel a hint of panic. The agent must have noticed this, because he smiled and told me to relax. Doing so was not going to be easy for me. As the agent unpacked his equipment, my heart pounded. I glanced at Agent Clark and he offered me a reassuring look. This did little to calm me.

The other agent explained the process, telling me what each of the several wires coming from the machine did. The agent would be reading my nervous system, which I had disciplined myself to control, though I wasn't doing the best job of it right now. I eyed the door. For just a moment, I considered making a break for it. I would find some peaceful place where neither the CIA nor the Revolutionary Guards could find me.

But then I remembered the executions. The hangings. The torture. My friends. And my resolve returned as never before.

The agent asked me to sit down and roll up my sleeves. He hooked the wires from the machine to my arms, wrist, fingers, and chest. Sweat formed on my forehead.

"You can relax, Wally," the agent said. "This isn't going to hurt."

Agent Clark moved into the second room of the suite, closing the door behind him. The other agent told me to look straight ahead. He sat to my right, adjusted himself a couple of times, and said he was going to ask some questions; all I needed to do was answer with a simple yes or no. He bent over, concentrating intently as a roll of paper extruded from the machine, his pen ready to make notations.

"Is your name Reza Kahlili?"

"Yes."

"Are you twenty-seven years old?"

"Yes."

"Were you born in Iran?"

"Yes."

"Are you married?"

"Yes."

"Do you work for the Revolutionary Guards?"

"Yes."

"Did they ask you to come here?"

"No."

"Did they help you with your travel plans?"

"Yes."

"Did they ask you to contact us?"

"No."

"Have you contacted the Guards since being here?"

"No."

"Have you told them about this meeting?"

"No."

I noticed that several of the questions seemed repetitive, with nuanced differences. I wondered if this was the agent's attempt to trip me up.

"Does your wife know you are here?"

"She knows I am in America but she doesn't know I am with you."

"Stay with yes or no, please. Does anyone know about your contact with the CIA?"

"No . . . well, yes . . . Well, not really . . . but FBI agents . . ."

He did not let me finish. "Only yes or no, Wally."

I was sweating heavily at this point. This made the places where the agent had attached the electrodes itchy. The agent watched me shift in my seat and then made a notation. I wondered how badly my obvious nervousness was hurting my chances.

The agent turned two pages in his notes, seeming to skip ahead. "Have you been inside Evin Prison?"

"Yes."

"Do the interrogators rape virgins before they're executed?"

"I . . . I didn't realize Agent Clark would be telling you . . ."

"Yes or no, please, Wally."

I swallowed as memories tumbled one after the other. Parvaneh's last look at me. Roya's letter. "Yes. They rape the virgins before they are executed because they believe virgins are sent straight to heaven."

"Wally, please, just yes or no. Did you witness this?"

"No."

"Did you witness tortures and executions at Evin Prison?"

In the hum of the air conditioning, I could hear Naser calling, *"Reeezzzza."*

I exhaled slowly. "Yes."

The agent turned back a couple of pages to where he had been.

"Do you work for the Revolutionary Guards as their chief computer engineer?"

"Yes."

"Did you acquire this position through Kazem Aliabadi?"

"Yes."

"Was Kazem Aliabadi a childhood friend?"

"Yes."

"Was Naser Hushmand also a childhood friend?"

"Yes."

"As far as you know, is Kazem loyal to the goals of the Revolutionary Guards?"

"Yes."

"As far as you know, is Kazem aware that you do not share his beliefs?"

"No."

"As far as you know, does Kazem consider you loyal to the goals and ideals of the Revolutionary Guards?"

"Yes."

"Have you taken an oath to remain loyal to the Revolutionary Guards, including a vow to become a martyr for the Ayatollah Khomeini?"

"Yes."

"Is Kazem aware that you took this oath?"

"Yes."

"Do you consider it immoral to break an oath to your friend?"

I felt a lump in my throat as a tide rose in my chest. My eyes brimmed with tears. I had left home a respected member of the exclusive Revolutionary Guards. I would return a *jasoos,* a spy betraying my country. I knew that if my father were alive and found out what I was doing, he would turn his back on me. I knew that my grandmother, who taught me to be a devoted Muslim and to be honest and trustworthy, would be ashamed of me.

Through the roar of blood in my ears, I heard the agent ask, "Would you like me to repeat the question?"

How could I be a spy if I could not hide my emotions and provide fast answers to provocative questions? I had joined the Guards with the purest intentions. I believed at the beginning of the revolution that the Islamic movement was fair and just, carrying the promise of a nation's salvation. Instead, I had witnessed brutality, murders, and lies committed in the name of God. I had witnessed the destruction of a nation. Because of this, I was about to embark on a life of treason. I was going to lie to my wife, lie to the people I loved most. I was going to risk their lives without giving them the chance to protect themselves.

"Wally?"

The CIA saw me as a godsend, an asset they needed at a time when they were struggling to understand the threat that Iran had become to them. If I was going to help them, they needed to know what made me tick. Yet I wasn't sure I could explain myself to them. How could I make them understand why I was risking my family and betraying my friends to save my country when I wasn't sure myself?

For the first time since I'd begun this journey, tears broke over the edge of my eyes and dripped down my cheeks.

"Wally," the agent said softly, "do you consider it immoral to break an oath to your friend?"

The question split my soul in two.

"Wally?"

Because the two people inside me had contradictory answers. And God would not send half of me to hell.

"Reza?"

2

THREE FRIENDS

1966

"REZA!"

I rubbed my eyes and opened them reluctantly. My grandmother, Khanoom Bozorg, was pulling the curtains to the side.

"Get up, son, it is almost eight o'clock."

"It's too early, Grandma. Please let me sleep some more."

"Naser has already come by the door twice. Don't you want to see your friends? Get up now. The guests will be arriving soon."

"They won't be here until noon."

My protests didn't carry any weight with her. Grandma gave me a pinch on my cheek and pulled the blanket off me before she left the room.

Today was Ashura, a day when Shia Muslims mourn the martyrdom of Imam Hussein, Shiites' third Imam, with solemn stories and great feasts. My grandmother was hosting Rowzeh Khooni, a ceremony of mourning. I awoke to a flurry of activity around the house. Grandma had begun preparations days ago and they continued now with fervor. With the help of family members and neighbors, she had the furniture moved out of the living area because she was going to be hosting so many people. Over my grandparents' Persian rugs, they'd placed colorful maroon and burgundy patterned cushions, with large matching cushions resting against the wall for added comfort. In this newly opened space, they could bring together more than a hundred guests.

I went to the kitchen, where Grandma had my breakfast ready. She made me hot tea and a piece of lavash bread rolled with butter and cherry jam, which was my favorite. The kitchen was a mess. Big copper pots filled with food sat on the floor. Grandma was an accomplished cook and a fine host, and she had prepared a feast for that day. She had even hired several servants in addition to the usual help because she wanted all of her guests to feel comfortable.

The aroma from the food she'd made wafted through the house— and probably through the neighborhood as well. She'd made *gheyme polo,* rice with yellow split peas and meat; *baghali polo,* fava beans with rice and veal shank; and *fesenjoon,* walnut stew with white rice. And she'd made enough to feed every guest for several days.

While my parents' house was only a few blocks down the same street, I spent most of my time at this point in my life at my paternal grandparents' home. I even had my own room there. Both of my parents worked, sometimes until late at night. Since I was the only child and since, at twelve, I was still young, someone had to take care of me. I loved spending time with my grandparents. Khanoom Bozorg always made my favorite food, told me stories, and had her maids clean my room and wash my clothes. I never had to do anything around this house—unless she was punishing me for doing something bad. Agha Joon, my grandpa, was like a second father to me. His favorite phrase was "*Pir shi javoon,*" "Grow old, young man." At the time, I wondered why he would wish a young person to grow old, but I would someday understand what he meant by this. And where Grandma could be strict, Grandpa usually found a way to get me off the hook with her when I was in trouble.

The reason I most loved being at my grandparents' house was that Naser lived next door. Naser and I had been friends for as long as I could remember. We grew up together, played together, went to the same school, and hung around together after classes nearly every day. My grandfather and Naser's father, Davood, were good friends even though there was a considerable difference in their ages. They enjoyed gardening and bird-watching together. They had pet canaries whose song they could imitate with their own uncanny whistles.

Davood adored his three children. He always bragged about Naser's grades and the artistic endeavors of Soheil, his younger son. He regularly claimed that Soheil would be as famous as da Vinci one day. With the birth of his only daughter, Parvaneh, Davood celebrated life anew. *Parvaneh* is the Farsi word for "butterfly" and Davood gave his daughter this name because she had brought color and beauty to his life. He always took the toddler along when he visited Grandpa. Naser's mom, on the other hand, was a private woman and rarely joined my grandparents' gatherings.

After I ate breakfast, I ran to Naser's house. We had plans to meet up with our friend Kazem. Naser and I were twelve and Kazem was a year younger; adult gatherings gave us a great opportunity to create mischief and we suspected we'd generate some today.

When I got to Naser's house, he was in his yard chasing frogs. I put my head between the bars of the iron fence that surrounded his house and called his name.

"Come on, let's go get Kazem."

"Wait, I almost have this frog."

He was zigzagging, jumping here and there in pursuit. He finally managed to catch the frog, and once he did, he ran toward me. His big brown eyes glinted in the summer sun. His smile widened as he extended his arms to show me his catch.

I scowled at him. "You're wasting time chasing frogs, Naser! The guests will be arriving soon."

Naser put the trapped amphibian in his pocket with a shrug. "Okay, Reza. Let's go."

He whistled happily as we walked. A fresh breeze from the mountains stirred the tall trees that lined our streets. Water from the snowmelt flowed through a creek that wove and tumbled its way through the thickets of raspberry and blackberry bushes in

Grandpa's backyard, creating a melodic brook in which Naser and I could splash.

We lived in an upscale neighborhood with lush foliage in the north of Tehran, the capital of Iran. My grandparents' house was at the end of a long, narrow street lined with gated properties on both sides. You could not see some of the larger homes from the street as tall brick walls or hedges concealed them. On our walk through this area, we always peeked through gates to take in the acres of impressive landscaping, ponds, waterfalls, and swimming pools. I felt very proud to live in a place this beautiful.

This area was close to the slopes of the Alborz mountain range. Nearby was the Sadabad Palace, built during the Qajar dynasty in the nineteenth century. Reza Shah lived there in the twenties. His son, Mohammad Reza Shah Pahlavi, Shahanshah, King of Kings, moved there in the seventies.

Kazem's house was only a thirty-minute walk from ours, but in many ways it seemed a world away. In his neighborhood, potholes dotted the asphalt streets, rotted wooden gates marked the entrances in the crumbling clay walls around the small homes, and only a few small trees stood along the sidewalks. The very same creek that ran past my grandparents' house wound through this neighborhood as well. But where Naser and I used the creek for frolicking, some of Kazem's neighbors used it for washing clothes.

Even at our age, it was impossible not to notice the difference in living conditions. Hungry kids sat on the street in torn, dirty clothes with flies buzzing around the dried crusts of dirt on their noses and eyes. Their mothers carried laundry in big aluminum bowls atop their heads. Women traded dried bread and a little change for a bag of sea salt, which the street merchants carried in donkey saddle packs. The merchant used the dried bread to feed his donkey and the change as his sole source of income. And while men in our family discussed whether to purchase American-made or German-made cars, men in Kazem's neighborhood owned old bikes or, like Kazem's father, a three-wheeler pickup truck.

The differences weren't only economic. Here, the women covered themselves under chadors, unlike the women in our family and many others in Iran who dressed in Western-style suits and fancy dresses, covering their hair with a loose scarf only on special occasions, such as mourning ceremonies or funerals.

As we drew closer to Kazem's house, we saw him with his mother escorting Mullah Aziz outside. Kazem's mother bent over and whispered something to Kazem, who stepped toward the mullah, took his hand, bowed, and kissed it. That was his way of thanking Mullah Aziz for teaching him the Quran. When he spotted us, Kazem didn't blush. He was not embarrassed to have us see him kissing a mullah's hand, as Naser and I would have been. In fact, he smiled with pride.

We'd met Kazem a year before on a hot summer afternoon. Kazem was the local butcher's son. Despite being only ten then, Kazem worked for his dad after school and during the summertime. Naser and I were playing soccer outside my grandparents' house along with a few other boys from our neighborhood when Kazem made a meat delivery to Grandma. Afterward, he sat on the curb and watched us play. He was short and skinny and wore his hair so closely cropped that his round head almost seemed bald. His dark, droopy eyes moved with the ball and every time one of us made a bad play, he giggled.

After this happened a few times, Naser threw the ball to Kazem and challenged him to show us some of his moves. Kazem jumped from the curb eagerly and started bouncing the ball on his feet ten, twenty times without dropping it. Then, in one fluid motion, he kicked the ball above his head and headed it back to Naser.

Naser and I looked at each other, amazed. Right there, we asked him to join our soccer team. Kazem happily agreed. His only caveat was that he could not play with us during the month of Ramadan because his mother insisted that he fast. I found it hard to believe that any kid would put religious obligations ahead of soccer, but we had no choice but to accept this.

"Mullah, may I kiss your hand," Naser said, teasing Kazem, as we made our way back to my grandparents' house.

With a grand gesture, Kazem presented his hand to Naser and said, "May God forgive you for your rudeness, son. You shall bow and kiss my hand now." Then he laughed.

Naser reached into his pocket quickly and put the frog in Kazem's outstretched hand. Kazem screamed and pulled away. The frog hopped to the ground and made his escape. Naser had to hold his stomach, he was laughing so hard.

"What is wrong with you?" I said, slapping Naser on the back. "Why did you do that?" I didn't like touching frogs, either, so I sympathized immediately with Kazem.

"Come on, Reza, you coward. You're both cowards. It's just a frog." Naser wrapped his arms around us, giving us a big hug.

In the middle of this we heard the clop-clop of a donkey. We turned to see Mullah Aziz passing us. His short legs were hanging off the sides of the animal and his sandals were bouncing on his feet. Naser pointed at the hole in the mullah's socks and the three of us laughed. I knew the mullah was on his way to my grandparents' home to perform the Rowzeh Khooni. This ceremony was a business opportunity for neighborhood mullahs. They lived in near poverty, so the fee they received for this occasion (the equivalent of a dollar or two) meant something to them.

Some Muslims, like Kazem's family, held the mullahs in high regard and followed their teachings closely. However, most people— my family and Naser's family among them—considered the mullahs nothing more than low-level preachers who helped them practice their faith and meet their moral obligations. Grandpa did not like the mullahs. I once heard him say, "These donkey riders should all be moved to the city of Qom, where they learned all this nonsense. They should be kept in a compound and only allowed to preach there." And then in a moment of terrible prescience, he added, "God forbid if they ever get the power to rule."

As soon as Mullah Aziz passed us by, we encountered a *dasteh,* a mourning parade of men in black clothes, marching down the alley carrying banners and singing torturous songs about Imam Hussein's martyrdom. We sat at the curb and watched as they moved along. The neighborhood women carried big pitchers of cherry sherbet and offered it to the men, who were sweating under the heat. As part of the ceremony, some men struck their chests with their hands and some rapped their backs until they bled with a special chain made only for the parade.

"What's wrong, Reza?" Kazem said when he saw my reaction to this. "Why are you making that face?"

I was nauseous. The funereal singing and the sight of so many backs covered with blood made me gag. I always tried to avoid a *dasteh*. I would try to stay inside if they came to our neighborhood, though they usually kept to neighborhoods like Kazem's.

I avoided answering Kazem's question because I knew his response to this sight was very different from mine. "We should be going now," I said, pulling Naser's shirt. "If we wait here for the *dasteh* to pass by, we won't get home in time. And look, Mullah Aziz is also taking off."

The mullah had been on the other side of the alley, sitting on his donkey, watching the crowd and playing with his prayer beads. Naser got up, looked toward the mullah, and pulled Kazem by his arm.

"Let's go," he said, pointing down an alley and smiling mischievously. "Let's get to the house before Mullah Aziz. I know a shortcut. This way, Reza! Kazem!"

We followed Naser, running. Breathless, we managed to get to Grandpa's before the mullah.

Inside the house, the guests were already there. The women sat in the living room and the men sat in the adjacent family room. Some kids were in the yard playing and the smaller kids were inside with their parents.

"Come on, guys," Naser said as he noticed the mullah's arrival. "He's here."

The mullah dismounted his donkey and tied it to a tree at the end of the paved driveway next to Grandpa's 1955 white Cadillac De-Ville. My grandfather loved that car and he made sure his chauffeur kept it in pristine condition. He would have been appalled to see the mullah's donkey pounding his feet and kicking up dust on the car.

Mullah Aziz made his way down the potted-geranium-lined path leading to the stairs up to the balcony entrance. While everyone else waited inside the house for the sermon to begin, the three of us hunkered down behind the Cadillac. I still did not know what Naser had in mind, but he seemed ready to burst with excitement.

Grandpa had opened the double doors to welcome Mullah Aziz. The mullah went inside and quickly took his place in front of the living room mantelpiece under a picture of Imam Ali, the Shiites' first Imam. Grandma had placed a special cushion for him there.

"Okay, guys," Naser whispered. "Kazem, you stay here in front of Agha Joon's car and make sure nobody sees us. If you see anybody coming, whistle twice. Reza, you come with me." Kazem agreed to join in reluctantly, obviously uneasy about doing anything that might victimize the mullah. As was usually the case with Kazem, he didn't volunteer to start mischief, but he didn't back away from it, either.

Naser and I crept toward the donkey. I grabbed the bridle while Naser untied the reins. The animal did not move. Naser gave him a kick in the leg; still nothing. I pulled his tail. The donkey turned his head and neighed at me.

"He isn't going anywhere," Kazem said, laughing.

Naser grabbed a small stick from the ground and hit the donkey on the back. That finally got the animal moving. With the donkey now free of his restraints and running, the three of us chased the hapless beast down the street, roaring with laughter.

"There goes the Mullah Aziz's 1965 Donkey-Mobile, down the hill in neutral," Naser said.

Once the donkey was gone, we ran back inside, thrilled with our success and determined to appear as innocent as possible.

Meanwhile, Mullah Aziz was beginning his work. After adjusting his turban a few times, he closed his eyes, lifted his chubby arms skyward, and opened the ceremony with *"Besmellahe Rahmane Rahim"*—"In the Name of God, the Merciful, the Kind." Then he began to tell sad stories of the Imam's martyrdom. The women found this mesmerizing. Within minutes, Mullah Aziz had them crying with his mournful performance. Meanwhile, in the other room, Grandpa was making fun of him and his delivery, whispering to my dad, "The son of a dog is telling the story of Imam Hussein like he witnessed the Imam's martyrdom himself."

With the women in a state of rapture, Mullah Aziz peeked at them surreptitiously. Rubbing his full black beard with his fingers, he moved his eyes around the room until he spotted my two cousins, Haleh and Mina. I learned that they'd earlier caused a stir when they entered the women's room because they were dressed so conspicuously. Mina was wearing a tight, short, light green dress and Haleh a black lace blouse and a miniskirt. Both girls wore red lipstick, green eye shadow, and rosy blush. As a concession to propriety, they wore thin see-through veils atop their updos. As Mullah Aziz came toward the close of his sermon, he glanced at my cousins again and winked at them. Haleh looked at Mina in shock and they started giggling.

Naser saw this exchange and wrinkled his nose. Naser had a huge crush on Haleh despite the fact that she was eight years older. "Stupid mullah," he whispered. "I hope he never finds that donkey."

After the mullah's presentation, the servants offered platters of food on a *sofreh,* a linen tablecloth spread across the floor. We filled our plates and ate in the yard. The mullah stayed inside, enjoying the large plate of food Grandma had prepared especially for him.

When we finished eating, we lay on the bench by Grandpa's fishpond and talked about our next soccer match. The guests had scattered in the yard. Some prepared to leave, some gathered in small groups talking, and some helped clean up. I had nearly forgotten about what we'd done with Mullah Aziz's donkey when I heard my grandmother's trembling voice.

"Reza . . . ! Reza . . . !"

She came over to us, biting her lip, hands on her hips, tapping her foot.

I looked at Naser and then Kazem. "How did she know it was us?" I whispered.

I knew I was in trouble, but I would not betray my friends. We had sworn an oath to be friends forever and never tell on one another. I ran back inside and hid behind my grandfather, though I had a feeling that even he was not going to be able to save me this time.

"Reza! I will give you a good lesson tonight," my grandmother said with ominous calm. "But now you go with your friends and find that donkey."

Though I hadn't ratted out my friends, she knew all three of us had been involved. She had the authority to punish only me, though, so I would withstand the worst of this. We went out to look for the animal and found him just around the corner by a gutter. He was probably very confused about his master's whereabouts. We brought the donkey back home, where my grandmother was apologizing profusely to Mullah Aziz for our behavior. This seemed to mollify him, especially when Grandma presented him with a big basket of food and fruit to take home.

My grandmother could have beaten me for this indiscretion and I really wouldn't have had any legitimate gripe. But the punishment she chose was far more humiliating than any beating—she made me help the women in the kitchen that night and then she made me clean up the garden the next day.

"You'll also be in your room for a few days. No soccer or outside playing," Grandma demanded.

"Khanoom Bozorg, that's not fair!"

"What you did to that poor mullah was not nice."

"But . . . but we have an important match coming this Thursday. Please, Grandma, I adore you, I do." I pouted and pressed my eyelids together. She left the room, letting my appeal for leniency go unanswered. The following Thursday, though, I not only played soccer, I also went to see a movie with Naser and Kazem after our game. Kazem insisted we see *A Fistful of Dollars* with Clint Eastwood even though we had seen it a few times already. We loved American movies, especially Westerns. We each had a favorite American actor. Kazem's was Clint Eastwood, Naser's, John Wayne, and mine, Steve McQueen. We even called one another by their names. We loved going to the theater, eating popcorn, and drinking orange soda.

One thing we didn't love was that before every movie started, we had to stand up to the picture of Mohammad Reza Shah, which appeared on the screen as the national anthem played. Although that night we got to the movie theater a little late, all of the people in the audience were on their feet to honor the picture of the shah. Naser put his two fingers by his forehead to salute me. I imitated the same motion to Kazem, and Kazem bowed to both of us as we all giggled. On the way home after the movie, Kazem drew his imaginary gun and shot at Naser and me. We acted as though he'd actually shot us and swayed back and forth in slow motion. "Clint, please don't kill us," we called as we fell.

Since the next day was a Friday, that meant it was time for another of my grandfather's weekly gatherings. Some Muslims continue the mourning of Imam Hussein's martyrdom for the entire month of Muharram, wearing black clothes and avoiding parties and music. But for most Iranians, like my family, life went back to normal the day after Ashura.

As soon as everyone arrived this Friday, Grandpa called upon the kids, lining us up in three rows from the oldest to the youngest so we could perform the national anthem:

> *Shahanshah e ma zendeh bada*
> *Payad keshvar be farash javedan*
> *Kaz Pahlavi shod molke Iran*
> *Sad rah behtar ze ahde basetan*
> *Az doshmanan budi parishan*
> *Dar saye ash asude Iran*

Iranian peyvaste shadan
Hamvareh Yazdan bovad ura negahban

Long live our King of Kings
And may his glory make immortal our land
For Pahlavi dynasty improved Iran
A hundredfold from where it once used to stand
Though once beset by the foemen's rage
Now it has peace in his keeping sure
We of Iran, rejoice in every age
Oh, may God protect him both now and evermore

Naser, Kazem, and I were in the middle row. Naser had his little sister, Parvaneh, on his shoulder. Parvaneh, only two at the time, was too young to sing the anthem, but she would mouth some words as if she knew the whole thing while moving her head so that her pigtails hit her in the face. When we made fun of her, she curled her lips, bent her head down, and frowned. Naser, who was very protective of his siblings, rolled his eyes at us. Meanwhile, Grandpa moved his arms like a world-famous conductor, pointing at us and bobbing his head with eyes closed. Anyone could see how much he loved doing this.

"Agha Joon, let the poor kids go play," Naser's father, Davood, said after a while. "Enough of Shahanshah."

Davood helped my dad fire up the brazier for the *chelo kebab,* ground beef and steak skewers with rice. While my grandmother always made the food for the big feasts, Friday lunches came from my grandfather, my father, and Davood. They would marinate the steak the night before. While one kept the fire going by fanning it constantly, the others arranged the meat on big metal skewers.

After lunch, we all assembled around the goldfish pond in the center of the yard. My grandfather had placed large benches there under the mulberry trees, covering them with Persian rugs. My grandmother made tea on the samovar and her servant served this and pastries to everyone.

Grandpa used the charcoals still burning on the grill to light his hookah and called to Davood to share it with him. As soon as Davood had his first puff, he started singing. Soon everyone joined in by clapping along to the song. While the girls started dancing, Naser, Kazem, and I climbed the walnut tree at the corner of the yard. From there Naser could follow Haleh's every move. My cousin's dark brown silky hair caressed her shoulders as she danced.

"Reza, she is so beautiful," Naser said with a sigh. "I will marry her someday."

Kazem let out a groan. "Here we go again—Naser's love story."

Naser scowled at Kazem. "How about you, Kazem? Do you have a good view of Mina from up here? She's wearing your favorite skirt, the shortest one. Hey! Look!" He pointed into the distance. "She's waving at you." Mina was talking to a guest on the other side of the yard.

When Kazem turned his head to see, Naser blew a raspberry at him and said, "Keep dreaming, man."

Kazem seemed a little embarrassed, but he recovered quickly. "At least I have a chance with her. Your big nose would scare away an ugly witch."

Sometimes when we were up in that tree, we shook the branches and watched the walnuts fall to the ground. We laughed every time a walnut hit Soheil or one of the other kids who were too small to climb the tree. When there were enough walnuts on the ground for everybody, we would climb down, gather the walnuts, and sit on the bench next to Grandpa and Davood. We listened to their stories as we hulled the walnuts. We knew that cracking so many walnuts was going to leave a black stain on our hands, but since it was summertime, we didn't care. We always left the biggest walnuts for Grandpa.

Around this time every Friday, Grandpa and Davood would start debating. My grandfather's recollections of World War II often led to animated conversations about the shah and the lack of political freedom in Iran.

"The shah has done wonders for our country," my grandfather

would say. "Look at all the modernization, the new high-rise buildings, and the universities. Women in Iran are free now. This is progress."

"You're right about that, Agha Joon," Davood would respond, "but we lack freedom of speech. We need democracy. The shah rules with an iron fist. God help those who stand up to him."

"That will change, Davood *jon*. He's been making changes all along. We have a good life. We're very prosperous because of his programs."

"What are you saying? We have more political prisoners in our jails than ever before. All our progress is meaningless if our basic rights are being denied."

My grandmother always found this talk annoying. She'd shake her head and say, "Bah, they started this again! There are kids here. They might tell someone at school that we talk bad about Shahanshah at home." She would turn to my dad and scoff. "I think Davood is looking for trouble."

This would lead to my father putting his arm around Grandma and saying, "Don't worry, Mother. They are talking about history and democracy. It is good for the kids. They learn to be open-minded."

My mother wouldn't agree. "Your mother is right. Some kids can interpret talk like this as disrespect to the shah."

Grandma would jump on this to reinforce her point. "They should teach these kids piety instead. That's how they learn to be good. It's through God and religion that we can teach these restless kids to be honest and trustworthy."

My parents were not religious people nor political. They did believe in God, but they thought religion kept people from discovering science and the purpose of being. "Religion mandates what to do and how to do it," my mother once said to me. "It stops your way of thinking and exploring your options in life." My mother always thought progressively. While most Iranian women chose to be housewives, she spent most of her time in a children's hospital as a nurse.

While my mother and father had similar perspectives on the world, my grandparents thought very differently from each other. Grandpa thought that man was all about his background and roots. He would say, "We are a nation of royalty with a rich history of kingdom." He spoke proudly of the rule of shahs over the centuries and about our rich culture of arts and crafts. His love affair with the Pahlavi dynasty started when Reza Shah-E-Kabir, known as Reza Shah the Great, took the reins of the country in a military coup in 1921 and confronted the Soviets, hoping to control Iran by helping rebellious militias in the north of the country. Reza Shah dethroned Ahmad Shah, the last king of the Qajar dynasty. He then chose the name Pahlavi for himself, becoming the first king of this new dynasty. My grandfather believed in Reza Shah's edicts, such as the order that any woman seen wearing a chador should be made to remove her veil. This was a direct insult to the mullahs and Reza Shah became the immediate enemy of the clerics, but he did not let up. He continued to Westernize Iran, building roads, bridges, railway systems, and universities.

Reza Shah's monarchy ended badly, however. During World War II, the Allies felt he was sympathetic to the Germans, and because of Iran's vast oil reserves, they attacked our country—the Russians from the northwest and the British from the west and the south. They conquered Iran and unseated Reza Shah. The British sent him into exile in Africa for the rest of his life, and they appointed his twenty-two-year-old son, Mohammad Reza Shah, the new king of Iran. The new shah continued many of his father's policies, but he was more moderate, allowing people to practice their religion freely.

My grandmother agreed with the shah's approach to religion. This irritated my grandfather. "Khanoom, we are Persians, not Arabs. Islam is not for us. We are the nation of Zartosht, Zoroaster. The British have long helped the mullahs to keep us entangled with Islam and keep us busy with Allah and his punishments while they take advantage of our oil."

"Agha, bite your tongue. Our belief in God is just. It has nothing to do with the British. You haven't learned anything about Islam. How did I spend so many years with such an ignorant person?"

I learned what I knew about religion from my grandmother. She showed me that Islam was a religion of honesty, love, respect, courage, and justice. She told inspiring stories about the Prophet Mohammad and Imam Ali. One of my favorites was about how Ali would go out at night in disguise to help the poor. Although a leader with the highest regard among his people, he led a life of hardship and deprivation, disdaining material wealth and comfort.

My grandmother's voice still echoes in my mind. "One day Ali's brother, who was a blind man, approached Ali, saying to him, 'Ali, you have control of the treasury. Why don't you share some with your poor brother?'

"Ali told him to come and take what he needed. Then, instead of giving his brother the coins he wanted, he placed a candle in such a manner that caused his brother to touch its flame. His brother cried out in pain, demanding to know why Ali had done that.

"Do you know why he did that, Reza? Ali was the ruler and the most honest, trusted man in the eyes of his people. He wanted to show his brother that stealing was a sin. He shouldn't take money he didn't earn. If he could not bear the pain of a little burn on his finger, how could he bear Jahanam's fire, hellfire?" She finished this story as she always did. "You must always choose right over wrong."

I loved both of my grandparents, but I secretly loved my grandfather a bit more. It was through his passion for his garden that I learned how precious life was. Grandpa spent most of his leisure time in the garden tending to his fruit trees, red roses, white jasmines, and several small pots of flowers. Every afternoon, he filled his watering can in the pond and, holding on to the back of his long robe, bent and carefully nurtured his beloved flowers, speaking fondly to them as he did.

"Agha Joon, why are you talking to your flowers?" I asked him once while he was doing this.

Grandpa turned toward me. "Reza, my son, there is life in flowers.

They are like humans. They have feelings. They are God's creation. Cherish them and they will flourish. Neglect them and they will perish."

I continued to learn from my grandfather as the years went by, even as the outside world became a bigger and bigger part of my life. Summers went by in a blur. Soon Naser and I, now seventeen, were preparing to enter the last year at our all-boys' high school, where we carried a heavy load: two-hour classes of algebra, chemistry, physics, history, English, and more. Kazem went to a different high school and still had the job delivering meat orders for his father. He received some teasing for this from some neighborhood boys. Most young people in Tehran didn't work. Only those who lived in poverty would allow their sons to have jobs. Kazem was not ashamed of working and he brushed off the taunting.

Meanwhile, Naser and I were having the time of our lives. Now that I was older, I spent most of my days at my parents' house. While my parents were at work, Naser and I smoked cigarettes and drank beer there. Kazem occasionally joined us when he was done with his meat deliveries. We hid our bottles of beer from him because we didn't want to subject ourselves to his lectures about temperance. They were worse than the lectures my grandmother gave me.

One afternoon, when the three of us sat on the deck off my room, Naser put out his cigarette and stood up. "I'm thirsty. Is there anything to drink?"

"We should have some 7UP and Coke in the fridge," I said. "Do you want me to go and get it?"

"No, I know my way around your house. You guys want some too?"

We both nodded. When Naser went inside, Kazem pulled his chemistry book from his bag, saying that he hoped Naser would help him prepare for a test the next day. Kazem needed to ace it to pass the course.

"He's got nothing to do," I said. "I'm sure he'll be able to help you. God, I hate chemistry."

Naser came back with three glasses on a tray. "Reza, turn off the lights. That'll keep the mosquitoes from attacking us."

I did so and Naser gave each of us a glass. As soon as I took a sip, I knew he was being mischievous. Under the dim light coming from the window in my room, I rolled my eyes at him. He raised his eyebrows and gestured to me to stay quiet.

"Kazem, have your drink," Naser said. "It is nice and cold."

Kazem got a paper from his bag and then picked up his glass. "Thanks, man."

Naser watched Kazem delightedly while I tried not to laugh. Kazem gulped the drink and then, like a cat sprayed with water, he jumped off his seat and spit the drink everywhere—including all over Naser. This caused Naser to jump as well. I turned on the lights and burst out with laughter.

"Man, you are so stupid," Kazem said, coughing alcohol. "What the hell was that?"

"We call it Shams. Shams beer. A product of our fatherland."

As soon as Kazem heard the word *beer*, he ran inside. We followed him and saw him try to wash his mouth under the kitchen faucet.

"Three times!" Naser said, still laughing. "Muslims should wash the alcohol off three times. Otherwise, you go to *Jahanam*."

Kazem was scandalized. "Shut up, Naser. Why did you do that?"

"Have some fun, man. You won't go to hell if you have a little fun in your life. It is just beer."

"Drinking is a sin. Don't you know anything about your religion? You should get a little serious about life, Naser. All you want to do is smoke, drink, and chase girls—and you are dragging Reza down with you."

Naser stopped laughing now. "What are you trying to say? That having a little fun means I'm not serious about life? You think the only thing a person can do is follow religious rules? And Reza can speak for himself. He is his own person."

"Stop this, you two," I said, trying to defuse the tension. "It was just a joke . . ." Kazem narrowed his eyes at me. ". . . a bad one.

Now you should start your chemistry homework before it gets too late."

I did not want Naser's prank to cause any trouble between the three of us, and I hated to choose sides. Naser apologized, but Kazem stayed angry for a while. Naser's helping Kazem prepare for his test ultimately allowed us all to relax. However, this night underscored for us that while we could enjoy soccer, watching movies, and going to my grandfather's gatherings as a trio, Kazem couldn't be a part of everything we did.

This, of course, didn't prevent Naser and me from doing those other things. Every day after school, we would go over to the nearby girls' school and watch the girls pour out into the street after their classes, some smiling and flirting with us. We would put our home phone numbers on pieces of paper to give to them. Naser had grown into a handsome, sturdy six-footer with a full head of black hair that he kept carefully styled in a Beatles haircut. The Beatles were very popular with young people in Iran at the time. Girls were crazy about Naser and he made jokes and winked at them. Although I was a little shorter and had a slightly lighter complexion than Naser, most girls assumed we were brothers. We had the same hairstyle and even dressed alike in Levis and black shirts.

Once in a while, Naser would steal his dad's red Chevy Impala convertible and bump the music up while we waited outside the girls' high school. To impress the girls, we always had a pack of Winstons handy and played songs by the Bee Gees, Bob Dylan, or the Beatles. We were soon dating some of those girls, taking them to the discos opening all over Tehran and clandestinely making out with them. We never worried about getting into trouble, though Davood would have been furious with us if he knew we regularly stole his car. My only regret was that Kazem couldn't join us in most of our exploits. "He will gradually understand that life is not all about praying and practicing religion," Naser would say when I mentioned this to him.

As I was getting ready for my high school finals, my dad, a civil engineer who had studied in America, talked to me about the importance of education. He said I should remain focused on my studies and that I should always dream big. He convinced me that I should go to America to study computer science because he believed that computers were the future and that the universities in America would train me for this future better than those anywhere else in the world. In the spring of 1972, with the help of my aunt, who lived in Los Angeles, I enrolled at the University of Southern California (USC). Although it was a dream for any young Iranian to go to America, I would have preferred to go to the University of Tehran with Naser, but my father's persuasion was forceful and I could not argue with him.

Before I left, my family and close friends threw a good-bye party for me. During the event, I sat on the bench next to the fishpond watching the crowd wistfully. The people there were an essential part of me. I looked at my grandfather's flowers. It would be hard saying good-bye to them, too.

Naser and Kazem came by and sat on the bench next to me. I wanted to hug them and let them know how hard it was for me to move so far from them, but I couldn't find the words. I wished at that moment that we could stop time. We sat there quietly and said nothing for a while.

Finally, Naser slapped me on the back and said, "Hey, don't forget about us here. Write and tell us how life is in America."

I wrapped my arm around him and I pulled Kazem in with my other arm. "I will write to you every day."

Kazem patted my shoulder. "Remember the first time we made an oath? It was here, right on this bench."

"Friends forever," Naser said.

I nodded. "We swore on our lives to remain buddies."

"To our graves," Kazem said, fighting to choke back tears.

3

COMING TO AMERICA

I HADN'T SEEN my aunt Giti since the last time she visited us in Iran, when I was twelve years old, but I recognized her immediately when I departed the gate at LAX. She was waving a little sign with my name on it and I saw tears in her eyes as I approached.

"Ahh, Reza *jon,* look at you," she said as she hugged me. "You are a grown man! I am so happy to have a dear family member with me now." Aunt Giti lived alone. She had moved to America many years ago when she was about twenty to pursue her education. A few years later, my dad joined her to go to college before moving back home. Aunt Giti continued her education, became a chemist, and had been back to Iran only a few times to visit.

I kissed her cheeks, and hoping to avoid an emotional outburst I wasn't prepared for after my emotional departure from home, I opened my carry-on bag to give her the Persian pastries Grandma had baked. "Khanoom Bozorg made these just for you. She said you should have some right away while they are still fresh."

We took a cab to her house. Aunt Giti sat close to me with her arm around my shoulders, watching me intently. While we talked, I occasionally looked outside the window to explore the new city that I would come to call home. We didn't have anything like the LA highway system in Tehran, but in many other ways the landscape seemed familiar. Even the sunny weather was similar to what I knew. I found this comforting, as I was still wary about traveling all this distance to go to school.

Despite her busy work schedule, Aunt Giti had taken care of all my paperwork for USC and had prepared the guest room in her Tarzana house especially for me. In order to allow me to learn the language as quickly as possible, she suggested we speak only English to each other. She also signed me up for intensive English courses at the local Berlitz school. Though I had taken the language in high school, I was hardly fluent, and I knew Americans would have a difficult time understanding me if I didn't improve quickly. I therefore spent long hours in classrooms with exchange students from Japan and Mexico just as inarticulate and homesick as I was.

I missed everything about home. I missed Naser and Kazem. I missed the Friday gatherings. I missed my grandfather's political debates with Davood. To substitute for some of this, I followed Iranian politics on TV, imagining what Agha Joon would say about the day's events.

When my first semester at USC began, I found myself surrounded by young people very rapidly speaking words I was still learning. Sometimes my head would hurt from concentrating so hard to understand people, but I loved this total immersion. I met a student named Johnny in one of my math classes and we became fast friends. He invited me to his place and I asked Aunt Giti if it was okay for me to spend the night.

"You don't need my permission, Reza *jon*," she said. "You are a big boy and just letting me know is enough. I trust you to do the right thing." This was my first experience of a significant difference I would discover between Iran and America—here, people weren't always looking over your shoulder. Here, they believed that if you were old enough to go to college, you were old enough to make your own decisions.

Johnny lived in a small three-bedroom town house in West LA with two roommates. One was his best friend, Alex. The other was a guy who was about to move out to live with his girlfriend. There was a party going on when I got there, and it was unlike any party I'd ever known—a long way from Davood's singing and Mina and

Haleh dancing in their minidresses with parents watching every move we made.

In no time, college girls and boys filled Johnny's place. With them were bottles of vodka, tequila, and beer, along with a thick cloud of cigarette smoke. Some people were smoking marijuana in the small balcony off the living area. It was the closest I'd ever been to this kind of drug. In Iran some young people smoked hash, but Naser and I were never around anybody who did so.

Before I knew it, I was making out with a couple of girls whose name I didn't even know. Soon one of them called another girl to join us.

"Hey, Molly, come meet Reza. He is so cute. He has this cute accent. Reza, say something."

Molly was a tall blond girl, wearing the shortest cutoff jeans I'd ever seen. Her red tank top was way above her belly button. She looked me in the eye, held my hand, and asked me to go to the balcony with her. The other girls were annoyed that Molly was taking me away from them, but they found the lap of another partygoer quickly enough.

I walked outside with the blond beauty. When we got there, she filled her cigarette paper with greenish leaves and lit it. She took a puff, and then passed it to me. My heart started pounding. I did not want her to know it was my first time, but I also didn't know what to expect. "Mari-joo-ana?" I said, grabbing the joint with my thumb and forefinger.

She burst out laughing. "They were right—you are cute." She ran her fingers through my hair. "We call it pot, sweetie," she said as she kissed my lips.

I don't remember much of what happened after that. I woke up on the floor next to the kitchen at four o'clock the next afternoon with a horrible headache, an upset stomach—and the desire to go to another party as soon as possible. I liked this new life very much.

After that, Johnny and Alex made me part of their group, which accelerated my learning of the culture and the language far beyond what any Berlitz class could. We hung out after our classes, talking for hours about the meaning of life while we blasted Pink Floyd and Jethro Tull. Before I knew it, I was contributing to conversations without having to think. I started getting, and then making, jokes in English.

To make my college life in LA complete, I needed a car. People without cars in this town were second-class citizens and I wanted no part of that. I pressured my father for one, explaining that because the city was so big and sprawling, cabs were useless. How else could I attend classes, living so far from campus? Aunt Giti seconded this and Dad agreed to send the money. Johnny suggested a red Mustang with mag wheels and he helped me get a driver's license. As soon as I bought my "study mobile," I started dating LA girls and experiencing everything this town had to offer.

At first I wrote regularly to Naser and Kazem about life in the U.S. I told them about college life, my red Mustang, my new friends, LA girls (this last part only to Naser), and how different America was politically. I told them how student protesters could burn the American flag and deface photos of President Nixon right in front of the police, who just watched. In Iran, if you insulted the shah or the royal family in public, the notorious SAVAK police would arrest you and throw you into Evin Prison. There they'd beat you and demand to know the names of your friends.

In one of my letters to Naser I included a picture of myself leaning on the hood of the Mustang with my arms wrapped around Molly's waist. "Check out these two babes!" I wrote on the back of the picture.

Although I included a picture for Kazem in the letter I sent him at the same time, it was Johnny and Alex who stood next to me in that picture. "I now have the real Clint and John next to me," I wrote on the back of that picture. "We are hiding our shotguns in the trunk! Ha ha!" I signed it, "Your friend, Steve McQueen."

Both Naser and Kazem found life in America fascinating. Their letters were full of questions, particularly about politics. I was surprised that they wanted to know so much about this. The Vietnam

War and Watergate dominated the news at this point, so these became the main topics of my letters. I also wrote about how student rallies protesting the war were more like social gatherings and about the stratification of the student body into stoners, jocks, Greeks (frat boys and sorority girls), and the rest of us.

Naser and Kazem were keenly interested in how Americans openly protested their leaders' policies. Naser found the American resistance particularly interesting while Kazem wondered if religious principle motivated Americans. I did my best to explain the subtle differences, knowing they both ultimately wanted proof that a society of free speech and protest could work.

Meanwhile, Johnny and Alex's roommate moved out and they were looking for someone to take his place. I started lobbying my parents to allow me to move in with them, explaining how it was important for me to be around college buddies to improve my language and study skills. How was I supposed to pursue my degree without a study sanctum close to campus shared with my fellow scholars?

My parents were suspicious at first. Alex and Johnny? Who are these people? What kind of families did they come from? After explaining that everyone who attended USC came from a good family and convincing Mom and Dad they were just the American version of Naser and Kazem, they approved.

I was part of a trio again, only this time all three of us partied and dated girls. I filled my new room with the posters of my favorite rock bands and half-naked women. I didn't have Grandma's maid coming into my room early in the morning to make my bed or clean up after me, and it showed. We had no rules whatsoever.

For the next three years, it was volleyball at the beach, football in the park, barbecues, road trips to Vegas, watching football games, and only occasionally cracking a book before going to the next party. Iran and my friends back home became a dimming memory. My letters to friends and family slowed to a trickle. I believed I was exactly where I wanted to be in the world.

Then, one evening in my senior year, I was watching TV when the phone rang.

Alex answered. "It's your mom. She sounds upset."

I put the phone to my ear and heard my mother crying. "Mom, what's wrong?"

"Your father . . ." she said, and my heart sank through the floor. Between sobs she explained that doctors had diagnosed my dad, a lifelong smoker, with lung cancer. He was in critical condition. He was only fifty.

"Reza, he is everything to me," she said, her voice trembling. "If something happens, I don't know what I am going to do."

I booked the first flight home.

I arrived in Tehran for the first time in four years, planning to take a cab home, but Naser and Kazem surprised me at the airport. When I saw that they were both dressed in black, I got very nervous, but I dared not ask why they were wearing this color, trying to convince myself that they had a reason for this that had nothing to do with my father.

Naser's hair was now short and combed back. Kazem's hair was slightly longer than his old buzz cut, but he was neat and clean, as always. Their dress was a huge contrast to my sandals, tight T-shirt, loose jeans, and long, uncombed hair. At that moment I realized how time had separated us and this pierced my heart. I grabbed both of them in my arms and started crying like a little child.

"How did you know?" Naser said. "Who told you?" He thought I was crying over the loss of my dad, not realizing that he'd just confirmed it for me.

"How is my mom doing?" I said, trying not to cry harder.

Kazem patted my shoulder. "She is devastated. But that's the way it is, Reza. Hopefully, she'll cope. It is so good you are here. It will mean a lot to her."

"I am so sorry, Reza," Naser said. "May God bless your father's soul."

Naser bent his head. I'm sure that when he did so, he noticed my bare toes.

I felt embarrassed by the way I looked. "I think I should get some proper clothes from my suitcase and change in the car."

On the ride home, we reminisced briefly about my father. I had a million thoughts about him running through my head. He'd encouraged me to live a full life. He taught me how to play soccer and how to swim. He helped me with school, telling fables about the tragic lives of boys who did not do their homework and the triumphant glories of boys who did. He made me promise never to waste my life or my time.

I looked out the window wondering if I was living up to that promise, considering how I'd spent most of my USC days. But I was immediately distracted by how much Tehran had changed since I'd been gone. Building cranes monopolized the skyline. Apartment buildings were thirty stories high. Pahlavi Boulevard, a cosmopolitan center with upscale shops and restaurants lining it, looked like a street in any big city in Europe or America. In four years, it seemed, Tehran had moved forward fifteen.

Naser started telling me how things had been while I was gone. Student protests in the universities had heated up with the number of SAVAK arrests climbing proportionately. Kazem said that the SAVAK arrested members of the clergy in the religious schools of Qom because they spoke against the shah.

The SAVAK was a security and intelligence organization the shah created in 1957 with the help of the U.S. military after the CIA helped overthrow democratically elected Prime Minister Mohammad Mosaddeq because he nationalized Iran's oil. Iranians were still angry about it. Nixon's support of the shah helped keep this wound open. The shah and Nixon were buddies. U.S. products filled Iranian store shelves. Our military was fully Americanized and trained. Iranian pilots helped fight the Vietnam War. The shah supported the royalists in the Yemen civil war that ended in 1970. Then, in 1971, he helped the sultan of Oman put down a rebellion at the bidding of the U.S. In exchange, Nixon visited Iran in 1972, and he allowed the shah to buy any American weapons he wanted. The U.S. saw advantages in having an autocratic monarch as an ally who would do the U.S.'s dirty work in the Middle East. Saddam was the Soviets' man. The shah was America's man.

While Naser was going to school for engineering (receiving excellent grades with little effort), he talked about politics and injustice constantly. Kazem, still struggling with his studies, was a full-fledged devotee of Islam. He mostly agreed with Naser's critique of the shah's policies, but he objected to the encroaching Westernization of the country because he saw it as a key contributor to growing decadence among Iranian youth—girls wearing miniskirts, drunks in the streets, and the preponderance of nightclubs and bars. Kazem and the other members of his poorer religious class were hurting financially, and the fabulous profits from oil had not filtered down to them. The shah's modernization had left Kazem's people behind while at the same time assaulting their moral principles.

As Naser pulled into our driveway, I grew anxious. My heart felt heavy because my father was not going to be there and I would never greet him again. When I saw my mother, we hugged each other tight and she cried hysterically. I tried to console her, but nothing could stop her sobbing. My grandfather and grandmother were there and they seemed to be suffering horribly from the loss of their son, but as my mother and I huddled close together, Agha Joon whispered, "Your son is here, be happy."

Kazem and Naser stayed up late with me that night. We talked about my dad and some of the more memorable events of our childhood. Before long, though, our conversation turned back to politics. Little time ever passed before one of these two veered back toward that topic.

"This tyranny has to fall," Naser said. "People are suffering. This is the twentieth century and we still live under a dictatorship. There is no freedom of speech. No freedom of the press."

Kazem nodded in agreement. "Many people still live in poverty while the shah's family and those around them are obscenely wealthy and stealing what belongs to the people. We have to bring justice to our society. We are becoming a nation of corruption and decay. We need to turn to our faith. Only Islam can rescue us and our country."

"But it's only through Dr. Shariati's view of religion and society that we can find our true selves in all human dimensions and fight tyranny and its moral decay," Naser added. I knew virtually nothing about Ali Shariati. Naser explained that he was an Islamic scholar, sociologist, and critic of the shah and the mullahs. Shariati was so popular that citizens who weren't even students overflowed his lecture halls to hear him speak.

At the time, I did not share Naser's keen interest in politics or Kazem's devotion to Islam. Their well-informed dialogues aroused my interest, but I did not have much to contribute. I had not until this moment understood the intensity of moral outrage against the monarchy. It made the American outrage at Nixon seem like a minor irritation. And maybe that was appropriate. After all, while Nixon had an enemies list, the shah had an execution list.

That night, I also learned about the most famous case of arrest and execution, that of Khosrow Golesorkhi, the Iranian Che Guevara. He was a Marxist-Leninist poet and journalist arrested for a plot to kidnap the shah's son. "In truth, he and other leftists had only speculated about it as a means to trade for the freedom of political prisoners," Naser told me. He also said that since the shah was courting the West and conscious about the declarations by the UN human rights committee on various issues, including the treatment of political prisoners, he allowed what he thought would be an open-and-shut case to be aired on television. The court permitted Golesorkhi to speak, ostensibly to recant his crimes. Instead, he spoke with stirring eloquence on behalf of the peasants laboring under the shah's land reform, comparing their struggles to those of the great martyr Imam Hussein himself and detailing the shah's crimes against humanity. Golesorkhi refused to defend himself; he would defend only the people. When asked if he would continue his terrorist activities against the shah, he brazenly said that he would.

"You know what Golesorkhi did when they took him to be executed? He refused the blindfold and stared his executioners in the face when they fired at him. He was a hero, Reza." Naser shook his head. "No man should live under oppression. You have to stand up for your rights."

Naser then recited a poem by Golesorkhi:

> *"On your breast lay*
> *the deep scar of your enemy*
> *but, you standing cypress did not fall*
> *it is your way to die."*

Both Naser and Kazem sat up with me until I fell asleep. They were by my side when I woke up. I was very thankful that they were there because sleep had caused me to forget temporarily that my father was gone. When I awoke and remembered, the grief overwhelmed me anew. I don't know what I would have done if I didn't have my dearest friends by my side.

Naser and Kazem remained with me during my father's funeral, when every vulnerability in me was exposed and raw. I was my mother's only son and I felt a great deal of responsibility for her, but I knew she would not allow me to quit my studies to care for her—especially since my father had so strongly wished for me to get a degree in America. She was secure financially, but I was not convinced that she could cope emotionally without my father. Kazem and Naser assured me that they and their families would look after her and check in frequently. They did this because they loved her and they loved me. They knew I had an enormous opportunity in America—an opportunity they couldn't have—and they wanted to make sure I made the most of it. This outpouring of support brought me light in these dark days. I could hardly believe that I had allowed myself to neglect my two best forever friends as much as I had the past few years.

I returned to California determined to devote myself to my studies and to do my father proud. Home would not leave my mind this time and letters from home took on new meaning. Naser wrote about the mounting opposition to the shah. In sending me letters, he risked arrest by the SAVAK, as they monitored communications in and out of the country. I admired Naser's bravery and the passion of his commitment to the Iranian people. One of Naser's letters came with copies of some of Shariati's books. Reading these changed my life forever.

Shariati reinterpreted Islam through the lens of sociology, reviving its original principle of social responsibility. He decried both the stodgy mullahs, who replaced scholarship with cant, and capitalism, which encouraged a human being to be a mere consumer, "an economic animal whose only duty is to graze." Shariati foresaw a new type of religious leader who modeled himself after Mohammad, one who earned his leadership not by tyrannizing people, but by inspiring the best in them. The Quran proclaims that God and the people are one. Thus, to know God's will the leader must look to the deepest longings of the people. This radically democratic interpretation of Mohammad's teachings invigorated me.

The Prophet and the great Imams were transformational figures, said Shariati. They were not conservatives. They were radicals. The essence of Islam was dynamic, vibrant, and revolutionary. Shariati reminded us of the radicalism of Hussein, who stood up against the tyranny of his ruler and was beheaded for it. His final words were "Dignified death is better than humiliating life." Shariati said that any modern Muslim who accepted injustice was living a humiliating life. He believed that if every Muslim lived by the example of Hussein, injustice on this earth would end.

Shariati practiced what he preached and this led to his expulsion from colleges, the banning of his books, his arrest, and his exile. The monarchy did everything they could to stop him from talking—yet he wouldn't let up. His words rang so deeply that Iranians like Naser were sending his books and tapes all over the world to those of us living abroad.

I must have read ten Shariati books. Often, I would break down and cry from the power of his writing.

> . . . My Lord, grant me such a life that on my death-bed, I may not be resentful of its worthlessness. And grant me such a death, that I may not mourn for its uselessness. Let me choose that, but in the way that pleases you the most. My Lord, You teach me how to live; I shall learn how to die.

Shariati taught me that I'd allowed the ridiculous mullahs of my youth and the hypocritical leaders of the clergy to disillusion me from the Islamic spiritualism and rectitude my grandmother tried to teach me. While corrupt leaders could bend religion to serve their purposes, the principles of God were always there, in the hearts of good people. I hadn't allowed myself to embrace religion because I let the wrong people color my opinions. Now Shariati compelled me to dedicate my life to the pursuit of righteousness.

For the first time since I was a boy, I began performing my prayers routinely. I set up a prayer rug in the bedroom of my LA apartment, and while they didn't completely understand it, Alex and Johnny were respectful of my needs. Shariati's clarity of thinking reminded me of what was best in the human heart: justice, compassion, mercy, and courage in the face of injustice. I began to believe that Shariati himself was the leader he called for in his writings.

Then, in July 1977, I received another letter from Naser:

Salam, Reza,
I don't know if you've heard the news about Dr. Shariati.
After his release from the prison, he was kept under constant
surveillance and he left the country for London last month.
Reza, I just heard he was murdered in his residence. Damn this

injustice. This is yet another killing under the dictatorship of our monarchy. But believe me, his death is only the beginning. He has moved many, and his odyssey will bring changes in our lives.

I'll be in touch!

Naser

My God, I thought, tears welling in my eyes, *Shariati pushed his principles all the way to his own death, just like Imam Hussein.*

I soon learned that assassins had killed Dr. Shariati in his daughter's home. Such cruelty was so dishonorable. I vowed that I would not allow his words to die in my heart, immediately joining the Islamic Students' Association (ISA) in Los Angeles. The swelling unrest and changes sweeping my country seized our attention. Farzin and Mani, my friends in the ISA, held meetings at their house. We knew that the political tension in Iran was building. People had started to criticize the shah openly. This led to the SAVAK turning Iran into something very close to a police state, which in turn drew the wrath of the international community. When Jimmy Carter became president, he denied U.S. aid to Iran in protest over the shah's human rights violations. Consequently, the shah, in an effort to show the West he was making progress toward liberalizing his policies, released a few political prisoners.

He also assumed, incorrectly, that these token gestures would stop the protests. But the movement against him was already under way.

Iranians felt ready to sacrifice.

We needed a leader.

4

SHAH RAFT: THE REVOLUTION

WHEN MY FRIEND Mani at the Islamic Students' Association called to ask me to come to a meeting in the fall of 1978, he had an almost uncontrollable sense of excitement in his voice. To say the least, this intrigued me. I skipped my evening class and instead jumped in my car and rushed to his house. When I got there, I found a group of young Iranian students listening intently to a man's voice on a cassette tape. I asked someone what we were listening to and he told me to be quiet before returning his focus to the speech. Realizing that this had to be what had gotten Mani so excited, I listened as well.

"A nation that doesn't have freedom does not have civilization. A civilized nation is one that is free. . . ."

Some in the crowd uttered, "Yes."

"There should be freedom of the press and people should have the right to their opinion. . . ."

The people in the room grew more excited and I wondered about the man who was speaking. I couldn't recognize his voice. Had he become an important figure in Iran while I was away? Did Naser and Kazem know about him?

"This shah, this Yazid, this servant of America, this agent of Israel, needs to be overthrown and kicked out of Iran. . . ."

Many erupted in shouts of approval. I grew more excited myself; I loved what I was hearing. The speaker was incredibly bold, even comparing the shah to Yazid, the ruthless ruler who had ordered the death of Imam Hussein. Iranians view Yazid as one of the most despicable human beings of all time.

"We need an Islamic government, independent of the superpowers, where all Iranians enjoy the wealth and not a specific few. We want to improve not only your material life but also your spiritual life. They have taken our spirituality. We need spirituality. . . ."

He was speaking for all of us—for Kazem's people, for Naser's idealist family, for my spiritual grandmother.

"In our government, clergy will not govern but help you with your spirituality. In our government, women will be free, and officials can be publicly criticized. . . ."

These were the words of Ayatollah Ruhollah Khomeini, the man who would change Iran in ways we could only imagine then. He was a stirring speaker, even though he was not a great orator. He spoke plainly and sometimes repetitively. Yet his voice radiated a steadiness of purpose. His appeal was not intellectual. It was primal. Over the next few minutes, I would discover that he had inspired a movement in Iran, one that passed his tapes through the black market all over the world as if he were a rock star.

I had so many questions about him. I sought out Mani and Farzin, who were talking to each other at the corner of their kitchen.

"Glad you made it, Reza," Mani said.

Farzin beamed with excitement. "What did you think of Ayatollah Khomeini?"

I shook my head in wonder. "I could not believe what I was hearing. He is a true leader. His message of political freedom and equality is stunning. But where has he been?"

Mani told me that the shah first imprisoned the ayatollah in the early sixties because of his strong criticism of the government before exiling him to Najaf, Iraq. The ayatollah had been calling for the fall of the shah ever since. He was now in France after fourteen years in Najaf, and he had begun to talk to reporters from all over the world.

In the ensuing days I learned much more about him. I found an interview he gave to Reuters where he said, "The foundation of our Islamic government is based on freedom of dialogue and will fight against any kind of censorship. . . . In Islamic Iran the clergy themselves will not govern but only observe and support the government's leaders. The government of the country at all levels will be observed, evaluated, and publicly criticized."

To a German reporter, he said, "Our future society will be a free society, and all the elements of oppression, cruelty, and force will be destroyed. Women are free in the Islamic Republic in the selection of their activities and their future and their clothing. . . .

"I don't want to have the power or the government in my hand," he told *The Guardian*. "I am not interested in personal power."

His speeches and interviews gained traction. Soon it seemed as though everyone associated with Iran in any way was talking about him. I started to write Kazem and Naser a letter about him, but before I could complete it, one arrived from Kazem. As always, Kazem started his letter with, "In the name of God."

Salam, Reza jon,

I hope my letter reaches you in good health and happiness. I am sure the power of our spiritual leader has reached to that side of the world too. There is a lot happening here. We are close to a free Islamic society. Thousands of people are demonstrating throughout Iran. People are burning the flag and the shah's pictures in the streets. Reza, I wish you were here. Naser and I have joined the uprising against the shah. Ayatollah Khomeini is the leader we need. We receive his manifestos and people in all parts of our nation, rich or poor, religious or atheist, man or woman, young or old, are sharing a common voice. It is time for the shah to step down. I will keep you posted. Meanwhile, don't just sit there, man. Join this holy movement.

Kazem

Even though most Iranians had enjoyed varying degrees of success under the shah, Khomeini's message resonated with a population weary of oppression and desperate for the political choice they felt the shah denied them. They believed Ayatollah Khomeini could make us not only prosperous, but also free. I heard more from both Kazem and Naser. They seemed thrilled about what was happening in our country and I looked forward to returning home as soon as possible.

The rising tide crested on January 16, 1979, when the shah left the country along with his wife and children. The state-controlled media reported that he was leaving to seek cancer treatment in Egypt, but, in fact, his army was in mutiny and his citizens were rioting. Iran was no longer safe for him and his family.

We gathered at Farzin and Mani's house to see the news on television, watching with unrestrained joy as the shah's departing jet rose into the sky. Mohammad Reza Shah Pahlavi, the leader of Iran since 1941, had abandoned the country he had inherited from twenty-five hundred years of Persian monarchy. The television showed us hundreds of thousands of Iranians surging through the streets carrying Ayatollah Khomeini's picture and yelling: "Shah *raft!*" *The shah is gone!* Cars drove through the streets of Iran with headlights on, horns blaring. In LA we loudly echoed this sentiment. I'd never witnessed such a passionate celebration, and I wished I could have been there with my fellow citizens.

Two weeks after the shah left, Ayatollah Khomeini took a French plane back to Iran. Watching from America, I imagined what it must be like for this seventy-eight-year-old man to step on his home soil triumphantly after fourteen years of forced exile. Millions of people gathered at Mehrabad Airport in Tehran to welcome him and to show their love and support.

After circling the airport for more than twenty minutes for security purposes, the ayatollah's plane landed. I watched as Khomeini approached the microphone after a fanfare of welcoming songs and introductory speeches.

"We have to thank all classes of people of this nation. For this victory up to now has been due to the unity of voice, the unity of voice of all Muslims, the unity of all religious minorities, unity of scholars and students, unity of clergies and all political factions. We must all understand this secret: that the unity of voice is the cause for success and we must not lose this secret to success and, God forbid, not allow the devils to cause dissent among your ranks. I thank all of you and pray for your health and glory and ask Allah to cut off the hands of foreigners and their cohorts."

With that, he left the microphone to greet the millions who had come to declare themselves to him.

Khomeini promised the nation that no one would ever have to pay for such public utilities as electricity, water, telephone, and other services. He promised political freedom. The clergy would only improve the spiritual life of the people and would not interfere with the government. He also said that the people's share of oil money would be delivered to their doorsteps. In his first major speech to a huge crowd in Tehran, he criticized the shah for his oppression, invited all Iranians to join the revolution, and promised a government run by the people and for the people.

Who could believe that any man could bring about the fall of the shah, king of kings? This unknown cleric had toppled the Persian kingdom simply by speaking to the people, as the Prophet Mohammad had. He vowed to kick the U.S.A. out of Iran, calling it "the Great Satan." The man was afraid of nothing. Many truly believed God was on his side. And so, apparently, did he.

While we continued our support of the revolution at the ISA, some Iranians still loyal to the shah gathered on the streets of LA and other major cities in America to protest the rise of Khomeini and to demand the return of the shah. To oppose this, we marched down the streets of the city carrying posters of Khomeini and shouting, with fists in the air, "God is great! Khomeini is our leader!"

Inevitably, the two forces met. During one of our demonstrations, we ran into a crowd of Shah supporters furious that we were backing the ayatollah. "We are Persians with so much pride and dignity," said a middle-aged woman carrying an Iranian flag in one hand and a picture of Mohammad Reza Shah in the other. "We don't need a mullah to rule our country. He will destroy our kingdom and its dynasty. Did you hear what Khomeini said when an American reporter asked how he felt going back home? *Hichi!* He said he felt nothing." She shook her head. "How could you have no feeling for your country?" She turned her back to our crowd and waved her flag. "*Dorood bar shah.* Long live Shahanshah. Down with Khomeini."

Inside Iran, the grassroots movement forming behind Khomeini was so powerful that shah loyalists declared martial law. Thousands of Iranians galvanized by Khomeini's return demonstrated anyway, and soldiers opened fire on them. Citizens took up arms, rampaged on military bases, broke open the armories, and passed out military armaments to the people. A week after Khomeini's arrival in Iran, Kazem and Naser called me together. It was the first time they'd ever done that.

"We were at the Eshrat Abad Garrison today," Kazem said. "We forced them to surrender."

Then Naser jumped in. "We each got our J-three machine guns, Reza."

They were shouting, laughing, and talking at the same time. They had so much energy that I could barely understand them. "Wait, wait, guys. What's going on? One at a time."

Kazem explained that they were among the demonstrators attacking the garrisons around the city of Tehran. They forced the shah's soldiers out to the street and disarmed them. Meanwhile, others entered the facilities and took away the soldiers' weapons.

"The victory is upon us, Reza," Kazem said.

This had been a risky operation, but they were triumphant. I could not believe that my friends were among those willing to sacrifice their lives for a free Iran. I was proud of both of them. Naser, a secularist intellectual, and Kazem, a religious devotee, were acting as brothers in a common fight. They were representative of all of Iran for that brief, shining moment—in perfect agreement and acting as one. Every faction and ideology—religious, liberal, secularist, Marxist, or Communist—had rallied under Khomeini's banner. Within a couple of months, the provisional government held a national referendum. The question: Islamic Republic, yes or no? The lack of other options caused some to raise their eyebrows, but in the heady aftermath of Khomeini's return, 98 percent voted yes.

On April 1, Ayatollah Khomeini declared an Islamic Republic that reflected strong, traditional Islamist values. As a concession to liberal powers in the country, Khomeini appointed Mehdi Bazargan as the first prime minister of the Islamic Republic of Iran to show that he was upholding his promise to keep his clergymen away from positions of political power. Bazargan was the head of the Liberation Movement of Iran. Ali Shariati had been among its founders, and the party dedicated itself to gaining freedom, independence, and democracy for the Iranian nation based on a modern interpretation of Islamic principles. The shah's regime had jailed Bazargan many times, but he and his party maintained a code of civil disobedience and moderation. In fact, Bazargan had objected to calling Iran the "Islamic Republic" and wanted to call it the "Islamic Democratic Republic." We had every reason to believe he would rule fairly and evenhandedly.

I couldn't wait to get home, and in June of that year I did. At age twenty-five, I had a master's degree in systems engineering and I was eager to lend my expertise to the revolution. My mother, still mourning the death of my father three years earlier, had moved into a condominium in a high-rise and I chose to live there with her.

The day after my return, Naser picked me up in the red Impala convertible we used to drive without his father's knowledge. Since Naser was using it all of the time anyway, Davood finally just gave it to him. His brother, Soheil, and his sister, Parvaneh, were in the backseat.

"We're going to pick up Kazem and then we're going to get ice cream for us and crème caramel for Parvaneh, since that's her favorite. We're celebrating."

"What are we celebrating, Naser *jon*?" Parvaneh asked. Although she was fifteen, she was small for her age and looked like she was no older than eleven. Her hair was still curly, though her pigtails were longer than I remembered. She even acted younger than her age, swaying her arm back and forth through the open window without a care in the world, trying to catch the wind with her hand.

"My best friend is back from America," Naser said, smiling and glancing over at me. "That is a good reason. And our country is free—that is a better reason."

"If it's free, why can't I go to the college?" Soheil said sharply. "I want to attend the College of Fine Arts at the University of Tehran, and now there is a rumor that they are closing down all the universities."

Naser gestured to his brother to calm down. "It's not going to be that way, da Vinci. If they do close the universities, it'll only be for a short while." We couldn't know then that Naser was being overly optimistic. The next spring, the government shut down the universities for several years in what they called a cultural revolution to eradicate Western influence on the universities and bring them in line with Shiite Islam.

After we picked up Kazem, we roamed around Tehran. Everything seemed different to me. Yes, there were new high-rises and new highways. But what struck me most was the palpable spirit of the people. Some handed out flowers and candies. At the traffic lights they flashed victory signs and congratulated one another. In coming days I would see people from different political groups gathering in the universities or at corners around town discussing politics and religion openly and in peace. It felt like the beginning of a Persian Renaissance. I was convinced that we would soon show the world how to integrate religious idealism with modern values, as Shariati had envisioned. I imagined a future of creativity and innovation led by religious principle.

It was great to be back with Naser and Kazem. We met at my place or at Feris, a small café on the ground level beneath Mom's apartment. These days, we talked about nothing other than the revolution. Both of them were already contributing. Naser graduated as a civil engineer and got a good job working for a private company. Meanwhile, Kazem had impressed so many people in the Islamic Students' Association with his dedication that the Revolutionary Guards hired him and quickly promoted him to the secretive Intelligence Unit.

Kazem had grown a beard with a mustache neatly cut above his lips like so many other religious young men supporting the revolution. Among ideologues unwavering belief was powerful. That quality of certitude, rather than scholarship, experience, or qualifications, had made Khomeini our leader.

"Reza, this is where you should be," Kazem said of the Guards. "Your expertise with computers and your faith in the revolution are assets. Do you want me to talk to my commander and see if there is an opening for you?"

I thought this was a good idea, as I had to land a job soon and I wanted to contribute. He quickly arranged an interview for me with his commander.

"They need you, Reza. The Guards are in the process of installing a computer system in their bases around the country and are now hiring. I told them that you are their man."

The next day, I went to the Guards' base in the south of Tehran. Kazem's commander, Rahim, had an office at the end of a long narrow corridor on the first floor of one of the four-story buildings that formed the base. Rahim was a short, chubby man. Like Kazem, he wore a full beard and a trimmed mustache.

"*Salam,* Brother. Nice to meet you," he said when I entered his office.

As Kazem had instructed, I brought the papers documenting my education in America, including my master's degree. Rahim did not want to see any of these and asked only a few questions about my knowledge and skill. Instead, he focused his questions on my activities in America and my devotion to Islam and our leader. He wanted to know who I stayed with and associated with in America. I told him about my involvement with the ISA, about how I came to support Ayatollah Khomeini, and how moved I was by his passion for Iran and Islam. I told him about my parents and grandparents and, to leave him with the best possible impression, I told him how my grandmother had taught me to be a devoted Muslim.

"I am looking forward to contributing fully to the revolution," I said.

"We are proud of brothers like you who are back from abroad to serve the country. We need your expertise desperately for the Guards. You can start right away and, *inshallah,* you will do your utmost for the revolution."

I began work immediately and Kazem showed me the ropes. We were happy to be employed in the same place. He had the respect of insiders, and he vouched for me at every turn. Kazem believed in me, and I was proud to have his respect. I felt as though fortune had shined upon me.

But soon a shadow descended. In the early morning of November 4, 1979, two months after I'd been hired, Kazem came to my office and said, "Come on, we're going over to the American Embassy. There is a demonstration going on in opposition to America allowing the shah into their country."

I got up from my desk immediately. All of us were angry that President Carter had given the shah sanctuary in the U.S. under the guise of getting him the best cancer treatment. We wanted our tyrant back here so we could put him on trial. I would happily participate in this demonstration.

We drove twenty minutes northeast to the U.S. Embassy. There we found hundreds of demonstrators gathered in front chanting slogans and carrying signs. They were mostly students, though I could see some older women in black chador veils. The press was there, of course, and men with megaphones incited the crowd. Emotions escalated to the point where most of the demonstrators began shouting, "Death to America!" Kazem joined in, lifting his fist into the air, and hollering, *"Marg bar Amrika."*

This made me uncomfortable. My years in America had been good ones and I had become quite fond of the American people. I was here to protest a policy, not call for the death of America. At the same time, though, I felt the need to express solidarity, so I chanted along with them. The chants of those near me reached a crescendo whenever news cameras were aimed in our direction.

"Reza, look!" Kazem said, pointing. I stopped shouting as I saw people climbing the walls and front gate of the embassy and dropping down inside. The only embassy guard I saw couldn't bring himself to shoot. He chose to run inside instead. Somebody managed to break the chain on the gate, and protesters swarmed onto what was officially U.S. property. I later learned that a woman had hidden a chain cutter beneath her chador. The intruders fanned out in different directions, as if they knew exactly where they were going.

I stood next to Kazem with mouth agape. This was not a rout. It was not an act of passion. It seemed too managed for that. The people who rushed in seemed to know one another and to know what to do. Military members of the Guards arrived quickly. I wondered how they heard about the break-in so fast. Then the Komiteh, the religious police recently given official status by Khomeini, came and promised to keep order. But the only thing they kept orderly was the takeover itself. Busloads of people arrived and joined the demonstration, another sign that this gathering was not spontaneous. Within minutes, the protesters controlled the compound.

I was uneasy at the cameras filming. Wasn't this against international law? I knew the media would display this all over the world. What if my face ended up on TV? What would Johnny and Alex think?

The protesters marched out of the embassy shouting, with their hands raised in victory signs as they brought out a blindfolded American with his hands tied. My stomach churned. I remembered visiting this very embassy to receive my student visa. The consul general received me so well that day. He even joked with me, encouraging me to pursue my studies but also have fun. Back then, not that long ago, Iranians and Americans shared a mutual affection. Americans had treated me as one of their own while I was there.

Now, all around me, I saw hatred spewing from the mouths of revolutionaries I thought were my brothers and sisters in a good cause. This shook me to my core. We could not respond to tyranny by tyrannizing Americans. We represented liberation, not kidnapping.

This wasn't the first extreme act I'd witnessed. Fanatics had blown up the mausoleum of the shah's father and replaced it with a public toilet. Hundreds had been put in front of firing squads without getting the chance to defend themselves by Ayatollah Khalkhali, the chief justice of the newly formed Revolutionary Courts, in response to the Kurdistan uprising. I'd read about the execution of the shah's military officers, even those who had surrendered honorably without firing a shot on their own people. Still, I had managed to convince myself that this was temporary mayhem after the revolution.

But witnessing this embassy takeover was a slap in the face. Here a fanatical minority was exerting its will on a reasonable majority. I had to allow myself to consider that the temporary mayhem might not be temporary at all. Radicalism seemed to be taking over. At that moment, I began to wonder if my visions for the future were nothing but illusions.

We remained outside the embassy until nightfall. Candles were passed among us. Smiling at me with his candle throwing a beatific glow on his face, Kazem told me that the whole takeover had been planned ahead of time with Khomeini's secret approval. The leaders of the invasion had even dubbed the embassy "the den of spies" for the media.

I didn't know how to tell Kazem what I felt about the radical actions we had just witnessed. I didn't see why loving Iran required me to hate Americans. Fortunately, he never asked me. My guess is that he thought I was as much of a true believer as he was. A purist like Kazem couldn't imagine how a fellow revolutionary would feel anything but joy at this moment. "This is the power of Islam," he said that night. "Even a superpower must kneel before it."

My candle kept blowing out in the breeze, and Kazem kept relighting it with his. I vowed to try to hold on to my faith in the revolution even though what was happening was not Shariati's vision for our nation. I convinced myself that Prime Minister Bazargan would not stand by and let this happen.

A couple of days later, Bazargan's cabinet resigned en masse in protest over the hostage takeover. The prime minister ordered the hostages released, yet the government was powerless to enforce its decrees over extremists who answered only to Khomeini and called the incident "the second revolution." Bazargan had no choice but to resign, humiliated. With his resignation, all hopes for a liberal democracy died. It was Khomeini's country now.

Never before had a Middle East leader made a major decision without considering how the superpowers would react. Here Khomeini displayed his first sign of genius for playing the superpowers against each other. Guards insiders told me that Jimmy Carter had instructed U.S. General Robert E. Huyser to order Iranian generals not to stage a coup to reinstate the shah. Carter's foreign policy team was worried about the Soviets taking over in Afghanistan and reasoned that nothing would hold more strongly against a Communist state in Afghanistan than an Islamist state in Iran next door. The Guards told me that Khomeini understood all this. But he wanted both capitalists and communists out, so he played to their hopes and fears, becoming the puppeteer of two superpowers. In the chess match of the Cold War, the pawn was manipulating the players under the rallying cry "We are neither capitalists nor communists. We are Islamists." This cleric was overthrowing kings, seizing control from superpowers, and fomenting revolution in Iran simply by talking. The madness he inspired in my fellow citizens chilled my blood.

The only revolutionary force that refused to turn in their weapons when Khomeini called for them was the Mujahedin. The People's Mujahedin of Iran was a religious socialist group formed in 1965 to oppose the shah. The Mujahedin based many of their beliefs on Ali Shariati's writings, including the assertion that Mohammad strove for a classless commonwealth. Naser sympathized with them as a reaction against the mullahs, and he began to spend time with students aligned with the organization. Anti-shah, anti-West, and fierce fighters, now the Mujahedin turned their violence against Khomeini, and could match him fanatic for fanatic. During the shah's reign, they'd gone so far as to assassinate U.S. civilians and military personnel working in Iran. Now they were demanding a share of the power, since they saw themselves as having contributed to the overthrow of the shah. However, Khomeini barred Massoud Rajavi, the leader of the Mujahedin, from running in the first presidential election, Khomeini loyalists concentrated attacks against the organization, and things got progressively uglier from there. The Mujahedin organized demonstrations that turned into clashes with the new government's forces.

The ideological split between the clerics and the socialists drove a wedge between Naser and Kazem that made our once friendly meetings a study in conflict avoidance. For a long time, they didn't confront each other, but when we got together for our New Year in March 1980, Kazem could keep his silence no more. He said that the Mujahedin's violence and demonstrations were desecrating the revolution. Naser countered that the heavy-handed governing of Khomeini's clergy was a betrayal of the revolution. The argument continued to escalate.

"Political freedom and power should be shared among different political parties," Naser argued. "That stupid referendum making Iran an Islamic Republic was a sham. They gave the people no choice whatever. What kind of choice do you really have voting either for or against it? You still get the mullahs ruling the country."

"Imam Khomeini is leading this nation into prosperity and preserving the rights of Iranians against the interference of foreign powers," Kazem responded. Kazem, and other followers like him, had begun to call Ayatollah Khomeini an imam, a saintly leader. "Islam is the only way to purity, and you're going to lose your soul if you're not careful, Naser. Islamic values should be instilled in people, and all the decadence the shah introduced should be abolished."

"Islamic values!" Naser protested. "What happened to the promise of freedom of dialogue? Is arresting the opposition and throwing them in prison for having different views part of Islamic values? I am sure you know about Khomeini's henchman, Khalkhali, executing all the army officers that served under the shah. You call that value—killing people without giving them a trial?"

"They had people's blood on their hands," Kazem said angrily.

I tried to arbitrate, pleading that they both had good points and that the revolution needed time. Neither listened.

"This is the beginning of fascism and you're an idiot for not seeing," Naser said to Kazem bitterly. "You are blind, Kazem, and people like you will cause this nation to suffer more."

My dear friend stood and headed for the front door, unable to stand my other dear friend's presence a moment longer. Before leaving, Naser turned to say something. But rather than doing so, he waved his hand in disappointment and whispered, "Forget it."

Then he slammed the door behind him and left.

5

THE INVINCIBLE IMAM

AS KAZEM AND I continued our work at the Revolutionary Guards base in Tehran, I became worried when he never spoke to me about that argument with Naser. I'd never seen the two of them fight like that before. They hadn't seen each other in a month and I wanted to get them in the same room so I could explain that the core ideals of the revolution transcended our differences. We just needed to give the revolution time to unite us in our shared commitment to a just society.

But I wasn't as certain about this as I had once been. When I traveled through the country, I saw the crack in my personal life mirrored in others. Many people were angry with their loved ones for their political beliefs. How could I have known then that this acrimony was only the barest hint of the horrors to come?

I decided to go to Kazem's office to talk to him about getting together with Naser. It was early in the morning and he hadn't arrived yet. I left a note for him to call me. An hour later, he rushed breathlessly into my office saying, "Reza, Reza, have you heard what happened?" He caught his breath. "The Americans have invaded!"

He said this with such joy that I wondered if I'd misheard him. Why would he be this thrilled about an American invasion? And then he told me.

"They've already been crushed! God created a sandstorm to defeat them! They crashed in the desert!"

"What are you talking about, Kazem? What crashed in the desert?"

"Helicopters, planes, everything. Brothers have already been dispatched to secure the area."

He turned a chair backward and sat facing me. "They came here on a mission to rescue the embassy spies. A sandstorm came up." Kazem took another deep breath. I thought he might hyperventilate. "The whole invasion fleet crashed in the desert."

"My God," I said in disbelief.

Kazem didn't hear it that way, of course. He interpreted my exclamation as praise to God. "*Allaho Akbar.* They were struck down as they approached Tehran."

I couldn't tell him I agreed with most Iranians, who wanted the hostages freed. As was so often the case now, I found myself measuring my comments in his presence. I never had to do that before we joined the Guards. I realized that broaching reconciliation between Naser and him would be fruitless at this point. All he could think about right now was the "miracle" that had happened in the desert.

When I got home that night, I found my mom glued to the TV, stunned over President Carter's attempt to sneak specially trained forces across the desert into Tehran under cover of night. I learned that the high-tech operation landed on a secret abandoned highway in the middle of the desert in Tabas, about five hundred miles east of Tehran. Immediately, a busload of poor families discovered them, driving up to stare at the helicopters and commandos with night-vision goggles. So much for sneaking into Tehran. The would-be rescuers took these forty-three Iranians hostage and searched their sparse belongings for any signs of threat.

Then the sandstorm came. Three helicopters were unable to take off because of this, forcing the soldiers to abort the operation. While refueling in order to flee, a helicopter crashed into a gigantic transport plane, igniting the ammunition and fuel in a fireworks display that rained bullets. Eight commandos died, scores more were wounded, and every vehicle received some level of damage. While Iranians slept in their beds, the weather defeated the greatest military machine in the world. The Revolutionary Guards didn't even know the country had been invaded until after the invasion had already failed.

My mother got up and turned down the volume on the television. "I don't know what to feel now. This is a treacherous act by the Americans. But what other choice have the mullahs left for them. The mullahs took innocent people hostage for no other reason than dirty political games. God help us all if these mullahs are always so lucky." She did not wait to hear my thoughts, turning to go to bed.

The next night, Ayatollah Khomeini claimed that God had created the sandstorm to defeat the Great Satan and called upon the people to go to their rooftops and shout *"Allaho Akbar"* at the heavens. Quickly, the swell of voices rose joyously in every corner of the city.

My mother was not home that night, so I decided to go up on the rooftop to see what was going on. It was an eerie scene. I watched as some neighbors turned out their lights, pretending they were not home while the Khomeini followers screamed *"Allaho Akbar"* into the night, their homes ablaze with light.

The feelings of those on the rooftops were abundantly clear. I wondered about those who chose to cower in the dark, though. Were they wondering how this ayatollah was able to accomplish the impossible so consistently? Less than two years before, he'd ordered a king from his throne. Then he made President Carter scurry to appease him. Now he was calling forth sandstorms to defeat our enemies and protect our cities. What more proof did they need that God was on his side?

Meanwhile, Kazem and Naser still hadn't spoken and the chances became dimmer that they ever would. In the months that followed, the clashes between Khomeini loyalists and the Mujahedin escalated to a terrifying pitch. Hezbollahi—"those from the Party of God"—attacked the meeting places and businesses of the Mujahedin, provoking just the sort of violence that the Guards needed to move in and violently pacify. At work I heard congratulatory talk among my brothers of their rounding up Mujahedin members and taking them to the dreaded Evin Prison, where the shah's SAVAK had once hosted torture sessions.

One day in June, I stopped by Kazem's office to talk to him about a minor work-related issue. I'd barely sat down when he said, "I think it would be a good idea if you talk to Naser."

"Naser?" I said, hoping he was asking me to broker a reunion.

"Tell him to stop hanging around people associated with the Mujahedin. He's going to end up in Evin Prison."

I swallowed. Kazem worked in the Intelligence Unit. He must have heard something. Was Naser's name coming up during interrogations?

"You know how stubborn he is, Reza," Kazem said, breaking through my skittish thoughts. "You need to talk some sense into him."

"He's just a sympathizer, Kazem. He's not involved in any demonstrations or any of the violence."

"You and I both know the authorities won't make that distinction. If he's arrested at a Mujahedin meeting, my brothers in the Intelligence Unit will treat him as any other betrayer."

"But can't you vouch for him?"

When Kazem broke eye contact, I detected worry in his voice. "He'll listen to you, Reza."

I rushed home, thankful that Kazem still treasured his friendship with Naser enough to give me this warning. I vowed that I would get through to Naser and make him rethink his actions. As soon as I got home, I called Naser and told him that I needed to see him.

He arrived at my mother's condo a short while later. When he entered and saw the look on my face, he knew immediately why I'd asked him over. "Kazem said something to you, didn't he?"

I motioned for him to sit down and sat across from him, leaning forward as I did so. "Kazem told me he still considers you a friend, Naser. He asked me to talk to you. You're on a dangerous path with these guys. I respect that you believe what you believe. I admit that some in the government are abusing their power. But the Mujahedin are not the answer, either. They are fighting for power, too."

Naser's eyes flashed anger. "Reza, have you forgotten what Shariati taught us? We must stand up for what's right, even at the cost of our own lives. If you don't say what you believe about this madman, you're complicit in evil."

I held out a hand, as though trying to reach through to him. "Look, this is not just about saving a friendship. Kazem works in the Intelligence Unit. He must have heard something specific—about you."

Naser stood up and paced around my mother's living room. "Look around, Reza. Everything is changing. Banning the opposition parties, shutting down the universities, attacking whoever disagrees with them. They're taking our rights away. They're arresting innocent people for nothing more than reading a flyer."

I tried to calm him down, attempting to soothe my own rattled nerves at the same time. "We're in a transition, and change is always difficult. Maybe you should be more careful. Things will get better, you'll see."

Naser took a moment before speaking again. When he did, there was pain in his voice. "I wish I felt the same way, Reza. I don't want to argue with you, but if people don't speak up now, it will only get worse."

We didn't say much to each other after that. It was obvious that I wasn't going to be able to change his mind, and if that were the case, I couldn't simply pass the time with him as though nothing was going on. An image of one of the carefree pranks we'd played as boys came into my head and tore at my heart.

Before he left that night, Naser smiled at me and said, *"Bi-khialesh."* He was telling me to let it be. Naser's courage, which I once admired, now seemed reckless. Writing letters in defiance of the shah's censors was one thing. Being seen with rebels targeted for torture by the government was another.

My mother had stayed in the kitchen the entire time Naser was at the apartment, not wanting to get in our way. Now she came into the living room with a cup of tea in her hand. She had a bitter smile on her face and she was shaking her head.

"Things will get better," she said in a tone that mocked the conciliatory message I had tried to send Naser. "For who? For the mullahs?"

I didn't say anything. The conversation with Naser had left me spent.

"I need to go to Agha Joon's. Please take me there."

I nodded, and we prepared to go. Before we left the apartment, my mother took a scarf and covered her hair. "A lifetime of freedom, and now I have to cover myself or be confronted by those Hezbollahi thugs," she said darkly.

In the elevator, we ran into one of my mother's neighbors. A retired teacher who once supported Khomeini, he looked at me with disgust because he knew I worked for the Guards. He smiled at my mother, though. "*Salam,* Mrs. Kahlili." He looked at the scarf on my mom's hair. "I hope to God that these mullahs will be kicked out of our country soon and we'll all be free."

Mom looked up and whispered, "Hope to God."

It had been only one year and four months since a million devotees met Khomeini at the airport and already many Iranians were hoping for the overthrow of his regime. Brigadier General Ayat Mohagheghi, a highly decorated air force commander, tried to turn that hope into action but he instead served as another example of the omnipotence of the imam.

I first heard of the incident the way I heard about most things: from Kazem. The public would learn about it the next day. I walked into a hallway to see Guards rushing about excitedly and ran into Kazem.

"What's going on?" I asked.

Kazem's eyes shone. "The air force pilots tried to stage a coup. But Imam Khomeini found out and squashed it! God is great, Reza. The brothers moved in to arrest these traitors. I'll keep you informed."

He rushed off to attend to his intelligence business, leaving me stunned.

I pieced together the whole story from bits and snatches of gossip among my brothers in the Guards. Iran's best fighter pilots and paratroopers, led by General Mohagheghi, planned to fly F-14 Tomcats from the Shahrokhi Air Base in Hamadan and bomb strategic military targets. They also planned to drop seven hundred and fifty pounds of cluster bombs on Ayatollah Khomeini's home in Jamaran, which was only a six-minute flight from the air base. Another team of officers was to take over the radio/television building in Tehran and announce that a new Western-style democracy was in control. The night of the coup, Guards stormed the conspirators' camps. Every officer arrested was tortured but refused to give the names of those few who escaped.

Khomeini was there to save the revolution once again. Later, the government radio station announced that the mother of one of the officers had turned them in, so loyal was she to the Islamic Republic.

The gathering at my grandparents' house that week was limited to watching the trial of those officers. Naser and Davood were there, as well as my mother and many of my aunts and uncles. My relatives wanted to pull out their hair from frustration over what might have been. "How can this happen?" my grandfather said. "How can professional air force pilots and decorated generals be outwitted by these mullahs?"

The inquisitors brought Mohagheghi before the cameras freshly beaten. Hojatoleslam Reyshahri, a theologian and the chief judge of the Military Revolutionary Tribunal, questioned him. Despite the general's unshaven face and haggard appearance, and though he faced torture the day before and the specter of execution the following day, he looked self-assured and movie-star handsome as he sat in a white short-sleeved summer shirt. Without shame, he explained why his duty compelled him to stage a coup.

"What right does this imbecile mullah have to act like the moral superior to a general?" demanded Agha Joon. "This pervert married the daughter of Ayatollah Ali Meshkini when she was nine!"

Reyshahri wanted the officers to confess that they were mere puppets in a plot by Israel or the U.S. They each stated that they acted on their own initiative, not out of corruption by foreign agents, but out of their sacred oath to protect the Iranian people. "My decision to participate in the plot stemmed from my disillusionment in the face of what was happening to my family and country," Mohagheghi said unwaveringly.

Those words resonated with me more than anything from Khomeini or even Shariati. Mohagheghi didn't plan the coup to attain paradise. He didn't do it to mimic Imam Hussein. He did it out of compassion for his people.

"Imagine," said Davood, finally breaking our somber silence, "if we had awakened that morning and heard these men had taken our country back."

"And killed the mullahs," my mother spat.

When the camera panned back to show all the unshaved faces of the officers, Davood said, "I wonder which one of their mothers turned them in?" his voice dripping with loathing.

My grandfather waved his hand angrily at the television. "It's the new propaganda these dogs are peddling, congratulating mothers who turn in their children and children who turn in their parents. Anyone who puts Khomeini above his own family is lauded as a hero."

"They'll even execute their own children if they're associated with the Mujahedin," Davood added.

I shot a glance at Naser, who was leaning back in his chair with his arms folded defiantly.

"It's all nonsense," Agha Joon grumbled. "No mother of an F-14 pilot would turn him in because she's loyal to Khomeini. It must have been the British who informed the mullahs."

"Here we go with the British again," said Davood.

Davood and Agha Joon had a long tradition of reading between the lines of state-controlled newscasts in search of the real story. Kazem, Naser, and I had many times listened to their debates for entertainment.

"It behooves the British to keep the mullahs in power," said Agha Joon, "so the country will go backward hundreds of years while they take advantage of our oil reserves. Keep people hypnotized with religion. Instill fear. You think the mullahs overthrew the shah by themselves?"

Davood shook his head. "It's not always the British. We have new superpowers now. I think it's the Russians. They always wanted to influence Iran, and they are one of the main causes of the shah's downfall. Now they are trying to protect this new regime."

Naser moved forward in his chair. "Why would the West—or even the East for that matter—want Iran to progress when they can take advantage of our oil while having stupid people rule the country? It's up to us to protect our rights and control our own future."

"The first step," my mother said, "is to get rid of the mullahs."

No one was addressing the elephant in the room: me. I was sitting on the couch, feeling sad for the officers, yet wearing a beard to show my commitment to traditional religious values and leaving for work every day as a member of the Revolutionary Guards. Every time my mother called those who still supported the revolution "donkeys," "jackals," "traitors," and "imbeciles," she was including me—whether she meant to or not—with those who supported the revolution. My mother was secular to the point of agnosticism. She did not pray. She was no fan of the shah, but she hated the mullahs. And there sat her only son, a sorry-ass symbol of tyranny.

Only Grandma had a smile on her face, walking in and out of the room serving food and then tea and dessert, telling everyone not to make themselves upset over politics. "This too shall pass," she said. "As all things do."

She was intervening on my behalf. Khanoom Bozorg was protective of me and gently inserted her kindness between her grandson and her daughter-in-law without angering anyone. She was proud of my education and the fact that I still did my prayers just as she had taught me.

"Say a prayer that the pilots will not be executed," she said, patting my cheek with her wrinkled hand. I remember smiling sadly at her kind face, knowing prayers of that sort were not answered anymore.

For the first time, I felt uncomfortable putting on my uniform the next morning. A beaming Kazem greeted me at work, eager to share the joy that God had stepped in to save Khomeini and vanquish the traitors. The rising confidence among my brothers in the Guards was palpable. They all knew they were going to heaven and they would be glad to die for Khomeini.

I sat amid the celebration vacillating between two forces—the invincibility of Khomeini and the humanity of my family—pulling my heart in different directions. Everyone I knew was committed to something. Only I was indecisive.

I later learned from one of my relatives in the air force that intelligence provided by the Soviets to Iran's Foreign Ministry had alerted Imam Khomeini to the coup attempt. Davood was right. Nothing happens in an oil-rich nation without the superpowers meddling.

When Agha Joon read in the newspaper of the execution by firing squad of every air force officer, he got up from his seat and walked in his garden, muttering, "Today the best of Iran has been executed by the worst." He then bent over, caressing one of his roses, and whispered, "How history hinges on the smallest details."

6

A FUNERAL AND
A WEDDING

MY GRANDFATHER'S HEARTBREAK grew deeper when Khanoom Bozorg passed away in the summer of 1980. My grandmother was the foundation of our family, and in that time of restless uncertainty, she was the one who held us all together. I knew I was going to miss her horribly and that many things would never be the same with her gone.

More than a hundred people attended her memorial service, including many I'd never met before. This shouldn't have surprised me. My grandmother loved people and she was always making new friends. She was also very proud of her home, so she was constantly having new people over. I tried to greet everyone who came to the service and to interact with them, sharing our memories of this vibrant woman. Ultimately, though, I chose to sit alone by the fishpond, grieving and thinking about everything she'd meant to me. Khanoom Bozorg didn't allow me to get away with much, but she made me a much better person than I ever would have been otherwise, and I knew I needed to consider the impact she had on my life and how I would carry her example with me for the rest of my years.

While I sat in silence, a young woman caught my eye. She was sitting next to my mother, engaged in conversation. And she was beautiful. So beautiful that I couldn't stop looking at her, even through the haze of my grief. Every time she smiled while talking with my mother, my pulse quickened. As the memorial continued, guests came toward me to offer their condolences, but I couldn't keep my eyes on those people; I was too busy searching for her.

Agha Joon, who was also in the yard welcoming and thanking guests, came over and sat next to me. He was an observant man and I was afraid that he saw me staring at the woman. This shamed me, because I didn't want him to think that I'd stopped thinking of my grandmother because of a pretty face.

"Khanoom Bozorg had a dream for you, Reza *jon*," he said, putting his arm around my shoulder. "She loved you even more than her own children. Do you see that nice girl next to your mom? Her name is Somaya." He smiled. "Her grandma and Khanoom Bozorg were close friends. Khanoom Bozorg had her in mind for you. She even talked to Somaya's grandma about you. You know how women are. All they want to do is to hook young people up with each other. That's a good thing, isn't it?"

I didn't know what to say to this. Fortunately, my grandfather wasn't looking for a response. He kissed my head, gave me a nudge, and said we should have a chat about Somaya when the moment was right.

Somaya!

On the way home, I asked Mom to tell me more about her. My mother said that Somaya's Lebanese father was a British citizen and that he and her Iranian mother split their time between London and Tehran, where her grandmother and most of their Iranian relatives lived.

As clichéd as it might sound, I fell in love with Somaya the instant I saw her. Thoughts of her filled my head. Over the next few days, I would call her name in my daydreams. Whenever I closed my eyes, I saw her smile. My stomach felt delightfully uneasy. I knew I needed to have her in my life.

I wasn't surprised when Agha Joon dropped by for a visit a few days later and announced that he would arrange a meeting with Somaya's parents while they were still in the country. He wanted to make Khanoom Bozorg's wish come true by asking Somaya's parents for their daughter's hand for me. I realized with horror that he planned to go *khastegari* for me. Going *khastegari* was like arranging a marriage. It was an old-fashioned thing to do and I did not want Somaya to think of me as an old-fashioned suitor. I told Agha Joon I was uncomfortable with this.

"Can't I just ask for her number?" I pleaded.

"We have to go *khastegari* first," he said, adopting the tone of the grand patriarch of our family. "I know Somaya's grandmother and her parents. They are very traditional, and to respect their customs we should tell them that your intentions are pure and moral. I know you've grown used to American ways, but this is the way it is done in this country. At least *some* families still do it this way. If her parents agree, then you can go out on dates, get to know her, and do it your *American* way." He patted my back, lifted his prominent eyebrows, and, with a big smile, made it clear that I had no other option.

Moheb Khan, Somaya's dad, agreed to the meeting and told Agha Joon they looked forward to getting to know me. On the day of *khastegari,* Agha Joon and Mom accompanied me to Somaya's grandmother's house. As part of the *khastegari* tradition, the intended bride did not attend the initial phase of the gathering. While we waited, Agha Joon regaled Somaya's family with stories about my limitless abilities and glorious plans for the future. This made me squirm.

"Reza *jon* is a family man, just like his dad. A good son to his father, he will be a good father to his son. As you know, he is a graduate from a fine university in California. USS, isn't that right, Reza *jon?*"

"USC, Grandpa," I said, embarrassed.

"Of course, USC. Reza has never wasted his life and he is destined to make a good living for his future wife, providing whatever she wishes."

I tuned out Agha Joon's ceaseless praise. All I wanted at that moment was to see Somaya. I'd heard that women liked their men to pass some kind of test to prove their affections. Certainly my bearing up to the embarrassment of my grandfather's bragging had to show the depth of my commitment to her.

When Somaya finally entered the living room carrying a tray of tea, the room went quiet. Gently and elegantly, she offered tea to each guest, from the oldest to the youngest. I could not stop looking at her, but she didn't look directly at me. She was wearing a green satin blouse that enhanced the dark green color of her eyes. Her long black hair shone like smooth silk around her neck, and her shy and innocent smile made my heart beat faster.

She came toward me with the tray and the last cup of tea, offering it without looking at me. Her smile was even more magical up close. I found her so captivating that I was afraid I would drop the tea and make a fool of myself. When I hesitated, she glanced up. I knew at that moment that the clever girl had noticed me admiring her at the memorial, somehow without ever looking back at me. The gleam in her eyes made me realize that I would be the luckiest man on the planet if I could convince her to be next to me for the rest of my life.

Our families met one more time and then, trusting that I was a responsible young man, Somaya's parents agreed that we could go out on dates. At first the dates took place in her grandmother's living room, but at least her grandmother allowed us to be alone. Somaya talked about her life and friends in England, saying that she mostly socialized with her father's side of the family. She visited Lebanon occasionally and finished school in London. But she adored her grandmother and longed to spend more time in Iran, as the rich culture and hospitality of the Iranian people fascinated her. I told her that I loved people who were multicultural. She smiled and said that she was glad we went *khastegari* first, as she also believed in the traditional ways. My grandfather found it especially satisfying when I told him about that last part later.

As I began to spend time with Somaya, I fell in love with her beyond my control. Eventually, her family allowed us to go out together, and I took her to parks, restaurants, and the movies. At some point, I realized that she had fallen in love with me as well and I knew that our marriage would be everything I could have dreamed.

To respect Grandma's passing and Agha Joon's grief, Somaya and I agreed to wait a year to get married. But Agha Joon insisted that because Somaya and I seemed so happy together, it would have been my grandmother's wish to see us marry sooner. I knew he wished the same. I also knew that since my grandmother's passing, my grandfather had been thinking more about his own mortality. While he didn't specifically say this, I believe he was worried that he wouldn't be at the wedding if we waited an entire year. That would have devastated me, so following his prompting, Somaya and I married only a few months after we first met.

Agha Joon insisted that the wedding take place at his house. This delighted both Somaya and me. We held a big ceremony in Grandpa's beloved garden and it felt as though new life were blooming in that spot where so many plants had flourished. I found this deeply encouraging. Despite the end of the ancient Persian monarchy, and despite the crisis after the revolution, the Iranian people could still fall in love and celebrate.

Everybody was there, just as when we were kids. Naser and Kazem attended, careful to avoid each other. That they declared a truce to be with me on this blissful occasion touched me. Although Kazem came alone, Naser came with his parents and siblings. He was also holding hands with a woman I'd never seen before. Though he hadn't said a word to me about her, they had to be serious if she was coming to an event like this with his family.

Naser and the woman approached us. He had a huge smile on his face. "So you finally tied the knot," he said, hugging me and kissing Somaya's hand. "Congratulations to both of you. Especially you, Reza. You are a very lucky man."

Somaya blushed. "We are both lucky."

Naser put his arm around his guest's shoulder. "This is Azadeh."

I shook her hand and said hello. Then I turned toward Naser. "And . . . ?"

"And we are dating." He glanced over at Azadeh with deep affection in his eyes, and this warmed me. When Azadeh complimented Somaya and her gown and started asking about wedding details, I pulled him aside.

"What's going on? Is it serious? I saw your mom and dad all over her. This looks like more than *dating* to me."

Naser laughed broadly. "I guess that makes two of us with a leash around our necks! She is such a great girl, Reza. I think I am in love."

Azadeh reminded me of my cousin Haleh, whom Naser had a crush on when we were kids. She had the same hairstyle and a similar smile. Naser had always been so casual about romance; it was amazing to see him looking at this woman with such devotion. I felt so happy that Naser was with someone who made him feel this way. I allowed myself to believe that maybe love could conquer ideology after all, and I wished at that moment for Kazem to find romance, too.

The party was joyous. Naser's father, Davood, as he had on so many occasions, sang for us and led us in dance. Naser and Azadeh danced together the entire night. For those hours, life was as simple and untroubled as it had been when we were children.

But the outside world would never allow this peaceful satisfaction to continue. The last hopes of shah loyalists had already been extinguished when Mohammad Reza Shah Pahlavi died of cancer in Egypt in July 1980. An imperial tradition that had begun in 500 BC with Cyrus the Great was now fully at its end.

"Allaho Akbar!" some people cried in the streets. "God is great!"

Agha Joon denounced this celebration of Khomeini followers. "Shame on this nation," he said, "to have the last king of kings die in exile like a gypsy."

And then on September 22, 1980, just two weeks after my wedding to Somaya, Iraq attacked Iran, raining bombs on several targets, including our city. I was at work with Kazem when several explosions shook the walls. Concerned that the ceiling would fall on us, we ran into the courtyard, confused. Soon, our commanders told us that Iraqi planes had attacked several Iranian airports to disable the air force's ability to launch. The bombs did minimal damage, however.

Soon after the invasion, Imam Khomeini appeared on television to announce, *"Etefaghi nayoftadah, dozdi amadah va sangi andakhte":* "Nothing important has happened." It was just a thief throwing stones. The country breathed a communal sigh of relief. However, the next day Kazem informed me that Saddam had attacked with six army divisions on three fronts. These divisions were, at that very moment, moving quickly into Iranian territory.

This news chilled me, though I could not have realized at the time that this would mark the beginning of an eight-year-long war. Or that half a million Iranians would die in the conflict before it was over.

The violent rivalry between Arabs and Persians was centuries old, stemming from the Muslim conquest of Persia, where Arabs defeated the Sassanid Empire, ending the dynasty of Sassanid and the practice of the Zoroastrian religion in Persia. Saddam seized upon our moment of vulnerability to launch his attack. Our government, having just executed all of the leading military commanders who served under the shah, had no trained generals, and it was using revolutionaries instead. In addition, we ousted not only the shah but his superpower ally with him. The American hostage crisis isolated Iran from the rest of the civilized world and the Mujahedin seemed determined to hurl our country into a guerrilla war. In the uproar and chaos, Saddam saw his chance to become the dominant oil power in the Middle East and to seize the oil fields near his border with our country.

Like all aggressors, Saddam claimed he was preemptively attacking in defense. His Sunni regime worried that the Islamic Revolution was spreading like an infection to the oppressed Shiite majority in his own country. In fact, an Iraqi version of Khomeini had emerged among the emboldened Shiites, a mullah named Muhammad Baqir al-Sadr, who preached the Islamic religion in a style similar to Kho-meini's. Saddam executed him as soon as al-Sadr's voice rose above the crowd. When the U.S. passed satellite intelligence to Saddam that suggested that Iranian forces would collapse quickly if attacked, Saddam launched his offensive.

The September 22 attack was our Pearl Harbor. Imam Khomeini asked every male Muslim who could walk to volunteer to defend God's government. Heeding the call were army officers, Guards, normal citizens, and—most fearsome of all—Basij, a paramilitary force with boys as young as thirteen. Two hundred thousand un-trained volunteers—a far larger militia than the number of trained servicemen we had—arrived at the front within months and met the Iraqi invaders. Since the Guards and Iran's soldiers operated sepa-rately, there was no coordination of movements among our troops. But we soon learned that Basijis—many of whom were adolescents infatuated with martyrdom—could not be defeated by mere tanks and machine guns.

A short time after the first Iraqi attack, the Foreign Ministry an-nounced they were closing the airports and that no one could travel outside the country except foreign nationals, Iranians studying abroad, and Iranians with residential status in a foreign country who had been in Iran less than six months. Those who qualified stood in long lines to secure permission to leave. Somaya's parents were anx-ious to get out of a country under attack, and I asked Kazem to call his contacts in the Foreign Ministry to facilitate their departure.

My in-laws did not want to leave their only child in Iran during a war that was intensifying every day. I could sympathize with them. I told Somaya that I would feel better if she left with her parents, and I promised that I would visit her in England as often as I could. She refused flatly, telling me that she did not marry me to leave in times of trouble. This made me cherish her even more, despite my fears for her safety and my concerns about whether I could do what was necessary to protect her.

I did not go to work the day Somaya said her tearful farewell to her parents. I knew she needed me to be with her while she dealt with this abrupt change to her world. We were renting a small house that came with a neglected garden, and Somaya had been spending most of her days tending to it and planting flowers. When her parents left, she went there and I joined her, watching her work and thinking of how much she reminded me of my grandfather when she did this. We spent hours in the garden that afternoon. When we were done, Somaya's face glinted with a wide smile. "It's so beautiful, Reza. I especially love the lilies." I was glad they had given her a measure of peace.

After dinner, Somaya sat on the bed quietly. I knew she was missing her parents. I sat next to her and took her hands. It was one of the first times in our marriage that we were alone completely. Her parents were gone, and the constant stream of family and friends visiting us was dissipating. I needed to be there for her. I needed to hold her in my arms and show her how much I loved her. I looked into her eyes, still not believing that someone as remarkable as she had chosen to marry me. I moved her hair away from her neck.

"You are so beautiful," I said, pressing gently on her hands. She smiled at me warmly, defining the dimple on her cheek. I kissed her neck and pulled her close to me. She closed her eyes. I wrapped my arms around her waist and caressed the heat of her skin.

"I love you," I said, kissing her again.

She started to respond when a loud whistle suddenly filled the air. Somaya jumped from the bed as if catapulted.

"Oh my God! There is an attack! Reza, get the radio!"

Startled, I ran to the kitchen to grab the radio and turn off the lights. On the radio, an announcer instructed everyone to get to a shelter, as Iraqi bomber planes were entering the sky of Tehran. I knew the Iraqi planes were going after military targets. But I also knew they wouldn't worry too much about hitting civilians at the same time.

We had a small cellar in our house but Somaya didn't feel safe there. She worried about being buried in rubble if the house took a direct hit. We rushed outside and leaned against a wall. This made even less sense than going to the cellar, but for some reason Somaya felt better there.

As we stood outside, it was ominously quiet.

I held Somaya's hand, her palm wet and cold. The heat I had felt only moments before was now gone from her body. I brought her close to me and she pressed me tight beneath the night sky, shivering. Then the shrill whistle of Iranian antiaircraft guns screamed only blocks away. That meant the Iraqi fighters were somewhere close by. Just that day, I'd promised Somaya's parents that I would take care of her. But how could I protect her from this madness? I looked at her innocent face illuminated by explosions and antiaircraft fire. She had stayed in this conflagration to be with me. If not for me, she would be safe with her parents in England now. I felt her chest beating hard against mine.

"I am okay, Reza. I am not afraid," she said as her voice broke. She was afraid, of course, but she was not a coward.

"I know," I said, "but I am *not* okay. Hold me tighter!"

This got a small reaction from her. She pinched me and told me to stop joking, smiling as she said it. I prayed to God to let this attack pass without any harm coming to her.

A loud blast shook the wall against our backs. I knelt down, pulled Somaya with me, and covered her body. We huddled in that position for the longest minutes of my life, as the explosions and missile fire continued.

Finally, the green siren announced the all-clear signal.

The attack was over.

For now.

That night, neither of us could sleep. Instead, we listened to reports on the radio with growing trepidation. The next day, I pleaded with Somaya to leave for London. I told her it wasn't too late, that Kazem would help her get out. She wouldn't hear of it.

In the midst of this, another war continued. The Mujahedin increased their violent fervor, attacking anyone associated with the

Islamic forces, including the Revolutionary Guards, the Komiteh (the revolutionary police), and the Basij. Officials of the Islamic regime were assassinated one after the other, some at the very base where I worked. Now Kazem and I were in no less danger than Naser.

At the same time, Hezbollah (Party of God) gangs of radical Islamists, sporting uniforms of dirty long beards and buttoned-up shirts, roamed the streets on motorcycles, brandishing sticks and chains, shouting *"Allaho Akbar"* and *"Khomeini Rahbar"* ("Khomeini is our leader"), and attacking people who did not adhere strictly to Islamic rules.

These rules were extreme, and few among us agreed with all of them. They included a dress code for women that required they wear no makeup and that they appear in public with a proper Islamic *hejab* covering their hair and body. Men could not wear shorts. Only married couples could be seen together in public places. Alcohol was banned. No parties or music were allowed, even within the walls of homes. Failure to follow these rules led to arrest and lashing in public.

The radicals called people who objected to the mullahs *mohareb,* or "those waging war against God." Khomeini issued a fatwa on the Mujahedin, calling them hypocrites and ordering their arrests. He asked people to inform authorities of anyone they suspected of belonging to that group. Neighbors began turning one another in, and I shuddered to think of where Naser's inability to censor himself would lead him.

Mainstream Iranian society cheered for neither the Mujahedin nor the clerical government. We were caught up in three wars: Iraq against Iran, the Mujahedin against the mullahs, and Hezbollah against the people. Our youth were slaughtered on battlefields and our citizens were rounded up, whipped, beaten, and humiliated as punishment for disobeying some arbitrary rule of decorum.

Somaya was constantly worried about me and I was beside myself with worry for her. She always wore a *hejab* in public and she adhered to the Islamic laws, but I never knew if this would be enough. It seemed that people were being arrested for no apparent reason.

The violence kept creeping closer to our home. One day, a cab dropped me off across from our house. I saw a Land Cruiser with the Komiteh logo there and this immediately made me nervous. The coming traffic kept me from crossing the street to the other side, raising my anxiety. Was Somaya in some kind of danger? As I waited, a motorcycle with two riders crept up alongside the Land Cruiser, and I saw the man on the back of the motorcycle throw a grenade through an open window of the car.

I flung myself to the ground as the car exploded thirty feet in front of me, raining debris and glass on me. I jumped to my feet as the motorcycle sped down a narrow alley. Among the dust and explosions, I ran to the Komiteh car and looked inside. There had been four men in there. Blood was splattered throughout the inside and three men were in pieces. One man, I believe it was the driver, actually managed to get out. He was severely disoriented, but through some odd effect of blast physics, his only injury was a bloody hand. In his other hand, he held a machine gun.

Somaya had heard the commotion and rushed outside along with many of our neighbors. She saw me by the destroyed car, my face covered with dust from the blast and with some drops of blood on my shirt. She rushed to me with tears.

"Reza, are you okay? What happened to you?"

I let go of the man I'd helped to the sidewalk, asking a neighbor to call for help. Then I took Somaya into our home. She was terribly frightened and I knew I needed to calm her down and let her know that we were going to be okay.

I just wasn't sure how I was going to manage that.

7

EVIN PRISON

ON JANUARY 20, 1981, the day Ronald Reagan became president of the United States, Imam Khomeini ordered the release of the American hostages. Americans celebrated this and saw it as the end of one of the most disturbing chapters in their history. Iranians of all ideologies celebrated as well. Khomeini's followers rejoiced in this final slap in Jimmy Carter's face, knowing that the hostage crisis had a great deal to do with his defeat, and seeing it as retribution for his support of the shah. They believed that sending the Americans home was a way to punctuate Khomeini's triumph over the world's biggest superpower. For other Iranians, including my family, the release of the hostages allowed us to hold out hope for better relations between the U.S. and our country. Perhaps, we thought, Khomeini was now ready to begin dealing diplomatically with the rest of the world and Iran could escape from its self-imposed isolation.

I worked every day at my office training Guards members in the use of computers. This work was challenging and it kept me busy. Although I saw Kazem at work all the time, Naser and I had not been in contact for quite a while. Marriage consumes time, love consumes attention, and war consumes both. Naser had Azadeh, who unfortunately hadn't helped blunt his increasing political activism, I was content to nestle in with Somaya, and Naser and I just never found the opportunity to get together. The three "battlefields" in Iran left a pervasive strain among all of us, but despite this, I reveled in the time I had with my wife. She was so full of energy and so loving that I found it possible to forget everything else when I was with her. For me, Somaya was the antidote to war.

"I want us to have three children," she said one afternoon as we sat in her garden.

"Why three and not two or four?"

"This way I can spoil them all."

I laughed at this. "You can only do this with three?"

"Three is the perfect number, Reza. Let me tell you how it works." She settled back in her seat, drew her legs under her like a little kid, and put her hair back in a ponytail. "You always adore your oldest kid because it is your first one. The third one is your favorite because you know he or she will be the last. So you spoil both of these. And you spoil the middle one because you don't want him to feel neglected."

Her reasoning brought a huge smile to my face. "Then three it is," I said, delighted that this would make her happy.

The phone rang and I got up to answer it. "Three spoiled kids," I said as I rose. "I hope I'll still get a chance to spoil my wife as well."

I winked at her and went into the house.

My mother was on the line. Her voice was frantic, pulling me immediately away from the reverie I'd just shared with Somaya. She was so upset that I couldn't understand her.

"Mom, what's going on?" I said nervously. "Are you okay?"

She sobbed and then gained a modicum of control over her emotions. "Reza, you have to do something. Naser, Soheil, and Parvaneh have been arrested."

I felt a chill to the depths of my soul. "Arrested?"

"Davood has not heard from them for a couple of months. He does not know what to do. They are in Evin Prison, and he can't visit them."

My knees started shaking and my entire body went numb. Fear raced through me. I had heard the stories about Evin Prison. Everyone had. If Naser and his siblings were there, they were in horrible straits.

I grabbed my jacket to go to Davood's house. Somaya came in at that point, saw my panic, and rushed toward me.

"I'll be back soon" was all I could say before I headed out the door.

When I got to their house, I found Davood and his wife, Mahin *khanoom,* hysterical.

"Reza *jon,* I know I should have called you earlier, but I didn't know what to tell you until now. We just learned that they've put Naser, Soheil, and Parvaneh in Evin." His shoulders shook and I thought for a moment that he wouldn't be able to keep speaking. The next words that came from his mouth were strained and halting, as though he could hardly bear to utter them. "They pounded on our door in the middle of the night and grabbed my children from their beds." He ran his fingers through his thinning hair. "I've been looking day and night to find out what happened to them."

Mahin *khanoom* had been crying while Davood spoke. Now she wailed. "God damn these shameless animals. They took my Parvaneh and my sons."

Everything about this seemed surreal to me. "I don't understand why they took them," I said, though I, of course, had an inkling of why they'd come for Naser. It made no sense to me that they would have taken the two younger ones as well, though.

"They took them for no reason," Davood spat. "Reza *jon,* please do something. Get my children back. They are innocent." He grabbed my arm. "They are in prison, Reza! Prison!"

"I'll do everything I can, Davood *jon.*"

He squeezed tighter on my arm. "It has been two months. Two goddamn long months! Reza, I have to see them. I need to know how they are doing. I want them back home."

I couldn't understand why he didn't let me know sooner. Even if he didn't know where his children were, he should have let me know they were gone. Was he distrustful of me—in spite of all our history—because I was with the Guards? Could he have possibly thought that I would side with the monsters who had stolen his children and my friends?

"I will talk to Kazem immediately, Davood *jon*. We will do everything we can. I promise."

"I need to see them," he said mournfully. "Please."

I rushed to work the next day, planning to catch Kazem as soon as he arrived. When I got to his office, though, he was already standing behind his desk reading some files. I told him the news and his face blanched. But his eyes showed no sign of surprise. It was as though he'd been waiting to hear this from the moment Naser started throwing his support behind the Mujahedin.

Regardless, Kazem stopped what he was doing immediately and started making phone calls. It took him some time, but he finally came to me with a name, Haj Moradi, to contact inside the prison.

The next morning, I picked up Davood in my car. He was nearly senseless with anxiety. I could barely reconcile the man sitting next to me with the one who'd led us in song and dance for so many years. I had no reference point for what he was going through. Considering how the simple prospect of discussing having children with Somaya had caused me so much joy, I could only imagine how eviscerated Davood felt by the crisis he now faced.

Evin Prison sits at the foothills of the Alborz Mountains in the northern section of Tehran. A tall redbrick wall surrounds it. There is nothing architecturally appealing about this compound. Its design had one obvious purpose—to strike terror in the hearts of those who approached it.

Things grew more ominous as we approached and heard the roar of a mob. Several hundred people had gathered in front of the huge iron gates. They were shouting and chanting, demanding to see their family members. Some of the women wailed in agony. As Davood and I got out of the car and tried to push our way through, the guards fired their machine guns into the air to quell the crowd. This led to immediate chaos, with people scattering, yelling, screaming, and running for cover. I grabbed Davood and brought him closer to the wall. We stooped down, covering our heads. I told Davood to stay pressed to the wall as I went inside to secure our visitation pass.

I entered a small office and approached the guard behind the desk. I showed him my card, and after he checked my name with the list of scheduled appointments for that day, he nodded and gestured me in. I noticed a tall tree in the courtyard as I went into the prison. From somewhere in my subconscious, an image flashed before me of Naser dangling from that tree with a noose around his neck. My trepidation increased a thousandfold.

I met Haj Moradi in the prosecution wing. I introduced myself and told him that Kazem sent his greetings. Then I watched in silence as Moradi called another prison guard and said with little emotion in his voice, "Take care of Brother Reza and see to it that his request is arranged."

Haj Moradi handed the guard a folder, presumably containing information on Davood's children. This man took me to a ward on the back side of the prison, one of the several buildings that segregated prisoners by the nature of their offenses. He told me that my brothers in the Guards' Intelligence Unit operated this one, where political prisoners were held. It was a nondescript space, clean and devoid of personality. I actually found some comfort in this. Unlike the outside of Evin itself, this ward didn't seem designed to intimidate.

But then we got inside the main hallway. Despite the Guards' best efforts to keep the prison clean, the stench of body odors and dank sewage assaulted my face and crawled up my nose. At first I heard no sound, which made the smells that much more overwhelming. Then distant screams and pleas for mercy cut through the silence. They echoed through the hallway from a floor below us. Moments later, I saw a line of blindfolded prisoners being led to a room. By this point, my palms were sweating and my heart was pounding.

The guard told me to wait in the hall while he arranged my visit with Davood's children. The sounds and the smells continued to swirl around me and I felt dizzy and aghast.

Moments later, I stared straight into the abyss. A group of armed guards emerged from a doorway. With them, a dozen teenage girls struggled barefoot down the hall. I went numb as they passed in front of me. These children seemed broken both mentally and physically. I could see that some were in shock. Some had tears rolling down their swollen faces. Others had blood caked on their skin. The rest seemed hopeless and resigned, an expression one should never see on someone so young.

I didn't think it was possible for me to feel more miserable than I felt in that moment. Until I realized that one of the faces was Parvaneh's. This stunned me so much that I fell back and had to brace myself against the wall.

The guard who had escorted me to this spot emerged then and I approached him instantly. I pointed to Parvaneh, pleading with him, "That's Davood's daughter and he's here to see her."

The man took my arm, pulled me aside, and whispered, "The order for execution is already in effect. Nothing can be done."

"But she is innocent."

This meant nothing to him. I wanted to rush forward, grab her, and pull her to safety. I wanted to plow through the guards imprisoning her and steal her from this hellhole. But before I could make a move, Parvaneh just lowered her head, totally defeated, and turned away. She never even acknowledged my presence. I have no idea if she knew it was me or if she just saw another tormentor when she looked into my eyes.

Tears welled up and I said a silent prayer, feeling damned by my helplessness. I stood paralyzed. Within minutes, dozens of gunshots echoed through the hallway from the distance. I heard a rush of birds in the courtyard flapping off toward the heavens.

And I screamed silently.

When the peal of the gunfire ended, the Azan, the call for the prayer, blared over the speakers.

"Allaho Akbar, Allaho Akbar . . ."

The guard who had just paraded Parvaneh and other girls in front of the firing squad joined others in his group in their praise of God.

"Allaho Akbar. . . . Ash-hadu anna la ilaha illallah. . . . Ash-hadu anna Muhammadan-rasool Allah. . . . Hayya ala-salat. . . . Hayya

alal-falah. . . . Hayya ala khair al-amal. . . . God is great. . . . I testify there is no God but Allah. . . . I testify that Mohammad is Allah's messenger. . . . Haste for prayer. . . . Haste for deliverance. . . . Haste for good deeds. . . ."

I forced myself to complete the arrangements for Davood's visit with his two remaining children. As instructed, I waited in a room in the prosecution wing, trying to make sense of what I had just seen, trying to believe that any hope remained. At last, a guard led in Naser and Soheil, and my heart dropped lower than I thought possible. Naser was hunched over, his arms hugging his rail-thin body tightly, trying to preserve body heat. His clothes hung loosely, mocking him. His face was so gaunt that his cheekbones seemed to be protruding obscenely. He was only twenty-six years old, but white streaks coursed through his jet-black hair. None of those streaks was there the last time I saw him, and I tried to force myself not to think about what had caused them.

Soheil limped in behind him, looking just as broken and dragging his foot as he walked. A livid scar stretched from his lower jaw across his neck. Again, I tried to avoid thinking about how he developed the scar and the limp, but it was becoming increasingly impossible not to imagine the torture inflicted on people I'd known and loved most of my life.

Straightening out the collar on my uniform, I marched past my escort in the hopes of gaining a few private moments with Naser. The guard lifted his hand to stop me.

"*Baradar,* you have to stay here."

I glared into the man's eyes. He must have seen the fury and desperation in my eyes, because he wilted back, allowing me to approach Naser.

My dear friend's bloodshot eyes engaged me for the first time since he walked into the room.

"Naser, I am here with your father. He will be here shortly. What have they done to you?"

I'm sure Naser realized that he did not have much time to talk to me. He leaned close and whispered through tears, "Reza, please get Parvaneh and Soheil out of here. I can't watch them being tortured anymore. This is unimaginable hell in here. These bloodthirsty animals raped Parvaneh in front of me. They made me watch as they twisted Soheil's ankle around in a circle. How can God allow this? I pray for my death every second. I can take all the torture they do to me, but I can't stand seeing what they're doing to my innocent brother and sister any longer." He paused for a moment, trying to gather his emotions. Finally, he continued, unable to stop his tears or the tremor in his voice. "I cannot forgive myself for not being able to protect my family. I don't know how I'm going to face my father. Reza, *please* get Parvaneh and Soheil out of here."

I put my hand around his head and pulled him close, whispering in his ear, "I will get them out, Naser. And I will get you out, too. I'll do anything for you. I promise."

The others in the room, including some of my fellow Guards, watched as our foreheads touched, but I did not care. I needed to offer Naser whatever comfort I could, even if it were only momentary release from the barrage of pain his jailers had been inflicting on him. I could not tell him that his little, blameless sister had only minutes before been paraded in front of me and then sent to her execution while I stood by helplessly. I held Naser close to me for a moment longer and then, as if sleepwalking, I walked back through the prison to retrieve Davood.

"Naser and Soleil are there to see you," I said when he looked up at me.

When I brought Davood into the room, I saw an expression on his face that will live in my memory for the rest of my life. It was an expression that said that he'd lost all faith in humankind in an instant.

"*Bebakhshid, Baba jon, bebakhshid.*" Naser and Soheil said these words together, apologizing to their father as though they were somehow at fault.

Davood melted into tears at that point. I thought I'd seen grief before. I even thought I'd experienced it when my father and grand-mother died. But what I witnessed here—the grief of a father an-guishing over his broken children—was far beyond anything I'd ever witnessed or felt.

Davood took both of his boys into his arms, and for ten minutes all he could do was cry. No questions; no words. Just crying as they hugged in a circle. I stood to the side, waiting to escort Davood back out.

One of the guards walked toward me and informed me that the visit was over. I gently reached under Davood's arm, telling him it was time to go. As we left, I took one last look over my shoulder at Naser. I tried to convince myself that I would find a way to help him, but the self-exhortations seemed hollow.

As soon as we left the room, Davood grabbed my sleeve and pleaded, "I have to see Parvaneh now. Please take me to her."

Telling myself that I was doing something merciful, I didn't let Davood know that his little butterfly had already flown off. Choking back tears, I said that the jail allowed only one visit, and then put my arm around his shoulder to guide him out. He allowed me to lead him, too weakened to do anything of his own volition.

We made our way past Evin's iron gate. Hundreds of people were still outside, but the earlier show of force by the prison guards had subdued their spirits. As we reached the car, Davood turned to look back at the forbidding building.

"Did you see what they did to my children, Reza *jon*?"

I nodded to him silently, knowing that I had seen more than I could even say, and knowing that what I had seen had changed me permanently.

8

COMMITMENTS

FOR THE NEXT couple of weeks, I pleaded with Kazem daily to use his connections with the senior people in the Guards to save Naser and Soheil's lives. When I'd told him about Parvaneh, he seemed sincerely sad—what human being wouldn't feel sad over the premature death of someone he used to tease and cajole when she was a little girl—but he continued to blame the Mujahedin for misleading young people and others into confronting Islam. It stunned me that he could not separate his grief over our friends from his outrage at a political nemesis. Why couldn't he simply acknowledge that the torture and execution of Parvaneh, a sixteen-year-old child, was wrong and unjust? And why couldn't he use the power he was amassing at the Guards to prevent unconscionable treatment for two other people he'd known and loved for more than a decade?

I continued to hope that Kazem would help free Naser and Soheil until the Monday morning when I walked into my office and Kazem asked me to come see him. Something in his voice told me that he wasn't going to tell me what I wanted to hear. I walked heavily to see Kazem in the building next door, as though I could avoid bad news simply by forestalling this meeting.

When I entered his office, Kazem looked up at me and pointed to the seat in front of his desk, indicating that I should sit down. The room was dim, the blinds were closed, and on the wall behind his desk, a picture of Imam Khomeini stared directly at me. I sat nervously, my eyes wandering to the folders stacked on Kazem's desk, the papers sitting on top of those, and the small flag of Iran Kazem always had there.

For what seemed like a very long time, Kazem did not say anything. He would clear his throat, but no words would come out. I tried desperately to convince myself that he wasn't about to deliver the worst possible news to me. Maybe, I thought, he was going to tell me only that there had been a delay in his efforts to free Naser and his brother. As Kazem continued to struggle to say what he needed to say, I felt growing tension and despair.

Finally, he stood and came over to my side of the desk, putting his hand on my shoulder.

"Reza, I just received a phone call from Haj Moradi at Evin Prison." He cleared his throat yet again. "A few days ago, an order was issued from high authorities and . . ." He took a deep breath before continuing. "Naser and Soheil were both executed yesterday."

As much as I'd come to expect him to say this over the past few minutes, the words hit me with unimaginable force. I felt the room start spinning and I had trouble breathing. I turned toward the Imam's picture angrily and stared at his eyes, silently cursing him. Then, bending forward, I put my head on the desk, crossed my arms around my head, and collapsed into myself. An image flashed in my mind immediately of the last time I saw Naser, at my wedding, when he was caressing Azadeh. He was dancing and laughing like there was no tomorrow.

"Reza, I'm going to marry her. I am in love. Now that makes two of us. . . ."

I felt Kazem's hands on my shoulders, gripping me tightly. "Reza, I am so sorry. I did all I could do, I swear."

I stood up. I needed to get out of this office. I needed to figure out how I was going to face the future that now lay in front of me. Before I could leave, though, Kazem hugged me and whispered, *"Lanat bar in Munafeghin."* Damn the Betrayers, the Mujahedin. He wiped a tear and shook his head. I'm sure he thought he was commiserating, but his sympathy felt hollow. Why wasn't he feeling this loss the way I was feeling it? Did all those years of soccer, Friday gatherings at my grandparents' house, and late-night homework help mean nothing? Was our oath of friendship just an empty promise to him?

"I need to go home," I whispered back, moving quickly toward the door.

I lived in a bubble of confusion for the next few weeks. What was happening to my country? Where was the revolution I—and Naser—had supported? I could not believe that young people like Naser, Soheil, and Parvaneh, the future of our country, were being tortured and executed. How could this possibly lead us to a better Iran? All Naser wanted for his country was to see justice. The revolution inspired him because he saw it as the end of a dictator's repressive rule. He truly believed that the revolution would bring us freedom. Instead, it snuffed him out.

I, too, had dreamt grandiose dreams about the revolution. I felt that Islam, the religion of honesty and hope, would bring justice and equity to all. But that revolution now had the blood of my best friend on its hands. In the name of God.

The guilt of wearing the uniform of the Revolutionary Guards weighed heavily on me now. I forced myself to go through the motions of working, but I did it bitterly, wondering if I were helping to destroy other futures with every computer I fixed and every Guards member I trained. Kazem kept a little distance because he knew he couldn't help me grieve. For the first time, I thought about leaving the Guards, but I didn't know where I would go or what I would do.

Somaya tried to comfort me, but even though her sympathy was genuine and her desire to help me was strong, she couldn't begin to alleviate my pain. One night, when I was sitting alone at my desk in the den, she came in, held me in her arms, and kissed my forehead.

"Reza, there are other people being arrested for no reason. I know a girl named Roya, who was just released from prison. She won't talk about what happened to her in there. A close friend of hers told me that she was not involved in any opposition group, but she was badly tortured anyway, and she is still in a state of shock."

This caught my attention. I wanted to know more about what was happening in that prison. My heart went to Parvaneh, her last look at me. The shame and defeat in her eyes, the confusion. I needed to talk to Roya. I needed to learn more about what Parvaneh went through, if only to help me understand what my brothers were becoming.

When I asked Somaya to set up a meeting for me, she hesitated at first. I knew my position in the Guards sometimes embarrassed her with her friends. These days, most people looked at a bearded man, especially in uniform, as a threat to their freedom. She tried to allay this by bragging about my knowledge and skill in the technical aspect of my job, but I knew some of her friends questioned how she could be with a man like me. In spite of her reluctance, Somaya agreed to connect me with Roya. This took some time because Roya didn't want to speak with anyone. In deference to her, I did not wear my uniform when she finally agreed to see me.

Roya kept her head down, her eyes fixed on her fingers, as she guided me inside her house. She was wearing the proper *hejab* but constantly checked her forehead to make sure her hair was not showing while we talked. She would not look at me, keeping her gaze focused on some distant spot on the floor.

"Roya *khanoom,* I know you weren't sure about meeting with me," I said delicately. "I completely understand and respect that. Please believe that I would never do anything to bring you more pain or sadness. I just want to know if there is something I can do to help fix the system."

There was an uncomfortable silence while she pondered my words. Then her head started moving slowly, side to side. Very quietly, she said, "Nobody can help." She paused and put a hand to her face. "Do you know what they did to Hamid?"

Somaya had already told me about Hamid, Roya's boyfriend. He was a member of the Mujahedin and the Guards arrested Roya and him at the same time. They released Roya after holding her for nearly a year, but they tortured and executed Hamid.

"*Na*, Roya *khanoom*, no, I don't know what happened," I said in the hopes that she would talk about it.

She said nothing for a minute. And then she spoke very softly. "It is not important. I am sorry I brought it up."

I needed to do something to reach out to her. "Roya *khanoom*, I am not part of any of this. I recently lost very good friends in that prison and I would like to know more about what is happening in there. What they are doing is inhumane. But I can't do anything if I don't know the facts."

Normally, I would never say anything like this to someone I didn't know well; it would be too dangerous. But I was trying to reassure her that it was okay to talk to me. I didn't succeed. She said very little and I left a short while later, feeling terribly empty.

Just before I left, though, I told her about Parvaneh, finishing by saying, "I need to know what happened to her, Roya."

I had hoped that my visit with Roya would help me get a grasp on the sense of hopelessness and fury I felt. Instead, it only made me feel more confused and impotent. A few days later, though, I received a letter. It came with no sender's information, and with the word *confidential* written sloppily across it. I rushed to my study and opened it.

Reza Khan,

I know what happened to your friend Parvaneh.

While I was in the prison, I wished many times that I could be free, that I could get out and forget about what happened in there. But now that I am out, I wish I were one of those girls who were lucky enough to go in front of the firing squad. They took everything from me in that prison. I have nothing left.

They killed Hamid. We had plans to get married and to have a family with lots of children. He was a good person, he believed in God and justice. In order to get his body back, they made his parents pay for the bullets they used to shoot him. He was missing an eye. They did terrible things to him—his arms and legs had broken bones protruding out. Every spot on his body had cigarette burns on it. Hamid's mother is now in a mental hospital. She lost her mind after seeing his body.

When I was released from prison, I rushed home to see my mother, but she wasn't there. She had a stroke a few months after I was arrested. I did not know I could cause so much agony and grief. I feel as though I killed her. Every day I blame myself for the pain I brought her. I prayed to God to let me see her one more time when I was in the prison. I asked God to send me home to her and let me put my head on her shoulder and cry, to ask for forgiveness. She was the only one I had. Now there was nobody to tell what happened to me. I had nobody to cry to. My mom was not there to hug me and tell me that it's okay—it's not your fault, Roya, it's not your fault to have a binamoos touch your body, private and sacred, which God forbids a namahram to see. She was not there to tell me—it's not your fault that they whipped you every day, beat your bare feet with cables. I could not tell her that I bled so hard that I would faint, never knowing what they did to my unconscious body.

When I was in solitary confinement, these filthy, evil men would come to my cell—every time a different rotten, dirty, nasty guard. Not even animals would do what they did to me. I am embarrassed even to say what they did. They raped me, but it was more than rape. They said the most disgusting things to me. When they were through, they kicked me in the back as hard as they could, threw me down next to the toilet, and told me, "You piece of shit, do your namaz now." Reza Khan, I am a Muslim. I believe in God, and my faith kept me alive in there. I did my namaz every single day, but these shameless people worship Satan, not God.

The day you came to see me, it was impossible to tell you what you wanted to know. But I have since thought about it a lot. I *thought about your friend Parvaneh. I felt you were sincere. I could feel the pain in your voice. Today when I woke up, I knew I was ready to tell you what is going on behind those bars—what happened to a lot of other girls like me and Parvaneh.*

Reza Khan, there are thousands of innocent young girls like Parvaneh being held in there. When I was finally released from solitary, they took me to a small cell, a cell designed for just a few, but which held more than thirty women. I had no complaints about being squashed in with these women. Seeing their tormented bodies and minds gave me the strength and the feeling that I was not alone.

Every few days they would call out names over the loudspeaker. We knew what that meant, and we would gather together, hold each other's hands, and pray that they would not call our names. But always at least one or two from our cell would have to go in front of the firing squad. We could hear the sound of the screams, the pleas for forgiveness, and then the gunshots filling the air.

They would line up the rest of us and make us hold one leg up for a long time. If you got tired, they would lash you on the tired leg and make you stand on it. All of us were crying. Some would faint from the pain and bleeding. Every day we had to undergo interrogation. I never knew what they wanted, nor did I know how to answer their questions. No matter what I said, they would hit me. One day, to answer their questions, I told them that I was not part of any opposition group and that I had no information. I said I didn't know anybody in the Mujahedin. They got more irritated when they heard the name of the Mujahedin. They cut my arm with a knife and told me that they would cut my throat the next time if I did not confess. The next day they sent me to a small dark room where another guard raped me.

This was the routine.

As disgusted and down as I was, I never lost hope. I thought about Hamid all the time. Every time I was tortured, every time I heard the click of my broken fingers, I thought of Hamid and the good times we had together and the good times we would have in the future. At night, I thought of my mother and how she would be happy when I came back home—how our life would be the same and how we would put all of this behind us.

One day they released me. Even thinking about it gives me shivers.

Haj Agha Asqar Khoui, a mullah who was in charge of guiding the prisoners to the Islamic path, became fond of me. In the third meeting I had with him, he told me of his interest in me and said that he would arrange my freedom if I agreed to become sigheh to him. I don't think I gave much thought to it. Being free was enough reason for me to make a bad decision. I made that decision not understanding that I had to give myself to another demented person; not understanding that I was committing myself to more torture and mental anguish by accepting the sigheh, by being temporarily married to a man who already had a wife or two.

For a few months, there was no physical pain, no beatings, no lashings, and no breaking bones. But I was disgusted with myself, of betraying myself, selling my pride to a mullah in return for my freedom. Was it really freedom? I did not know at the time. I did not know the heavy price I had to pay to get back to my life. The only life I knew.

Nothing is the same; it won't be the same for anybody that has been in that damned prison.

Today is a different day for me. Last night I had a dream. I saw my mother, Hamid, and my father, who died many years ago. They were all waiting for me behind Evin Prison's gate on the day I was to be set free. I ran toward the gate as fast as I could to embrace them, to tell them that I was free at last. But before I could get out, the gate closed and I was stuck in that cursed prison.

Reza Khan, I no longer can carry the burden of this guilt. I know what Parvaneh and many other girls and boys inside Evin Prison experienced. No one can help; no one can change our lives.

I wish I had been shot dead in there. I can no longer go to that dirty mullah every week and pretend that being out of that prison is freedom.

I can't live like this anymore. You are <u>habs,</u> a prisoner, forever. This is what's happening to every prisoner in there. This is what happened to Parvaneh.

Roya

Roya had hanged herself shortly after mailing the letter.

9

THE PRAYER

ROYA'S ULTIMATE ACT left me feeling lost. Her death, the deaths of my friends, and the executions of many more innocent young men and women had left a hole in my heart. I would never forget what happened and I would never forgive those responsible. I remembered the sound of the call for prayer at the prison right after they shot Parvaneh. How could these people stand in front of God and praise him after the unspeakable crimes they'd just committed?

I knew I needed to do something, but I didn't know what I could do or whom I could talk to for help. I knew only that my desire to act and my sense of helplessness were warring inside of me.

One rainy afternoon, I was sitting in my study looking out the window, staring at the sky, still hoping for an answer. I felt the raindrops were God's way of telling me he was as devastated as I was. Somaya's knock at the door interrupted my thoughts. She entered the room and placed a tray of food on my desk. She rearranged some books and papers to make room for the tray, picked up the tray from that morning that I'd left untouched, and said, "Reza *jon*, you should eat something. I am so worried."

I had not spoken to her much in the days since Roya's death, nor had I gone to work or left my room. Before she left with the tray, Somaya's eyes went to the floor where my *sajadeh* lay. "Do you want me to fold your *sajadeh* and put it away, or do you still have to do your afternoon *namaz*?"

I looked down to where my prayer rug, my holy stone, and my

prayer beads lay. I had not done my *namaz* for days. I rubbed my eyes, looked at Somaya, and said, "No, dear, I was about to do my prayers."

She smiled sweetly; the dimple on the side of her left lower cheek gave her perfect round face a delicate highlight. The sparkle in her eyes revealed the satisfaction of her attempt to bring me back to life. Before leaving, she said, *"Ghabool bashe."* May God accept your prayers.

I let the blinds down and sat before my *sajadeh*. I moved the little rug a bit more toward *Ghebleh*, Mecca, and worked its corners to make sure it sat properly on the floor. Then I put the prayer beads on my side and I sat on the rug in front of the holy stone. I raised my arms toward the sky.

"God, tonight I am doing my prayer differently. I am not following the routine and rules of *namaz*. As much as these Arabic words sound gracious and comforting, I have to talk to you in my own language. I need to tell you about my true feelings. I believe in your power. You are my creator and I have felt your presence throughout my life, but I have to make a confession. If what I am seeing in my country is Islam, then I no longer believe Islam to be the religion of honesty and sacrifice. I feel what is happening in my country is wrong. I feel the killings and crimes happening in your name are unjust. How can I watch all these atrocities? How can I watch people being slaughtered and not be able to do anything? How can I forgive myself for not being able to deliver the promise I made to Naser, to rescue him and his brother and sister? I cannot witness Parvaneh, Roya, and thousands of girls like them being held behind bars, their hearts ripped to pieces, and do nothing. How can I believe Khanoom Bozorg's stories anymore? I don't believe that the Islam preached by Khomeini and his men represents true love and munificence. They kill for their own survival. They use you as a shield, an excuse. How can I stand by and watch while they demolish our proud history and civilization? We are a nation with a rich and vibrant culture. They are taking us back to an era where the barbarous acts of Mongols left nothing but bloodshed throughout the land. God, I am scared. I can no longer remain quiet and watch my country disappear into a morass of evil.

"God, I admit I am helpless and am begging you for guidance, as you represent true love and justice and I believe in you and your power."

I folded my *sajadeh* and put it away. Then I went back to my desk, opened the drawer, and reached for Roya's letter, hidden with an old picture of Naser and me posing next to Davood and Agha Joon. I stared at the picture, unfolded Roya's letter, put the picture inside it, and put it back in the drawer.

As I closed the drawer, a thought came to my mind that I'd never considered before. God had clearly put it there as an answer to my prayers. I realized with sudden clarity that there was only one thing I could do to honor the spirit of my lost friends and all of the other innocent victims. I needed to go back to America, to the one other place I'd ever called home. America was one of only two true superpowers in the world, and I was convinced that Americans didn't really know what was happening inside of Iran—and that if they did, they would do what they could to free us. Someone needed to tell them about the atrocities.

I was that someone. I believed this now with every fiber of my being and I needed to act on it.

Feeling emboldened and feeling that I had to set things straight with the people I loved, I decided to make two visits I'd put off for too long. The first was to Davood, whom I had not seen since I dropped him off after our ill-fated trip to Evin Prison. On the way back that day, he barely spoke. But as he got out of the car, he turned his face away from me and stared into the distance. In a broken voice he said, "How can you wear the uniform of such a murderous regime, Reza?" He left without another word.

That question left a scar on my heart, a scar that grew more livid as I came to understand that I had no acceptable answer for it.

Mahin *khanoom,* Naser's mother, opened the door for me when I arrived at the house. She was barefoot and dressed in black and she looked much older than her age. She showed me no sign of recognition, though when I asked her permission to enter and see Davood, she took me to his room.

Davood was lying on his bed. The lines on his face were deeper, longer, and more defined; his gray hair drooped over his forehead to one side. When he tried to smile to be polite, I could see that the effort nearly overwhelmed him. Had he forgotten how? Or did he now think of me as one of the enemy?

I bent toward him and kissed his wrinkled, warm, and fatherly hand. "Davood *jon,* I am here for your forgiveness. . . ." I was not sure if he was listening to me. He stared at a wall in front of him. But whether he was or not, I needed to tell him how I felt. "I am so deeply sorry. I wish I could change everything. I wish I could carry all your pain. I wish I had the power to bring back the peace you and your wife deserve. I wish I could bring back your children. Davood, I am not happy with who I have become. I am not happy with what has happened to us. Please forgive me, *pedar jon,* if I caused any pain to you. I am sorry, Davood *jon.* You are like my own father and I can't see you like this."

He hadn't looked directly at me to this point, but when I spoke to him, calling him "dear father," something he would never again hear from his own children, he turned slowly and made eye contact through his tears. His expression warmed. He put his hand over mine, tightly clasping it. As his sleepy brown eyes fixed onto mine, I felt the blessing under his fatherly touch. He then closed his eyes and, with a tender smile, fell asleep.

Davood died two days after my visit, his heart unable to bear the burden of so much grief.

A rage brewed inside me. I couldn't tell Davood that I was going to use the uniform he despised to avenge his son's unjust death in prison. I couldn't tell him that with this uniform I was going to burn and bury Parvaneh's filthy murderers. His death was another sign from God that my mission was necessary. I needed to save other fathers from the misery that had killed Davood.

With new resolve, I approached Kazem, intent on involving him in helping me. I was going to give him a problem, and let him come up with the solution. Agha Joon had told me that doctors had diagnosed my aunt Giti with Parkinson's disease, and that he wished a family member could attend to her during this difficult time. I now realized that I could use this event to take the dangerous steps I needed to take.

"Kazem, I just had a call from Agha Joon. My aunt Giti is in declining health and needs to go to a rest home. Agha Joon says it is time for me to pay back my dues. Since she provided for me during my stay in the U.S., it is my duty to go there and take care of her needs." I shook my head. "He's put me in a very awkward position."

Kazem considered this for a moment. "I think you should help her, Reza. You owe her for all she did for you. We have to take care of our relatives."

"But I am not sure how to go about it. I can't just leave work. I have no idea how long I'll need to stay there."

"Don't worry, Reza. I will talk to Rahim and take care of it."

"You are a true friend, Kazem. You have always been there for me." I swallowed my pride to be able to continue. "I never got to thank you for your efforts to rescue Naser. I knew you would if you could. Naser went a different way. You were always right that the Mujahedin manipulate our young people and that Naser did not see that."

"It is sad what happens to these people. They are turning to these stupid opposition groups. For what? We have everything that God wants us to be in our Islamic government and they still allow themselves to fight against his rules!" He shook his head and said nothing more, never mentioning Naser by name or acknowledging the loss of our friend's innocent siblings. I let that pass, as I needed him to help me with my travel plans.

I called Agha Joon first to let him know that I would be able to travel to America. Then I went on the second trip I needed to make: to see my mother. The relationship between us had become strained and I had to fix that. The last time we talked was when she called me to let me know that Davood's children had been arrested. It was no longer unusual for this much time to pass between conversations because it had become nearly impossible for us to talk without offending each other. My decision to join the Guards had driven a wedge between us. The last time we were in a room together, a discussion over the president at the time, Abolhassan Banisadr, turned into an ugly argument. Banisadr had been elected the first president of the Islamic Republic of Iran in January 1980 with almost 80 percent of the vote. He was a liberal counterpoint to the mullahs, someone Khomeini tolerated because he offered the illusion that the clerics hadn't taken complete control of the country. More than a year after Banisadr's election, people like my mom, who were so disappointed with the Islamic regime, saw him as the only hope for a free Iran. Although Khomeini had approved of this election as a concession to liberal powers in the country, Banisadr had taken to giving stirring speeches on the virtues of freedom and self-governance, criticizing the mullahs for their torture and execution of the opposition. He never directly challenged Khomeini, but incendiary slogans shouted by his crowds, such as "Free us from the mullahs!" were deemed acts against God.

My mother was among those who shouted this from the crowd. She participated in Banisadr's rallies with much enthusiasm. I was secretly proud of her and I supported those courageous souls demonstrating on Banisadr's behalf, but I did not want anything to happen to her. I tried to stop her from joining the rallies, especially after club-wielding Hezbollahi had beaten other demonstrators and the Guards had fired on the crowds—and especially after my best friend and his siblings lost their lives for doing less. She mistook my concern for her as being anti-Banisadr and our words became bitter.

With the hope that I could reconcile with my mother, and a wish that her motherly instinct would recognize the purity of my intentions, I knocked on her door. When she opened it, she just glared at my beard and then left the door open and walked into the living room.

"I am going to Los Angeles to take care of Aunt Giti," I said as I shut the door and followed her in. She turned up the television and sat on the couch.

"They are destroying our only hope," she said as she stared at the TV. The broadcast showed a report about the rising opposition of the clergy against Banisadr.

"Things are not going to stay like this, Mom. I promise." I was sure in my mind that I could make a difference with my plan. She glanced at me, got up, and turned off the television.

"Reza! I don't know how someone like you, who never cared much about this religious nonsense, can suddenly come back from America and devote himself to a man like Khomeini. Do you even realize that what they are doing is inhumane? Do you see what is going on around you? Do you even care about Naser and what happened to him?"

Every accusation she had made carried a sting, but this one struck me right in the heart. I got up to leave.

"Your father and I had high hopes for you. We thought we raised a man."

I slammed the door and left her house. For her safety, I had to bite my tongue and let my mother be ashamed of me. To tell her what I was about to do would put her at even greater risk. But now I was even more passionate about my mission.

I will prove it to you, Mom. I will prove it to you that you raised a man, not a coward.

I waited a few days for Kazem to get back to me about Rahim's reaction to my travel plans. At that time, the government didn't permit ordinary citizens to travel because of the war with Iraq, and I needed his approval to secure the necessary authorization. When Kazem called me into his office, I thought he was going to give me an answer.

"Come on in, Reza," he said, motioning me to sit. He was behind his desk signing papers and reviewing some files. After putting the folders to the side, he looked up and said, "Thank God Imam Khomeini finally reclaimed the position of commander-in-chief from Banisadr. It's about time. We can't afford a president who is weak on war. This is a serious time in our movement. Our enemy, Saddam, is wreaking havoc on our soil and Banisadr is drawing up a truce and negotiating the terms to end the war." He shook his head.

I knew then that Banisadr was in trouble. The mullahs did not intend to allow his verbal insurrection to continue. Nothing had so galvanized the population behind the mullahs as this war, and no one, not even the president, was going to interfere.

"Kazem, have you talked to Baradar Rahim yet?" I asked with hesitation.

"Is everything okay, Reza? You don't seem to be yourself."

"You know how Agha Joon is. He's been calling me nonstop. He is so worried about his daughter." I tried to compose myself. "He is afraid to lose her, too. He's already lost his son and his wife. And now Aunt Giti is sick."

"Of course, it is a hard time for him. I did talk to Rahim and he is looking into it. I mentioned it was urgent."

I thanked Kazem and left his office, frustrated at the time this was taking, but feeling satisfied that he was at least trying to help. Rahim, however, had other things on his mind. In the days following my conversation with Kazem, the parliament impeached Banisadr for standing in opposition to the mullahs. The brothers in the Revolutionary Guards, including Rahim, were ordered to invade the presidential palace to arrest and kill the deposed president. They didn't succeed at this, as Banisadr went into hiding and later managed to escape to France with Massoud Rajavi, the leader of the Mujahedin. They did manage to arrest several of Banisadr's friends and associates, and they executed them.

My anxiety level was rising. The loss of Banisadr, the only liberal in a position of leadership in Iran, meant the country was moving even further from the ideals of the revolution. I needed to act and I now had a plan, but I couldn't do anything without permission to travel. I couldn't push Kazem any harder than I'd already pushed him without the risk of raising suspicion. On top of this, Agha Joon kept pressuring me to go to LA to attend to my aunt.

On June 27, a week after Banisadr's impeachment, I ran into Rahim in the hallway of our building. He waved and gave me a short "Hi" as he passed by me.

I found this simple gesture deflating. Apparently, my request was of little concern to him. Weeks had passed since I asked Kazem for his help. With the crisis escalating in the country, it looked less likely that Rahim would approve my travel. I was about to enter my office and rethink everything when someone called my name.

"Baradar Reza!"

I turned my head. It was Rahim.

"I need to see you. Tomorrow I am busy attending a meeting, but come to my office the day after tomorrow and we will talk." He started to walk down the hall. "By the way, bring your passport."

I went home anxious to let Somaya know that I was finally getting my permission to leave. Rahim's asking for my passport was a good sign, as I needed the authorization to exit stamped in my passport. Somaya told me that she was happy for me, but I could hear the sadness in her voice.

"Why don't you go to London and visit your parents while I'm gone? I can arrange for that. And then we can come back together."

"Reza, you need this trip. I know you're going because Aunt Giti is sick, but you also need to get away for a while with everything that has happened." She smiled. "Don't worry about me. My grandma is having a surgery on her back and I promised my mom I would take care of her."

I held her in my arms and told her how deeply I loved her. She was the purest soul in a country gone mad and I felt lucky to have her.

When I went to work, I saw Kazem and told him about my

planned meeting with Rahim, thanking him again for arranging everything. That night, Ayatollah Beheshti held a high-level meeting at the Islamic Republic Party (IRP) headquarters. Beheshti was the head of the judicial system and the second most powerful man in Iran next to Khomeini. Rahim and several Guards members from our base attended this meeting, which was why he couldn't meet with me until the next day.

That night, while in my study, I grabbed my passport to make sure I didn't forget to take it with me. Then I pulled out Roya's letter and Naser's picture. I looked at Naser and then my eyes flicked to my grandfather. I thought about how Agha Joon always used to say "Grow old, young man" to us. I finally realized what he meant by this: Every person has the right to grow old and be part of this world. No one should be allowed to take that from anyone.

Somaya came into the room. "I am a little tired. I am going to bed. I'll leave the light on."

"I am almost done here. I am coming to bed in a little bit."

I put the picture and the letter back and checked to see that the passport was in my pocket. As I did, a loud blast shook the house. I ran out of my study and screamed Somaya's name. She was already outside the bedroom, running toward me, asking about the explosion. She rushed to the family room to turn on the television while I tuned in the radio.

"Do you think it was an attack by Iraq?" she asked anxiously.

"I don't think so. There is no siren or power outage. Let me make some phone calls."

I called Kazem, but there was no answer. I then called Agha Joon and Mom. They had not heard the blast. We spent the rest of the night fearing what would happen next, unable to sleep.

The following day at work, I learned that a series of powerful explosions rocked the Islamic Republic Party's headquarters where Beheshti was holding his meeting. Chaos spread through our unit. I went looking for Kazem, but he was not around. I rushed to Rahim's office. He was not there, either. Only then did I remember that Rahim had been at the meeting. I hurried back to my office and made a dozen calls to find out what I could.

I learned that this was a well-orchestrated attack. The assailants had planted bombs throughout the adjoining area to guarantee the greatest amount of devastation. Beheshti and more than seventy other party members died that night—among them cabinet ministers, deputy ministers, and parliament deputies. Many Guards members had been injured. Rahim was one of them.

I was devastated. Nobody would be trusted enough to leave the country now. Meanwhile, Khomeini, fearing a coup, ordered the Guards and the Basijis to surround the military bases. He named the Mujahedin the perpetrators of the attack and ordered the execution of many political prisoners in retaliation.

The Khomeini regime used this tragedy, as they did with all calamitous events, as a vehicle for public relations. They immediately claimed that seventy-two people died in the attack, calling them martyrs and comparing this incident to the martyrdom of Imam Hussein and his men, also seventy-two in number. The mullahs added a dramatic flair to the story when they spread rumors that Beheshti had told the crowd just prior to the explosion that he could "smell heaven."

A few days later, Rahim came back to work with a broken leg. He and Kazem came to my office, Rahim on crutches and Kazem helping him navigate.

"Baradar Reza, I did not forget about you," Rahim said as he handed his crutches to Kazem and sat in a chair. "I hope you have your passport with you. Kazem told me how close your family is and he has great respect for your grandfather. I have talked to the authorities and, with my concurrence, they are allowing you to travel."

Kazem winked at me.

"But Baradar Rahim," I said, "I know this is a very sensitive time in our revolution. If I am needed here more, I would rather stay and serve my country and our imam." I said this shrewdly, knowing Rahim had already made his decision and wouldn't change it, but also knowing that he would remember my willingness to stay and therefore have no suspicions of my reason for going to America.

All that was left now was for me to board the plane. The morning of my trip, the dawning sun cast a persimmon glow on the white marble of the Azadi ("Freedom") Tower as I headed to the Mehrabad International Airport in Tehran. I felt a tang of bitterness in my throat, remembering that this beautiful monument was built to commemorate the twenty-five hundredth anniversary of the Persian Empire. The Ayatollah Khomeini changed the name after the revolution from Shahyad Tower, for the shahs of Iran. The original intention of the tower was to remind Persians of their great history—the history that made my grandparents so proud. I heard Agha Joon's voice saying, "This is the land where Cyrus the Great ruled one of the largest empires the world had ever seen. He brought dignity and respect for all to this great civilization: a land where the first charter of human rights was introduced, a land where women were respected, where slavery was abolished, and a land where the Jews were free to return to their native land at the end of Babylonian captivity. This was the Persia where poets, philosophers, and scientists were the bedrock of national pride, where religion was based on three simple premises: good thoughts, good words, and good deeds."

Once on the plane, I had a moment of panic. How could I be thinking of doing such an insane thing? There was still time to change my mind; I hadn't yet committed a single treasonous act. I could simply go to LA, help Aunt Giti as promised, and then return. But then I thought of Naser, Soheil, Parvaneh, Davood, Roya, and the countless others the revolution had stolen from us, and my resolve returned. As the Iran Air 747 climbed into the sky, I noticed that the cake-frosting snow spreading unevenly across the Alborz mountain range to the north looked vaguely like the San Gabriel Mountains that guard Los Angeles, except for the occasional distinctly Persian buildings that dotted the landscape. I knew that once I landed in Los Angeles, my life would change forever. Like thousands before me, I was going to America seeking help, seeking hope, and above all, seeking freedom. The freedom that the Islamic government had promised once and then so shrewdly taken away.

In response, I had to commit treason against an outlaw regime, a thugocracy. I had made up my mind to deliver every secret I knew about the Guards and ask the American authorities for help. I could not allow fear or anything else to deter me.

10

CODE NAME: WALLY

THE LONG APPROACH to Los Angeles International Airport started with our descent somewhere to the east and south of the great sprawling Los Angeles Basin, near San Bernardino. It had been a grueling twenty-hour trip with a few hours' layover in Frankfurt, but a warm feeling came over me as I went through customs. The woman checking my passport asked why I hadn't brought my family along, and this simple, friendly question was so devoid of political subtext that it soothed me. She probably extended this courtesy to everyone, but her generous smile made me feel truly welcome.

I grabbed a shuttle for the short ride to the Sheraton hotel on Century Boulevard, arriving behind a line of limos dropping off members of a wedding party. Scenes like this had become rare in Iran since the revolution banned parties and alcohol. If the regime caught people committing these indiscretions, they laid them out in public, stripped off their shirts, and thrashed them with a whip.

I couldn't sleep that night, anxious thoughts cycling through my head. Was I doing the right thing? Would it make any difference? Would anybody care? Would the Guards catch me? Would they hurt my family? Was I losing my sanity? I needed to draw strength from my memories of the people who had suffered and the realization that so many continued to suffer.

This is what you have to do for your country. This is the only way to bring democracy and fairness to your people. This is your duty, Reza!

I tried to quell my uneasiness by thinking about the kind of information I would pass along. I knew of names and positions of the Revolutionary Guards' commanders. I knew of their connection to other radical Islamic groups and their plans to export their dangerous Islamic beliefs beyond Iranian borders. I had taken notes in my head of all the meetings I attended with Kazem, and I could quote details verbatim.

The long night finally ended with dawn over the Pacific Ocean. Before heading out, I contacted my aunt to let her know I was in town. She insisted I stay with her, but I told her that since I had plans to see some old friends, it was better for me to stay in a hotel. I promised I would take care of her while I was there, though. I knew I owed this to both her and my grandfather.

Aware that there was a good possibility an Islamic agent would be watching me, I tried to act as normal as possible. I did not trust Rahim, my commander. How could I possibly trust him or anybody associated with the regime? Returning to my old stomping grounds from my college days, meeting up with old friends, and going to my aunt's on a regular basis would provide the perfect cover for my travels around Los Angeles.

I called my college friends Johnny and Alex to set up a time to get together with them at the Horse Shoe Bar of Tom Bergin's Tavern in the Fairfax area of LA. We used to meet there after the USC football games on Saturdays. We always staked out the first booth to the right of the front door, as it was the best spot in the restaurant. When I got there this time, I discovered that "our" booth still featured paper shamrocks with our names on them.

Chris, the bartender, surprised me when he recognized me. He pointed to the table where my old roommates, Johnny and Alex, sat.

I felt an immediate rush of good old memories. The red Mustang with mag wheels, the LA girls, and my old girlfriend, Molly. How I had embraced that carefree life for a few years until my father's death. How Naser and Kazem had brought me back to reality upon my return home. I wondered how different my life would have been if my father had lived and if I had stayed with Johnny and Alex and my American life. Would I have been a happier person if the revolution in Iran had been nothing more than a news item to me?

"Reza, look at you, man," Johnny said, interrupting this wave of thoughts with a smile as he hugged me. "What's with the beard?"

The question, and, in fact, the entire reunion, had a surreal quality to it. How could I reconcile the easy college life I shared with these men with all the changes in Iran that had caused me to grow the beard? Would Johnny understand if I explained it to him? I decided not to try. Instead, we reminisced.

"It is the new thing. Everybody grows a beard these days in Iran," I said as I hugged him back.

We talked for a while about our lives after college. Johnny told me about his wife and his two-year-old twin boys, and about how being a father had changed him. Alex was still with Suzan, whom he'd been dating since our USC days. I told them about Somaya and showed them a picture of her.

"Wow, she is beautiful," Johnny said.

"How's everything back in Iran?" Alex asked. "We've been watching the news and it seems like a lot is going on."

As much as this was an invitation to talk about my true feelings, I did not divulge much. I said only that we were in the midst of a transition and that I believed things would get better.

As we caught up, we fell into our old, familiar rhythms. It was as though no time had passed since we last saw one another. But I knew that wasn't true. I'd gone through the equivalent of a lifetime since leaving California.

I did nothing more than visit with my aunt and get in touch with old friends for a few days. Then it was time to contact the U.S. authorities. I wanted to reach out to the CIA. I found that thought intimidating, but I knew they would take my information seriously. They weren't listed in the phone book, but the FBI was. I knew of their offices in the Federal Building on Wilshire in Westwood, a short distance from USC's crosstown rival, UCLA, and not too far up the I-405 freeway from where I was staying. After looking at myself in the mirror and summoning up my courage, I took a deep breath and picked up the phone.

Contacting the FBI was easy enough, but getting to the right person took some doing. "I'd like to talk to an agent in charge of international matters," I told one person after another. "I have some confidential information about Iran that is important." The experience was frustrating and was quickly becoming discouraging. *Maybe,* I thought, *this isn't such a good idea after all.* Finally, after an hour of bouncing from one person to the next, I managed to schedule a meeting with two agents for that afternoon.

I gave myself plenty of time to get to West LA. As the cab took me there, I looked out the window and remembered that the last time I took this ride up I-405, I was on my way to Westwood for a college party. I felt as though I were on top of the world then. Would I ever feel that way again?

The streets outside the Federal Building brought back less happy memories. This had been the scene of several pro- and anti-Iranian demonstrations during the revolution. A few of us from the Islamic Students' Association would join the demonstrations supporting Khomeini and clash with the shah's supporters. There had always been a number of television cameras present. I now suspect that there were quite a few Islamic agent cameras present as well.

I decided not to go directly to the Federal Building but instead maintained my deception by calling a friend and meeting him at the popular Mario's Restaurant. From the entrance to Mario's you could see down Gayley one way and down Weyburn Place the other. If anyone had followed me, I would know, since I kept careful watch on my way to Westwood. I finished my lunch, bid good-bye to my friend, left through the rear exit, ducked into the parking structure across the alley, and went out the other side onto Veteran Avenue. It was a long walk down Veteran to Wilshire, where the FBI building is located. It would have been impossible for anyone following me to remain hidden. Still, I didn't go directly to the building, instead turning down Wilshire and coming in through the rear.

Once I registered at the front desk, two officials escorted me to a twelfth-floor conference room. One man introduced himself as Special Agent Cully Madigan and the other as Al Mancini. I gave them my name and immediately wondered if I should have used an alias. They offered me a cigarette, which I declined, and water, which I accepted. Strangely, I was not in the least nervous. I think my hosts were more anxious than I was, which made me realize that mine was not the kind of call they fielded every day. I was, after all, Iranian. The FBI, I would come to realize, was not an international agency. Most of the people they dealt with were Americans or foreign nationals from Eastern bloc countries. Men of my color were not yet their main concern. Little did they know how much that would change.

After exchanging pleasantries, we finally got around to discussing my reasons for contacting them. It was awkward at first, because they seemed confused about what I was telling them. I told them I held a position in the Revolutionary Guards in Iran and had access to information that was critical to both of our countries. To my astonishment, they kept calling the Revolutionary Guards "the Red Army," obviously confusing the mysterious Iran with the more familiar Soviet Union.

Again, I had misgivings. If these agents weren't even aware of what was going on in my country, why would they care about any information I had to give them? They jotted down everything I said, but it was obvious this was not an area of their expertise. When they asked if I could show anything to prove my claims, I took out the documents I'd brought with me. The documents, embossed with the official Revolutionary Guards' emblem, included a payroll list with the names of high-ranking officers and internal orders from several base commanders. Some of these orders had my name on them. I explained each, and they nodded as I did so, but the documents were all in Farsi and neither agent spoke the language.

I also had a picture of Mohsen Rezaei, the commander of the Guards, in his uniform behind a podium speaking to a large crowd.

Armed guards stood in the corners, and behind him stood Kazem, Rahim, and me. The agents' interest sharpened when they saw this, and they started asking more questions. They asked if they could keep the documents to verify them. I told them I was worried about confidentiality, about where the documents were going, and about whether I would get them back. Madigan assured me that the entire matter would receive only the most top-secret treatment and then suggested that I keep a low profile.

"We'll get back to you in a few days," Madigan said. "We need to sort a few things out. There are some people we need to talk to."

"What people?" I asked innocently enough.

Madigan locked my documents in his attaché case. "We'll contact you in a few days, Mr. Kahlili."

They escorted me out, thanked me for my time, and took note of my hotel on Century Boulevard.

"The Sheraton? Yeah, I know the one," Agent Mancini said. "How about you move out of that hotel into another one? Let me suggest the Shutters in Santa Monica. It's right on the beach and has several exits. Take a couple of cabs to get there. We'll call you very soon."

The next few days were full of uncertainty. On the one hand, I knew there were Islamic agents in the U.S. watching Iranians who entered the country. Kazem had told me once that the Guards had their agents keep an eye on the members of the opposition outside Iran and closely monitor the Guards members traveling abroad, as they knew that foreign intelligence services were looking to recruit operatives. On the other hand, I was worried about getting myself into some difficulty with the FBI if they didn't believe my story.

Trust between Americans and Iranians ceased to exist after the embassy takeover in Tehran. I had been at that takeover—though I certainly didn't have anything to do with the taking of hostages—which meant that they could have had pictures of me there. The FBI could have received my overture to them in any number of ways. The worst possible scenario was that they and their counterparts in the CIA would view me as an Iranian spy attempting to infiltrate their ranks by walking right through their front door with some preposterous proposal about giving them the Guards' secrets. I could only hope that the documents I gave them would prove that my intentions were the ones I stated.

Mancini's suggestion to move to the Shutters hotel did a great deal to persuade me that they believed me. If they thought I was lying to them or if they thought I was trying to spy on *them,* they wouldn't have made any effort to protect me. The room overlooked the beach, which provided diversion. For the next few days, I stayed in this pleasant room, but the hours couldn't pass fast enough. One minute I would call myself crazy, the next a hero for trying to figure out a way to help Iran. I tried to distract myself by watching TV or spending time on the beach, occasionally ordering room service. But the waiting was nerve-racking. Whenever my anxiety rose to the point where I thought I couldn't take it, I reached into the left-side pocket inside my jacket where I kept Roya's letter wrapped around Naser's picture. Without unfolding it, I pressed it to my heart and reminded myself of why I was there.

Finally, four days later, Madigan called and directed me to a Holiday Inn a few blocks away. I could have walked there, but I chose a cab instead, irritating the driver who had waited over an hour for the fare just to drive a few hundred yards. He started complaining, so I had him drive a circuitous route just in case someone was following me and then gave him a generous tip. Even that didn't seem to appease him.

I climbed the stairs to room 303 as instructed, and Mancini and Madigan greeted me. Another agent sat at a table by the window. He stood up and said, "Glad to meet you, Reza. I'm Patrick Barry." He had a handshake that reminded me of Agha Joon's, who would always shake with both hands with a tap or two on the shaker's hand to give reassurance. In my mind, I repeated words from my grandfather to bolster my confidence: *"Life is like a river. At times, we must flow with its current and enjoy the journey. But when it reaches a fall, if you don't fight against its current, you will fall, too. God has given us strength and his blessing to go through the rough times and keep our faith alive, Reza."*

Agent Barry didn't give me his title, but it was clear he was in charge. We talked for a half hour, rehashing much of what I'd already covered with the other two agents. I assumed he was taping the conversation. We discussed the documents I'd brought with me to the previous meeting and he told me that a translation confirmed that these documents were real. Barry then mentioned the deputy commander of the Guards, a man named Reza Movahedi.

"We're a little concerned about how current these documents are," he said. "We've been told that there's a new man in that position."

"Oh, no. I assure you that Movahedi still has that job," I said, wondering who was passing them bad information. It wouldn't have surprised me if the Guards had sent agents to the U.S. specifically to feed the Americans with the wrong details.

At that point, a door opened and another man entered from the adjoining suite. He was much better dressed than the other FBI agents were. I guessed his age to be early forties.

"This is Mr. Clark," Agent Mancini said, coming to his feet. I stood at the same time, not sure what was going on and measuring my five-eight height against his six-two or so. Clark seemed to fill the room.

"Steve Clark," the man said, smiling and holding out his hand. "United States Central Intelligence Agency. It's a pleasure to meet you, Mr. Kahlili. Did I say your name right?"

"Yes," I said. He had a firm handshake and penetrating eyes. "It's a pleasure to meet you as well."

That was the last meeting I would have with FBI Agents Madigan, Mancini, and Barry. Clark's arrival now aligned me with the CIA.

I liked Agent Clark from the beginning. He had a relaxed manner about him, and he took my proposal seriously. We talked that first day for a couple of hours after the FBI agents left, but the conversation was more general than I expected. We reviewed the information I'd given the FBI, and he asked several more questions about the structure of the Guards and its leadership. He was much better informed about what was going on in Iran than the FBI agents had been. He asked if he could keep the documents I'd brought from Iran, and I agreed. Feeling a connection to him, I showed him Naser's picture and Roya's letter, and I told him her story. I told him how they tortured and killed young girls, in God's name, and before their execution they raped them because they believed that if a girl dies a virgin, she will go to heaven, and they wanted to deny them this reward. I explained how Asadollah Lajevardi, the head of the Iran Prisons Organization, created this atmosphere of terror to keep the prisoners frightened and submissive. Iranians knew him as the "Butcher of Evin," not only because of the thousands he killed, but for his practice of draining the blood of prisoners about to be executed to use the plasma for soldiers injured in the war with Iraq. He left his victims with just enough blood so they were conscious as they faced the firing squad.

I met with Agent Clark, whom I quickly began to call Steve, several times over the next few days. Each time, we took extreme measures to ensure that no one was tailing me. I would take two cabs to our designated meeting area, which changed every time, and then I would walk the last couple of blocks.

Steve listened sympathetically when I became emotional. He accepted my words without overreacting. I was relieved to be able to talk freely at last as I discussed the Guards and the nature of my position in the organization. My hopes grew with every meeting.

And then Steve said something that completely shocked me.

"Reza, I am touched by your painful story and I can feel your sincerity in wanting to help your country." Steve paused, looking me in the eyes. "But you could help the most if you went back working for us."

I froze in my chair and could not come up with any response. Even though I had initiated this process, I never thought that the CIA would ask me to be a spy on their behalf.

"I know how hard it must have been on you to take the huge risk of coming here and contacting us. Believe me, we are grateful for that. But we need your help if we are going to help your country. You will be our eyes and ears in Iran."

I hadn't come here with the intention of becoming a spy. I thought I would pass some information to the Americans and that they would take over from there. But now I realized how little they knew about what was going on in my country. They needed so much more than I'd brought with me, and if they didn't get it from me, they might not get accurate information from anyone.

"I will do it," I said hesitantly.

"That's exactly what I wanted to hear," Steve said, rising from his chair and patting me on the shoulder. "By the way, we've assigned you a code name. From now on, we'll be calling you Wally."

11

TRICKS OF THE TRADE

WALLY.

I repeated the name to myself.

Even though I knew from the moment I boarded the plane to America that my life was going to change forever, hearing this code name drove home the point that it would truly never be the same again. The idea that I now had a CIA code name brought all kinds of words to mind: *traitor, secrets, deception, suspicion, lies.* And these words weighed heavily on me. My parents didn't raise me to be a traitor and a liar. But they did raise me to believe in a higher good and to understand that destroying evil sometimes required us to do things we never would have imagined for ourselves.

My relationship with Steve grew into a comfortable daily exchange between two businessmen—whose business happened to be espionage. Steve seemed steady, direct, and honest. He was a well-grounded man, quick on the uptake. When I was with him, I felt comfortable and what we did felt natural. I didn't feel doubts and fears about the turn my life had taken when we were working together.

Hotel meetings turned out to have too many logistical complications, so Steve told me that we would continue our sessions at a safe house deep in the mountains above Malibu. I had to take a bus or cab to a predetermined location, walk a couple of extra blocks, and meet up with Steve. From there, we would continue to the safe house together.

The night before our first meeting at this new place, I examined all of the bus routes I was to travel. I memorized the information Steve provided about shopping centers along the way, which stores had back doors, which had big reflective windows, and where the restaurants were. All of this would help me if I needed to avoid having someone follow me. As it turned out, I would put this to use immediately.

At the first bus stop on the way to the meeting, I lined up with other passengers, checked the number on the bus against a printed schedule, looked around for street signs, and checked a map against the schedule. I looked very much the tourist. Just before I got on the bus, I asked the driver about various bus routes, hanging back to allow the other passengers to board.

One man wearing a baseball cap pulled low lingered behind me. He had a rolled-up newspaper in one hand and he kept the other hand in his pocket. He definitely set off my radar.

"Will this bus take me to Fox Hills?" I asked the driver, thinking quickly.

"Fox Hills?" the driver asked as though my question made no sense. "You're on the wrong side of the street, young man. Take the bus on the other side."

"Thank you."

I casually crossed the street and caught another bus going in the opposite direction. The man with the baseball cap followed me. This sent a surge of adrenaline through my body as I struggled not to look at him. In my early meetings with Steve, he taught me some "spy tricks," including how to lose a tail without being obvious. I did my best to remember his lessons now. I got off the bus at the Fox Hills Mall and wandered the stores, constantly checking reflections in the windows for the man in the cap. Heart pounding, I entered a bookstore. I picked up a magazine and stood reading it for a while as Baseball Cap wandered up and down the book aisles. After some time passed, I put the magazine back in the rack and left the bookstore.

I took several other evasive measures, but after each one, I soon spotted Baseball Cap again. My mind raced with the implications. I had to call Steve. I found a phone booth in the mall and dialed his number, but there was no answer.

I hung up, checked the number, and dialed again. Baseball Cap was across the mall talking to an old woman. He seemed to be asking for directions, as the woman pointed north and then west. Baseball Cap nodded and the phone kept ringing.

Dammit, Steve, pick up.

Frustrated, I was about to put the handset down when Steve finally came on the line.

"Steve, it's Wally. I'm being followed."

"Followed?"

"There is this guy who followed me from the bus stop to the Fox Hills Mall."

"Okay, Wally, stay calm. Just go back to your hotel."

"But what if he follows me there?"

"Do what I have taught you and try to lose him. I will call you in a few days to set up another meeting."

I started to ask another question, but Steve had already hung up. This made me feel very alone and very vulnerable. *Maybe I should just abort the whole enterprise and fly back home.* If spy work was this dangerous in America, how much more dangerous would it be when I returned to Tehran?

When I went outside of the mall, I found Baseball Cap at the bus stop, probably waiting for me to make my next move. Steve's suggestion to go back to the hotel was not going to work, so I went back into the mall and slipped into and out of several stores, ultimately trying on random outfits in a May Company dressing room for twenty minutes. When I finally came out, Baseball Cap was gone. It appeared that the evasive methods Steve taught me paid off.

Relieved and satisfied, I decided that instead of going back to my hotel, I'd go out to Tarzana, where my aunt Giti lived. What better way to throw off my pursuers than to act as normal as possible?

Aunt Giti lived in a neighborhood made up mostly of expatriate Iranians. Some had been around as long as she had and many more fled Iran when Khomeini came to power. I took a cab to the San Fernando Valley and asked the driver to drop me off a couple blocks from my aunt's home so I could walk the rest of the way and keep my eyes open for anyone following me.

"Bia tu, azizam," Aunt Giti exclaimed when she saw me at the door. "Come in, my dear." Hearing her speak Farsi with so much affection in her voice brought me an ache of longing, a reminder of the easy days of my earlier time in California when I didn't have to lie and I didn't have to look over my shoulder. This made me homesick for the home I once had, and I took my aunt to a nearby Persian restaurant on Ventura Boulevard, a popular gathering place for the local Iranians. I didn't care if anyone followed us there. I was just another Iranian visitor on family business. This was the closest I had felt to normal in days.

As we ate, Aunt Giti handed me a couple of brochures her doctor had given her explaining the progression of Parkinson's disease. "Reza, I dread what this insidious disease is going to do to me, but I've come to accept it. It's hard saying good-bye to all I have here. But I will be happy and safe if I move to an assisted-living home."

I wasn't nearly as convinced as she was. Though one of the purposes I'd had in coming to America was setting my aunt up in a new residence, I wondered if this was really best for her. "But, Khaleh Giti, all of your family members are in Iran. You should be among them. We'll take care of you. I will take care of you myself. . . ."

She interrupted me by shaking her head. "Don't, Reza. Don't make it harder for me. You know I would never return to Iran. It's not the same there anymore." She caught herself before the conversation turned more intense, smiled, and continued. "I wish your father were alive so he could see what a fine young man you've become."

I knew then that her decision to move into a care home was final and that discussing other options would be heartbreaking for both of us. I did what I could to make this easier for her, taking several days to arrange her move and put her house on the market.

When I dropped Aunt Giti at the assisted-living facility, she handed me a picture of her and my father on the Golden Gate Bridge. "This is the first summer your father was here. When he came to America, he told me he wanted to see this bridge more than anything else." She managed a difficult smile. Smiling was much tougher for her now because of her illness. "After he saw that magnificent bridge, he told me he wanted to be an engineer. And that's what he became. He was that kind of a man. He dreamed of something and he pursued it."

She closed her eyes for a long moment before continuing. "After he moved back to Iran and married your mother, and, of course, you were born, he continued writing me letters and talking about you, Reza. He told me he had big dreams for you. He loved you so much." At this point, she lost any semblance of control. She burst into tears and hugged me closely. "I am glad you came here, Reza. I am so proud that you cared so much that you left your wife to help your sick auntie. Your father was right—you are a great young man." I held her for a long time while she cried. Then I helped her settle into her new home and promised I would visit her again before I returned to Iran. As I left her that day, I couldn't help but feel a certain measure of shame. Yes, I'd come to her aid at a critical time in her life, but I'd used her as a smokescreen for my real activities in the U.S. Would I have been such a "great young man" for her if her needs didn't match so seamlessly with my larger agenda?

It took Steve the better part of a week before he set up another meeting. On my way to our rendezvous, I noticed the same man again, wearing a different outfit and a different hat. I changed a few buses and managed to lose him with my very last transfer. This left me with a certain sense of accomplishment, but a far stronger sense of foreboding. I suspected that the Guards already knew of my contacts with the CIA. If that was true, my family was doomed.

But when I met Steve at the rendezvous point in his car, he was beaming. "Congratulations! You used your tactics to shake a very skilled operative."

"Excuse me?"

"I assigned one of our people to tail you to see if you could spot him and shake him without panicking. You acted like a pro. You're learning your lessons well, Wally. Just keep it up and never let your guard down. You'll stay alive longer."

I didn't really need *that* reminder.

After a ten-minute drive through Pacific Palisades, we climbed up Las Flores Canyon to Piuma Road and the safe house. It was one of the most beautiful drives I'd ever made. Eucalyptus trees lined either side of the one-lane road that rose rapidly toward the top of the mountain. At the end of a driveway that approached from the rear of the house, a panorama opened up revealing a sparkling Pacific Ocean with the Channel Islands to the north all the way to Catalina Island and the Palos Verdes Peninsula to the south. We exited the car and approached a small wooden A-frame house whose front was all glass.

The interior furnishings were minimal, but the spectacular view was so diverting, I temporarily forgot why I was there. Several places in my country were this beautiful, and thinking of them now fortified my resolve. I wanted Iran to be beautiful for everyone.

Steve sat me down and we got to work, my appreciation of the setting soon forgotten. He took copious notes as we talked about the Guards: about how the regime formed them to protect the country and the revolution and to neutralize the regular army—and its many sympathizers—that had operated under the shah, about their training, the size of their forces, and their armaments.

"I knew several Guards members who traveled back and forth to Lebanon through Syria," I told him. "They complained about the cowardice of the Shia Muslim militias in Lebanon fighting the Israeli occupation. They weren't satisfied with the Israeli death toll."

"What's the Guards' involvement in Lebanon?" Steve asked.

"They introduced training, arms, money, and, most important, the idea of martyrdom."

Steve sat forward. "Tell me more about that."

"Muslim youth in the Middle East are being brainwashed by the mullahs to think that sacrificing their lives for Islam is the greatest glory. Those who choose martyrdom are promised the highest place in heaven next to Prophet Mohammad and the great Imams."

Steve said the CIA was concerned that Khomeini was extending his tendrils of control into surrounding nations. I informed him that Khomeini had already accomplished that goal. The Guards had established headquarters in both Syria and Lebanon, where they conducted the command and control of various radical groups, encouraging new recruits to carry out terrorist activities in order to achieve the rewards of martyrdom. Even where Khomeini didn't control governments, he reigned in the hearts and minds of frustrated zealots who wanted to regain the past glories of Islam by force. Khomeini wasn't merely the Supreme Leader of one nation; he was proclaiming himself the anointed head of the One True Religion who took orders directly from God.

"And anyone who dares to oppose Khomeini or the ruling clerics is defined as *mohareb,* those waging war against God. The Revolutionary Courts deal with them. These men believe that torturing the opposition to obtain a confession is proper. If a prisoner dies during torture this is fair and just, and comes under the auspices of Islamic law. Virgin girls have been raped prior to their execution so they would not go to heaven. Armed demonstrators are killed on the spot. There are no exceptions, not even for the wounded. Thousands of *mohareb* have been summarily executed without giving them a chance to defend themselves."

Steve shook his head and then looked at me with an odd expression.

I guessed what he was thinking. "These are the people who will deal with me if I am caught," I said.

He smiled wryly.

I went on to explain how Syrian diplomatic facilities and chan-
nels were at the disposal of the Guards. On Khomeini's orders, plane
after plane delivered arms and personnel to Syria to promote a new
Islamic state. Often the Guards' convoys received Syrian diplomatic
license plates so they could operate in Lebanon without interference.
At other times, the Guards were chauffeured in Syrian diplomatic
cars. This effort created Hezbollah, which grew with the full financial backing of Iran, quickly becoming a major force in Lebanon.

Steve continued to pepper me with questions, taking me in many
different directions. A conversation about where I worked wandered
into questions about my friends and family, about my education at
USC, and back to Iran and the Revolutionary Guards. This led to a
discussion about who I worked with, and I finally mentioned a difficult subject for me: Kazem. I told Steve about the nature of our relationship and about why we continued to be friends, though things
were not the same between us as they had once been.

"You know, Steve, I don't know if I can trust him anymore. I suspect he was involved in Naser's arrest. I wanted to leave the Guards
after what happened to Naser and stay away from Kazem. I decided
to stay on because I needed him to help me with my mission. He has
a lot of contacts in the Guards and he can make things happen."

I told Steve about our childhood. He smiled as I recounted the
mischief we'd gotten into. But as we continued to talk, he began
to understand how friendship took on a different cast in Iran when
ideologies conflicted. In America, two friends could hold opposing
political views and it would amount to no more than perhaps some
heated arguments. In Iran, it could result in the arrest and execution
of a friend—with his brother and sister thrown in for good measure.

Sensing my sadness in relating these stories, Steve suggested we
stop for the day. I appreciated this. I was tired and I needed to refresh
myself. We planned another meeting for the next day. That night in
my hotel room, I felt relieved. Talking to Steve about Kazem had removed a heavy burden from my shoulders. Trust in another man was
something I hadn't experienced in a while.

The interviews with Steve went on for four to six hours each time we met over the course of a month or so. I hadn't intended to stay in America this long, and I had to lie repeatedly to both Somaya and Kazem about the "complications with Aunt Giti's arrangements" that were keeping me here.

On our last day together, Steve asked me about the hostage crisis at the U.S. embassy.

"Here's what we know," he said, pulling out a folder and beginning to read from a report.

I quickly interrupted him. "No, that's wrong."

"How can you be sure?"

"I was there."

"You were *there*?"

"Yes."

"But you were a member of the Guards then."

"Of course."

He paused to absorb this. "So this wasn't some grassroots student uprising?"

"Not really. I did not know it then, but an order had come down from Mousavi Khoeiniha, a radical clergy member. The Islamic students' body developed a plan for the takeover and Khoeiniha presented it to Ayatollah Khomeini for his approval."

Steve's mouth dropped open. "I thought Khomeini didn't know anything about it. I thought he was just supportive after the fact."

I shook my head. "Kazem told me afterward that once the plan was approved by Khomeini, the students, who called themselves *Daneshjooyane Musalmane Peyro Khate Imam,* Islamic Student Followers of Imam's Line, arranged for the demonstration. Guards and intel members posed as students among them."

"I can't believe this!"

"The plan was to demonstrate against the U.S. for allowing the shah to stay in America. The protesters demanded the shah's return to Iran for trial. But in truth, Khomeini's clerics had already assigned individuals to facilitate the takeover. They had even chosen the name

Den of Spies beforehand, so that after the takeover, they could feed that to the press and claim the embassy was the center of spy activities against the clerical regime."

Steve looked down at his folder. "So our best intelligence is wrong."

"They laugh at you and call you cowboys, Steve. They watch your news shows and laugh."

"Amazing," said Steve, scribbling notes. "What was their ultimate goal for this action?"

"Khomeini hated America. He wanted to sever ties with the U.S. while at the same time making you look weak in the eyes of the world. This would strengthen the position of the radicals within Iran and punish President Carter for allowing the shah to stay in the U.S. They held the hostages long enough to ensure that Carter lost the election. In doing this, Khomeini went beyond unseating the king of Iran. He toppled the president of a superpower. Could there be any greater proof that Khomeini is God's instrument on earth?"

Steve understood the point I was making. "They really believe that stuff, don't they?"

"They really do."

We then had a long discussion about the three branches of the armed forces formed after the revolution in Iran—the Revolutionary Guards, the Komiteh, and the Basij. The Palestinian Liberation Organization had trained some of the Guards' commanders and these commanders were active in guerrilla warfare in Lebanon before the revolution. Steve wrote furiously as I related the details of the Guards' organization. I even sketched out an organizational chart of the various officers and their responsibilities. Then I talked about the Komiteh, the police force formed by the mullahs whose job it was to provide security and ensure strict adherence to proper Islamic behavior. And I told him about the Basij, or People's Army, the volunteer paramilitary force consisting primarily of teenage reprobates deployed throughout the main cities to confront any uprisings among the population. The regime recruited most of the Basijis from very poor families in small towns and villages. They taught them the virtues of martyrdom, gave them minimal training, and handed them machine guns to intimidate people in the cities. Steve knew very little about either of these organizations.

I told him about an incident with the Basijis that involved a prominent doctor and his family from my neighborhood. The Basijis spread throughout the city, especially at night, setting up checkpoints and searching cars for guns or members of the Mujahedin. At the same time, they, too, demanded adherence to proper Islamic behavior. For example, a man and a woman had to be married if they were in a car together unless they were family members. Two Basijis would routinely stop cars at random to interrogate the occupants, while two others would take a position nearby behind trees.

This particular doctor had taken his wife and two teenage daughters out to dinner when the Basijis stopped them on their way home. The teenaged militiamen were rude and insulting, and they scared the doctor's wife and girls. The doctor objected and he slapped one of the offenders in an effort to defend himself and his family. After all, these people interrogating them were young teenagers who should have been showing respect to this decent man. When the doctor slapped the Basiji, the others behind the trees opened fire, killing the man while his loved ones watched.

As I told this story, the outrage I felt when I first heard about it returned. When I finished, Steve massaged his writing hand and said, "Wally, we've covered a lot. Let's take a break and have some lunch. We should get away from this for a while."

Steve was right. I hadn't realized how drained I was feeling, how much emotional energy I was expending, until we took some time away. We sat on the balcony and ate in the warm afternoon breeze. Relaxing at last, I thought of Somaya and about how much I missed her and looked forward to seeing her again.

"You're smiling, Wally. Why's that—not that it's not a good thing."

It was comforting not having to hide what I really thought. "I was thinking about my wife. I wish she were here now. She loves nature and warm weather."

That afternoon, Steve and I talked about our families. We discussed the difficulties of lying to our loved ones. Steve's wife thought he was a contracts supervisor in charge of telemetry systems acquisition for the FAA. This provided him with the cover to travel and be away from home for long periods. He made sure he'd chosen an occupation that was too technical to discuss with anyone who knew him well.

I told Steve that I thought Somaya was the most beautiful woman on earth. He smiled while I told him how smart and caring she was and when I called her "the prettiest angel I'd ever seen."

"Then you believe in angels too?" he said with a laugh.

The thought sent pangs to my heart. While I did believe in angels, I'd come to believe in devils as well. I'd seen them at Evin Prison.

"Let's go back to work," I said. "I have a lot more to tell you."

Back in the living room, Steve pulled out his notebook and said that we should wrap up soon. He asked me to focus on areas I thought were most valuable to him. Torrents of stories and facts rushed through my mind. There was so much to say. We discussed the Foundation for the Deprived, which had seized the assets of people who worked for the shah's regime. They were responsible for the thousands who fled the country in fear of reprisal. This included minorities such as the Jews and the Baha'is. Since the mullahs don't recognize Baha'i as an official religion, they executed and imprisoned hundreds of practitioners and prevented thousands of others from getting jobs, education, and any opportunity. The Foundation for the Deprived seized factories, homes, money in banks, and personal belongings.

"Do your people know what they do with this money?" I asked Steve.

He shrugged.

"They fund terrorist groups through charitable organizations. The Revolutionary Guards supervise all of the transactions."

"Jesus, Wally, this is great stuff. Please go on."

"I learned through Kazem and my commander, Rahim, that the Chinese are providing military training for Guards members on a base in China and that the Soviets are setting up the intelligence apparatus and security infrastructure for the mullahs. They are responsible for introducing torture, polygraph tests, and truth serum injections at Evin Prison. And this is not just for high-ranking enemies of the state. This is where they take all political opponents, from journalists to teenage girls."

"Really."

"They don't just punish crimes, Steve. They punish thoughts. Torture and truth serum are ways to find out what you really believe in your heart."

"It sounds like the Inquisition in Europe."

"Except much more sophisticated and systematic."

"This direct contact between the Soviets and the Guards—did you see this or just hear about it?"

"I witnessed the Soviets' political attachés and businessmen in high-level contacts with the Iranian government while visiting several ministries with Kazem."

Steve put his notebook on the coffee table, took a sip of water, straightened his back, and looked at me. "Wally, you have no idea how helpful all this information is to us. Believe me, your total candor is very much appreciated."

It was rewarding to know that what I was telling him was having such an impact on him. I knew that I had information the CIA could use, but I didn't realize until Steve started debriefing me how uninformed the U.S. was about the ayatollah's activities in the Middle East. The thought made me realize how valuable my contribution would be—and how savagely the Guards would punish me if they ever caught me. That morning, on the way to the safe house, I thought I'd noticed another tail.

"Hey, Steve, did you assign someone to follow me today?"

He froze. "Why do you ask?"

"Well, the reason I was late was that I thought I was being followed."

Steve said nothing, only staring. This made me very uncomfortable and I started talking quickly to cover my nervousness.

"At first I thought I was mistaken, but after taking a few diversions, I noticed the tail was still there. It took me an hour to lose him."

At that moment, Steve turned into someone else, confirming for me that whoever followed me that morning worked for an organization other than the CIA. His jaw hardened and his voice became stern. "I want you to be completely aware of the consequences if things go wrong, Wally. The United States government will deny any relationship with you. There won't be a navy fleet coming to your rescue. I'm sorry to be so blunt, but it's absolutely necessary. Do I make myself clear?"

It took me a moment to answer. Maybe Steve had two people inside him also: the Steve who liked me and the Steve who would sacrifice my family and me for his cause.

"I understand."

Steve's sudden transition jarred me. As did the news that this was going to be our last meeting of this sort. He told me that my training would continue in London and that I needed to take a lie-detector test. I was surprised that he hadn't asked me to do this earlier, but I guess it truly mattered to the CIA only now that they were about to share some of their spying secrets with me.

He handed me a slip of paper with information about my new contact. I stared at it and wondered if Steve's empathy had just been keen professional interest. After all, training the Iranian patsy who would deliver dangerous secrets to his department would garner him accolades from his colleagues and boost his career. His safe, secure American career.

I swallowed my rising resentment and reminded myself of what I had already accomplished by reporting the madness to someone who could do something with the information. I had told him things I had never told anyone. I had trusted him, utterly. And at that moment, in spite of his shift in attitude, I was certain he trusted me.

My days in California were coming to a close. But my training was not. Next I would go to England, where I would truly learn how to be a spy.

TRAINING FOR ESPIONAGE

THE AGENT ADMINISTERING the lie-detector test at the Hacienda Hotel loosened his thin necktie. He seemed as tired as I was. It had taken him several hours of questioning before he felt satisfied with my answers. He unhooked the wires from my body, packed his bag, and then left me alone with my thoughts. The only sound in the room was the fan of the air conditioner. I felt drained, exhausted, and alone, thinking about Steve's earlier admonition and about how completely unprotected I was. I wanted to return to Somaya immediately, but at the same time, I feared what proximity to me might do to her. I was putting her at terrible risk simply for the sin of loving me.

I didn't feel like a hero. I felt like a traitor and, worse, a bad husband.

Then Steve entered—the "friendly" Steve—smiling broadly as he informed me I had passed with flying colors. This time, I couldn't muster enthusiasm for his pride in me. In the time that had passed since our sobering conversation, I couldn't stop thinking about the look on his face when I said I thought I'd been followed. The look said that if someone had been following me, the CIA knew nothing about it.

"Let's talk about salary," he said jovially, clearly not on the same train of thought as I had been.

I was surprised at the mention of money. We'd never discussed it before. I knew spies received compensation, but that had never been my motive, so I didn't think to ask about it. Steve offered me $2,500 a month. This was probably the bare minimum by American standards, but it was a good amount with the exchange rate in Iran. Without even considering negotiating, I accepted.

Steve offered a few options regarding getting the money to me. The first was a cash delivery, which I rejected because it would be difficult to explain my having so much cash if someone found me with it. Another option was to set up an account in another country, where one of the CIA's shell companies would deposit the money every month. That worked for me. He offered to have proof of deposit sent to me anywhere I wanted, but I declined. I wanted to reassert our relationship of trust. The CIA would have to trust that I would deliver important information to them, and I would have to trust that they would make deposits for me. We agreed to set up the account in London; I would need to memorize the details.

Once we finished this conversation, Steve stood. "Good luck, Wally," he said, taking my hand in a firm grip.

"Thanks," I said, less steadily than I would have liked. With no further words, I left for my hotel.

I never saw or heard from Steve again.

Once I packed my bags, I called the FBI agents I had originally contacted to say good-bye. My journey into this new life had started with a random connection to these men. Now, for good or bad, I was about to embark on the path I first stepped onto with them. The two agents put me on the speakerphone and both were gracious. Agent Mancini said he truly hoped to see me back in the States soon and wished that God would bless me in my endeavors.

Before I left, I went to see Aunt Giti to say good-bye. Once again, she told me what a good man I'd become, and once again this left me feeling like something of a fraud. I hugged her tight before I left. This would be the last time I'd ever see her. She died several years later and I never got the opportunity to visit her again.

I spent the sleepless twelve-hour British Airways trip to England practicing my new job in my head and thinking about what I would have to do. From this point on, I would be leading a double life. Half of me would continue to be a loving, devoted husband and a loyal member of the Revolutionary Guards. The other half of me would be reporting every salient fact about the Guards and would be putting everyone I loved in mortal danger. I wasn't sure I would ever be able to reconcile these two selves. I prayed for guidance and hoped my actions would have some meaning.

London was typically dreary when I arrived—overcast, hazy, and gray. It fit my mood. I checked into the Park Inn by Hyde Park as the CIA had instructed me. The hotel sits on the northern edge of Hyde Park, with easy access to the Tube, London's subway, and within walking distance of most of the tourist spots. It's close to the Marble Arch, which stands on the site of the Tyburn gallows, where grisly executions—many of people who opposed the government— took place centuries ago. The irony of this was not lost on me.

I passed by Marble Arch nearly every time I went out. I learned that the executions gave rise to a couple of familiar English phrases. The term "one for the road" originated here because the executioners allowed a condemned man to have one last drink at any alehouse en route to the Tyburn gallows. The same experience led to the phrase "on the wagon" because the guards minding the prisoner had to remain on the wagon that carted the prisoner while he had his last drink, and they were not allowed to imbibe while they were on the job.

When I settled in at my hotel, I called Somaya's parents. I told them that since my connection was through London, I decided to stay for a week to meet with some old friends and to pay them a visit. I found some small comfort in talking to them about Somaya. Thinking about my wife always made me smile, though I could no longer think of her without wondering about the future I'd created for us and of the lies I would be living. Her parents asked me about the friends I was seeing—yet another lie I hadn't prepared in advance—and insisted that I stay with them. They were quite upset when I politely declined, but I held steadfast. I couldn't allow them to become suspicious of my comings and goings.

I didn't do a particularly good job of mollifying them with my excuses. This led me to wonder yet again how equipped I was for a life of espionage. If I couldn't even come up with convincing lies to tell my wife's parents, how would I function as a professional liar under the watch of the Revolutionary Guards, who searched for spies in every turn of phrase?

After this, I went to a public phone booth and called my new contact. A few hours later, a soft-spoken woman came to my hotel room, introducing herself as Carol. She was a smallish American dressed in a brown outfit with knee-high boots. I assumed she dressed this way to blend in with high-end shoppers on Park Avenue or Oxford Street. I liked Carol right away. She was calm and reserved, and I found her presence reassuring. This feeling increased dramatically when she spoke to me in Farsi, which surprised and warmed me.

"You know, Wally, I lived in Iran for a long while with my parents when I was younger," she said when she noticed my reaction. "My father was a military attaché."

This meant a great deal to me. It meant that she would have a good picture in her mind of life in Iran before the revolution and that she would sympathize with what we had lost.

"I have lots of good memories of Iran," she continued. "Iranians are very hospitable. I made some good friends. I am grateful for the time I spent in your country." She talked about places she visited, making me feel as though I were having a conversation with an old friend and catching up on what we had done while we were apart. Of course, this was only an illusion. Carol had my complete dossier and knew everything there was to know about me and why I was there.

Although she spoke Farsi, we talked mostly in English. We'd been together for more than an hour when her smile dropped and she locked onto my eyes.

"Wally, you don't have to do this. You can quit right now and it will be okay."

Her saying this surprised me. Since my last meeting with Steve, I had felt as though there was no turning back. But what Carol was saying was true. If I wanted to walk away, I could do so without consequences—assuming, of course, that the Guards were not already aware of my activities. The fact that I could do so didn't matter, though.

"I'm in this, Carol. I need to do this. My decision is firm and final."

Carol's expression softened. "I had a feeling you were going to say that."

We went over the training schedule and Carol stressed the importance of my taking every precaution to keep my destinations secret and secure. Losing someone in a crowd was a little easier in London than it was in LA, but I would still have to be cautious.

My in-laws lived in the Mayfair district, which was convenient since the safe house was in the same area. Several means were available for me to get there: the ubiquitous black cabs, the Tube, or even a walk across Hyde Park or down Park Avenue. I usually walked because it allowed me to take in the surroundings, distinctive for their combination of new and old architecture. If I suspected that someone was following me, I altered my route slightly and dropped in for a visit with my in-laws. They were always delighted to see me, although it also meant that I would have to endure their further pleas for me to stay with them and provide my fumbling reasons why I couldn't do this. The safe house was down a narrow alley filled with several small shops that had attached flats. It was easy enough to duck into one of the shops to obscure my destination.

Carol had asked me to meet with her in a café in the Mayfair district. This made me nervous in a completely unanticipated way. Rather than worrying that an agent of the Guards would see me, I was more concerned that my in-laws might find me with Carol. How would I explain being with another woman? Although she was at least ten years older than me, she would still raise Somaya's parents' eyebrows.

We went from the café to the safe house immediately. I didn't ask her why we went to the café in the first place because I felt I needed to trust her. When we got to the house, she said, "Are you ready for your first training session?"

"I'm a little nervous, but I'll be fine," I replied, feeling more than a little apprehensive. But in a sense I was excited as much as I was nervous. I thought of James Bond movies and I had to smile thinking of myself filling the role of Sean Connery or Roger Moore. It was the first moment in a long time when this life didn't seem like a burden to me.

There were two American men waiting for us in the safe house. David was a young man who was to teach me how to write messages to Carol from home. Joe was a man in his midforties who would teach me how to receive code messages from the CIA. I worked half a day with each of them. These sessions turned out to be nothing like the James Bond movies and I certainly did not get a magic pen or a multitasking watch.

"You are getting this fast," David said after my first session with him. I found it easier to figure out how to send messages than to learn how to receive them.

The classes reminded me of being back in school. In the ensuing days my instructors presented me with a lesson and then gave me a test to see how well I absorbed what they taught. Although at first it seemed a little hard and confusing, I caught on quickly, and I discovered that I had a natural affinity for deciphering code. In all, the training lasted less than a week, filling me with new skills—and the new anxieties that came with having these skills.

For the final exam that I "had to pass," I received the coded message "Welcome to the CIA, Wally. Carol will be your contact from here on out and she will take good care of you." When I deciphered this, I knew I'd mastered this skill with Joe. David then challenged me to respond, using the methods he'd taught me.

"I am glad I have joined the CIA and I am looking forward to working with the agency to help free my country from the tyrants," I coded back. David deciphered this and then shook my hand.

"You are a natural," he said as he congratulated me. "Working with you was a pleasure." He gave me a package containing all of the documents I needed for my communications and I said good-bye to the two trainers.

Carol walked me to the door and put a hand on my shoulder.

"Be very careful, Wally."

I nodded. "I will be."

"Don't do anything that could bring harm to you or your family."

I offered her a bittersweet smile. "That's a little bit of a challenge in Iran these days."

"Just remember, Wally, if you need anything, I'll be here for you. Just let me know with your letters. I will do my best to guide you with my messages."

I went back to the hotel to pack. After being away for nearly a month and a half, I was headed home. I would be going back a different man than when I left, quite literally. Once I started packing, a wave of emotion struck me unexpectedly. I just started sobbing. I sat on the bed next to my suitcase, wiping the tears from my face. It had been relatively easy to maintain my resolve during my debriefing and training. But now that I was going back to Tehran, the force of what I'd agreed to become overwhelmed me. From the moment I set foot in my country, I would be living outside of the world around me. Though I would be involved in the lives of people who loved me, I would be, in many ways, alone.

I lay down on the bed, though I knew I wouldn't be able to sleep. To try to bolster my courage, I thought about Naser about how he witnessed the devastation laid upon his sister and brother. I thought about Roya and the degradations she suffered from soulless men. I thought about Khomeini, who characterized himself as a representative of God, yet was so power hungry and greedy that he caused the most brutal acts to be committed in his name.

None of it helped. I couldn't let go of the fact that I'd convinced myself that my only option was to become a betrayer of my country.

I had agreed to give sensitive secrets to the Americans. And while I believed that people like Steve and Carol had good intentions, I had no illusions about America's foreign policies. Those policies had sometimes caused pain in the world and especially in the Middle East. Ironically, the CIA, my new employer, was responsible for orchestrating the coup known as Operation Ajax in 1953. Funded by the British and U.S. governments, Operation Ajax removed the democratically elected prime minister of Iran, Dr. Mohammad Mosaddeq. He was responsible for nationalizing the oil industry and eliminating the British monopoly on Iran's oil. The CIA also helped set up the shah's SAVAK police, who tortured and executed the opposition. The SAVAK model for treating prisoners continued at Evin under Khomeini. Therefore, the very organization I was entrusting with my secrets had actually contributed to the atrocities I was trying to end. Would they change course this time and help me help my country?

I believed they would for two reasons. One was that while America's history in foreign affairs was hardly spotless, it was the country that had liberated the world in World War II. I truly believed they could come to the rescue again. The other was that in the face of all my confusion over my role and the fate of my country, I knew one thing absolutely: the people of Iran could never win without America's help.

None of this helped me to sleep that night. But it did allow me to hold my head high when I stepped onto the plane the next day.

A SPY RETURNS HOME

HEATHROW AIRPORT WAS crowded with midday travelers queued up to go through the checkpoints. Because of persistent attacks from the Irish Republican Army, security measures had been high in England for many years by this point. When I got through the long line, I joined a multitude of fellow Iranians milling about the lounge waiting to board Iran Air flight 710.

It was common knowledge among Iranians that Revolutionary Guards agents made note of every individual traveling to and from Iran. They scrutinized every flight coming into and going out of the country as if the future of the clerical government hinged upon their doing so. I knew I needed to be extra cautious to stay under the radar and to avoid arousing suspicion. Fortunately, this was becoming second nature to me, and I boarded without incident.

Sitting in a window seat, I flashed back on everything I'd experienced in the past month and a half. From my initial meeting with the FBI agents to my final test in London, these days had changed me overwhelmingly and permanently. When in the midst of this the thought of my wife came into my head, the fact that I'd redefined "normal" on this trip shook me and caused an ache in my heart. I had half expected to feel relief to be going home when the plane lifted off, but instead all I felt was anxiety. I was Reza/Wally now. I was no longer the husband Somaya sent on this trip, no longer the son my mother believed she'd figured out, and certainly no longer the Guards member my brothers thought me to be.

My thoughts stayed fixed while the landscape passed beneath me as we traversed the European mainland, then over the Danube River and the Adriatic Sea, the scattered mountains of the Taurus range, and the rugged peaks of the Zagros Mountains of my own country. The captain finally broke my reverie by announcing that we had entered Iranian skies. The clouds parted as if to proclaim a new beginning. The hills shone with shades of verdant green and golden browns—beautiful, God-given scenery. A reflective band of water shimmered like stained glass, and soon familiar glimpses of life appeared—a farm, a village, a city.

The seat belt sign flashed and I tried to cajole myself to stay in the present. I thought about Somaya waiting to pick me up, and this time the thought filled me with excitement. I'd missed my beautiful wife terribly and maybe fully realized how much I missed her only now that I was about to see her again.

But first I needed to go through customs. Once again, anxiety seared me. Everything could fall apart in this instant.

All of the passengers on the plane received equal scrutiny. Still, I felt invisible eyes watching me specifically, and the tension built. *Remember, you are a member of the Revolutionary Guards,* I repeated continuously as I headed toward the front of the line.

As I did, I heard all tourist interviews start with the same question: "Where are you coming from, and what are your plans for your visit?" The first question for all Iranians was "Where have you been, how long did you stay, and what have you brought back?"

When it was finally my turn, I answered, "America and England. Visiting family. I don't have anything to declare."

One customs agent stamped my passport while another opened my luggage. My heart started beating harder as I watched him leaf through the layers of clothes. What if he found the codebook the CIA had given me? What if he knew the purpose of those papers in my luggage? My breath nearly caught when he picked up the picture frame that had the codebook hidden in it. He kept the frame in his hand while he continued searching. Then he found the military book I'd purchased on the trip.

"Why do you have this?" he said, his eyes sharp, his voice accusatory.

Not wanting to sound intimidated, I adopted my own officious tone. "It is a gift for my commander in Sepah-e-Pasdaran."

The agent's expression changed to a faint smile. Or perhaps it was a smirk. Regardless, he quickly put everything back in my suitcase, saying, "There you go, *Baradar*." He closed my luggage and waved me through.

No one else approached me.

No one pulled me aside and said, "We know where you've been, Mr. Kahlili. We know who you talked to, *jasoos*. Come with us."

I felt the tension drain from me as I walked through the terminal to my waiting wife. Somaya looked even more beautiful than the picture in my mind, and my heart leapt when I saw her. Even though she'd covered her hair with a black scarf, her face brought life and strength to me. Was it her eyes or the way she looked at me? Was it her lips or the way she smiled at me? It didn't matter; when I saw her, I knew I was home.

All I wanted at that moment was to run to her, to hug her and pull her so close that we could become one. But it was not appropriate to hug and kiss anyone—even your wife—in a public place in Iran anymore. Instead, when I got close to her, I wrapped my arm around her shoulder and whispered, "I missed you so much. I am so glad that I have you in my life." She patted my back and smiled, saying, "I missed you, too." Though I desperately wanted to cling to her, I pulled my arm away and we walked through the exit like two strangers who had just met.

I managed to maintain a happy face until we got home. But as soon as we walked into the house, I held Somaya in my arms and a rush of emotion poured from me. I could not control my tears and I'm sure this worried Somaya horribly.

"Oh! Reza, are you okay?" she said, holding my face in her soft hands.

My emotions were still so overwhelming that I couldn't speak.

She wiped my tears from her face. "I never want you to leave me again."

I knew that I needed to get hold of myself. I couldn't let her think that anything was wrong beyond my missing her and my having had a long and difficult trip. "I feel bad for Aunt Giti," I said at last. "She's so sick and I hated leaving her alone in that facility. I wanted her to come back with me, but she insisted on staying."

Somaya smiled at me tenderly. But I also thought I caught a glimpse of something else in her eyes. Something that said she knew I wasn't telling her everything. It might have been only my imagination, but I realized at that moment that I would continue to envision reactions like this from her as long as I continued lying to her.

We talked for a while about the time we were apart, and I caught her up on how well her parents were doing in London. Somaya told me how lonely she'd felt without me and how hard it was for her to deal with this loneliness, even though I had not been away that long.

"I was almost happy for my grandmother's back surgery, though I know that is awful," she said. "Taking care of her kept me busy and kept my mind away from how hard it is for me when we are apart." She smiled at me. "I don't want to give you a big head, but I simply can't be away from you." She kissed me and held me tight. Being with her in this moment was the best I'd felt in a very long time.

That night, Somaya and I made love passionately, surprised when the first rays of light signaled the coming of a new day. I held her in my arms, wanting this precious time to last forever.

But it was necessary for me to return to work. I tried to anticipate the day ahead of me and what my coworkers would say. I considered questions they might ask and attempted to have ready answers. I was operating on no sleep, so I knew I wasn't going to be at my best under any circumstances.

Returning to my Tehran office filled me with emotions that ran from trepidation and fear to bravado and enthusiasm. On the one hand, I was Wally, a spy working for the world's largest intelligence agency. On the other hand, I was a member of the powerful Revolutionary Guards carrying out my duties as if my allegiance to Ayatollah Khomeini and his clerical regime were the most important thing in my life. Duality defined me now.

In my role as Wally, I would gather facts and information that only an insider with my connections could possibly access. There was an inherent danger to that. The regime was always on the lookout for spies, and when the United States took action on the information I would be providing, a red flag would surely go up among the Revolutionary Guards. How long could this go on before they traced the leaks to me?

As Reza, a member of the elite Guards, my role was to look and act the part of a devout Muslim enforcing all the new rules laid down by the mullahs. A full black beard was a mandatory accessory to the Guards' uniform, and I sported one along with every other member of the Guards. The image of a scowling black-bearded Guards member in uniform mustered fear and garnered respect. Playing the part of a zealot did not come naturally to me, and there were times I had to do things I dreaded: cautioning young girls to cover up, barking at kids for not displaying proper Islamic behavior, taking on the persona of a fanatic. Back in Iran now, I knew I would have to try to convince myself that doing these things allowed me to maintain my role—and maintaining my role allowed me to contribute to the downfall of the organization to which I so fervently imitated allegiance.

Once I entered the base, I went straight to the office of Rahim, my commander. He greeted me, shook my hand, and then we kissed on each side of the face, as is the custom among Iranians.

"How is your aunt, Brother Reza? Were you able to move her into a home?"

"Brother Rahim, it was your help that made it possible. May Allah repay you many times over." I went on to explain the situation with my aunt and that she was now living in an assisted-living facility.

"So what else did you do, Brother Reza? Where else did you go?"

"I visited some old friends from college. They were very happy to see me again. I also went to London and visited my in-laws on the way back."

I did not go into any detail, as I was already getting nervous. Hoping to cut the conversation short, I presented the gift I'd bought for him in the U.S. because I knew he would love it. Titled *Jane's Weapon Systems,* it was an impressive volume with color pictures showing virtually all of the weaponry used anywhere in the world at the time. This was the book that had distracted the customs agent. Rahim received the gift appreciatively, telling me that he was always looking for books and magazines on military equipment, which I knew because Kazem had told me this about Rahim months earlier.

I left to go find Kazem. As soon as I walked into his office, Kazem jumped up to greet me. With a grand gesture, he announced, "Reza, my dearest friend, world traveler and mystery man. Back from the United States at last," and slapped me on the back.

We hugged and kissed the sides of our faces. As he sat behind his desk, he added with a wide smile, "You didn't give away all of our secrets to the CIA while you were there, did you?"

The words stunned me and it took every bit of my strength not to let the shock of it show. For a brief moment, I thought my knees would buckle. But, of course, Kazem was only joking. Had the Guards known of my betrayal, they would have arrested me the moment my plane landed.

"Of course I did," I said, recovering quickly. "To go all the way to America and not have a conversation with the CIA would have been crazy. And while I was at it, I had dinner at the White House." We laughed together, but this failed to temper my uneasiness. We talked for a few more minutes—something innocuous about work—but all I could think was, *This is how it is going to be from now on. I won't even be able to have a simple conversation without being on guard and on edge.* I knew I'd created this life for myself. I even knew that I desired this life because of the benefit it offered my country. But it was going to take me a while to get used to it.

I prepared my first letter to Carol that night.

[Letter #——]
[Date:————]

Hi, Carol:
   1—I am back safe and sound.
   2—My family is well.
   3—Today was my first day back at work.
   4—Rahim and Kazem were happy to see me back.
   5—I will look for your messages.

Wish me luck,
Wally

BROTHERS IN ARMS

Hello, Wally:
We received your first letter.
We are happy you are back safely.
Our team is very excited.
Please confirm receipt of this message.
Please take care and stay safe.
Carol

Receiving the first message from Carol was thrilling, yet it un-nerved me, as it was an unintended but firm reminder of the torture and death that would await me if the Guards ever discovered what I was doing. While I'd considered how my decision was going to affect Somaya, being home with her, feeling her close, and feeling her love made it exponentially clearer what I was risking with my activity. As with all young couples, we had made plans for our future together. We wanted a family. Had I compromised that?

"Don't take any unnecessary risks," the CIA mandated. "Don't put yourself in danger. Be aware of your surroundings. Hide every-thing." Routinely switching on a light late at night might arouse sus-picion, so I used a small covered desk lamp in my study that was not visible from outside the house. Once in my study, down the hallway from our bedroom, I would quietly close the door and feel my way over to the table where the radio was.

Sitting alone in the near dark with headphones over my ears, I toyed with the frequency control, twisting the dial and picking up chatter all along the band. Back and forth, back and forth, up and down, up and down—just like my life now. An enormous number of codes crossed over the air. It was an international cacophony a linguist would love—German, Hebrew, French, Arabic, and even Farsi. As tense as all of this made me, I had to smile. The spy world was active and I was now in the middle of it.

The CIA's messages started Friday promptly at 3:00 a.m. The coded transmissions were not always easy to understand because they sometimes overlapped or were obscured by static. After a while, though, the garbled voices became easier to decipher.

I utilized the method I learned in London. First writing down the messages carefully, guessing at a couple of them, and then using the codebook, I deciphered them. Soon I recognized that these transmissions started with "Hello, Wally," which I found enormously exciting. It was like passing a club's initiation rite. This particular club—the CIA—had quite an exclusive membership, and I was just starting to wrap my mind around the idea of my being allowed to enter.

In time, my body clock adjusted in anticipation to my early-hour foray into the undercover world. Soon, I could awaken without an alarm at two thirty. Somaya accepted the pretext that I was getting up then because my best ideas for projects for the Guards came to me at night. She soon grew accustomed to my nighttime "insomnia." I even prepared a bit of disinformation regarding my listening to the radio while wearing headphones. If she ever came down to see me doing this, I would tell her that the Guards wanted to know what the English versions of Radio Free Europe and Voice of America were saying, and that they'd charged me with this mission.

Destroying the evidence of the deciphered messages was imperative, so I employed a technique they'd taught me in London. I folded the pages on which I'd written the messages in an accordion shape, taking an inch from one side and then the other, and placed them one by one in an ashtray. I then lit these and they would burn down without smoke. To complete the cleanup, I would flush the ashes down the toilet.

To let Carol know a message had come through successfully, I had to write an invisible letter the way David taught me in London. I made sure I followed everything I had learned. In another lifetime, I would have found it laughable that I was sitting in the near dark writing invisible messages. In my role as Wally, however, it was anything but funny.

I numbered each letter so Carol would know if she failed to receive one.

[Letter #———]
[Date:———]

Dear Carol:
  1—Received your message successfully.
  2—In a few days, I will be traveling to the front for a week.
  3—I will not be here next Friday. Do not relay a message. Start from the Friday after.
  4—There is a major offensive planned in the Dezful-Shush area.
  5—Should anything happen to me, please find a way to help my wife through my in-laws in London.

Wish me luck,
Wally

It was the duty of every member of the Guards to serve, in either a military or support role, in the battle against Saddam Hussein's army. Rahim sent Kazem, me, and three others to the Dezful-Shush region to fulfill this duty only a few weeks after my return from my trip out of the country. The war with Iraq had continued to intensify. Having taken advantage of the turmoil in Iran during the revolution, Saddam's army easily conquered and occupied many of the border areas. The tide was turning, though. More than two hundred thousand Revolutionary Guards, Basijis, and members of our regular army were cutting through Iraq's defensive lines, surrounding them and capturing thousands of POWs. The Basijis sacrificed themselves by walking through minefields to clear a path for the Guards or by tying bombs to their bodies and throwing themselves under Iraqi tanks to blow them up. While it took remarkable dedication to do something like this, each also believed that God would reward him for being a *shahid,* a martyr, like Imam Hussein. Each was convinced that heaven and all of its promises were awaiting him.

The mullahs used the legend of Imam Hussein to prepare the teenage Basijis psychologically for their martyrdom before every offensive. Shortly after we arrived on our first night, I witnessed this for myself. I sat on the barracks floor with other Guards, along with many young Basijis and their commanders. A hush came over the room, the lights were dimmed, and, with the sound of *"Ya Allah,"* everybody stood to welcome the speaker.

The mullah told Imam Hussein's story, climaxing with a retelling of the battle in Karbala, Iraq, where the Imam demonstrated his bravery by becoming a martyr. I'd been hearing this story since I was a child—how he fought for Islam; how he sacrificed his life for his religion; how Hussein and his band of seventy-two fearless warriors fought against an army of thirty thousand and never wavered; and how, just before he died, he exclaimed, "Dignified death is better than humiliating life"—but it still brought me to tears. While it would be nearly impossible for Westerners to understand how this story moved us, it charged us with deep emotional courage. While singing *"Ya Hussein, Ya Hussein,"* we would strike our chests as a display of devotion to Imam Hussein and in remembrance of his suffering.

The night felt incredibly tense to me. My heart was with all these brave young men and boys who deeply believed they were fighting for their country, for their religion, against this unjust war of Saddam's. Their parents and their families were proud to place their souls in God's hands. Upon their martyrdom, their leader, Imam Khomeini, would congratulate their families for their dedication to

Islam, reminding them of the promise of heaven's open gates and the welcome embrace of Hussein, the Lord of Martyrs. However, it was difficult for me to believe that this was the best way for us to utilize our country's youth.

The next morning before dawn, Kazem tapped me on my shoulder. "Reza, it's time. We need to do our morning *namaz* and leave."

Our job today was to help transport the Basijis behind the front lines. We loaded them, laden with their gear, into big trucks, and then convoyed them toward the front with headlights off and only the moonlight as a guide. The sky was clear and full of stars.

In our truck were brothers Mohsen and Madjid, ages thirteen and fourteen and probably no more than a hundred pounds each. We'd met them the night before at the mullah's sermon. The boys were very quiet now, unlike the night before, when they were full of energy and fooling around like kids their age do. Kazem and I had talked to them for a while after the ceremony. They were from a rural area near the city of Mashhad, and they were the only two boys in a poor family with five kids. They left school for *jebheh,* the war front, after their teacher, a mullah, decreed that it was the duty of every Muslim to go to *jebheh* and become a *shahid.*

"I will kill as many Iraqi soldiers as I can," Mohsen had said last night as he squared his shoulders with a big grin.

Madjid, the older one, wrapped his arm around Mohsen and said, "We will conquer Karbala and have *namaz* at Imam Hussein's shrine."

Now I could not take my eyes off them as the truck took us to our destination. Both boys had their heads down, saying a prayer, and both wore a *"Ya Hussein"* red bandana around their shaved heads. My stomach roiled as I watched them.

"Are you okay, Reza?" Kazem said, looking at me in a quizzical way that I, of course, interpreted as suspicion.

"I'm fine. I think it's just the bumpy road making me nauseous."

Of course it was the road—the road to an uncertain destiny. What was waiting for Mohsen and Madjid at the end of this road?

Who would come back? Who among all of the teens in this truck would see another day?

"Brothers, get out," the commander ordered when the truck stopped. The Basijis exited the trucks and lined up in groups, as instructed. Hundreds of children ready to defend our country. I couldn't help but think about their families, and about how little these boys had seen in their short lives.

"God, please save them!" I whispered.

"Baradar Reza, pray for our forgiveness," Mohsen sputtered, as he looked at me with his head tilted halfway up. His group's mission was to blow up a bridge behind the enemy lines.

Once we'd deployed the Basijis, we went back to the base behind the front lines and waited anxiously. For several hours, the violent sounds of gunfire, artillery, mortar shells, explosions, and screams of *"Allaho Akbar"* filled the air. Reports from the battle were slow to come, though, until I heard a commotion throughout the base.

Kazem ran up to me. "Reza, good news! The offensive was successful. We have destroyed fifteen tanks so far and have taken many prisoners."

"Is there any news of the Imam Hussein Battalion?" I asked desperately. I wanted to know if Mohsen and Madjid's mission was successful.

He shook his head in disappointment.

I knew that meant that I would not hear the news I wanted to hear. I went outside the bunker to smoke a cigarette, wiping my face before anybody could see my tears.

Just before *maghreb azan* (the evening prayer), Ibrahim, one of the Basijis from the Imam Hussein Battalion, came back to the base. I rushed toward him.

"Baradar Ibrahim, where is everybody else?" I asked.

He looked at me wearily and said, *"Baradar,* they all fought bravely, but . . ."

"Khaste nabashin, Baradar," someone said to him in passing, praising him for a good job.

I regained Ibrahim's attention. "What about Mohsen and Madjid? Where are they?"

Ibrahim couldn't hold my gaze. "We could see the bridge. There was one more hill between us as we descended. The Iraqis were waiting for us, hiding at the bottom of the hill. I had fallen behind and I could see bullets flying, the screams and shouting. The bloodshed was everywhere. Our kids fought back so bravely, but Mohsen was the last one standing. Iraqi soldiers surrounded him and they ordered him to drop his weapon and surrender. Instead, he opened fire while shouting, *'Ash-hadu anna la ilaha illa Allah; ash-hadu anna muhammadan-rasool Allah'* [I testify there is no God but Allah; I testify that Mohammad is Allah's messenger]."

Mohsen, the youngest brother of five children, along with his brother, Madjid, died that afternoon.

I knew their sacrifice was going to stick with me a long time. I also knew that it was going to cause me to reflect on what I was doing. How did my espionage fit into a world where boys gave their lives to defend a country whose government I'd vowed to undermine?

Because of the efforts of so many like them, the Iraqi army was eventually defeated and chased back into its own territory, where it was now defending against Iranian offensives. The Iraqis left behind horror stories of the crimes they committed, raping women and killing civilians. Rahim told me of one small border town where an Iraqi commander ordered all civilians to gather in the city square, women and children included. Iraqi tanks surrounded them and opened fire, slaughtering every single person. Our military executed many Iraqi POWs in retaliation for those crimes.

At this point, Ali Khamenei was president of Iran. In June of 1981, Khamenei had survived an assassination attempt by the Mujahedin when a bomb concealed in a tape recorder exploded, leaving him paralyzed in his right hand. The Iranian people elected him president in October of that year, after the assassination of President Mohammad-Ali Rajai by the Mujahedin in August.

Someday, of course, Khamenei would succeed Imam Khomeini as the Supreme Leader. I had heard from Kazem and others that Ali Khamenei regularly came to *jebheh* to review the troops, and that he was at least as much of a zealot about raising the flag of Islam across the world as Imam Khomeini. It was during this conflict that we learned that he believed we must continue to wage war until we destroyed all nonbelievers. This included, of course, the destruction of Israel. Ali Khamenei also wanted Jerusalem and the return of one of the most sacred mosques and holiest places to Muslims, the Masjid al-Aqsa.

The regime made it their mission to topple Saddam. The Iraqi leader had offered peace after our forces had pushed him out of our country, but Khomeini roundly rejected this. The mullahs now harbored Ayatollah Mohammed Baqir al-Hakim, an outspoken Iraqi opponent of Saddam, and gave sanctuary to his supporters. The mullahs in Iran and Iraq had a long history of cooperation through their seminaries in Qom, the hotbed of religious activity in Iran, and Najaf in Iraq. They instructed the Revolutionary Guards to help Ayatollah Hakim create the Supreme Council for Islamic Revolution in Iraq (SCIRI). This quickly became one of the most powerful political parties in Iraq and it continues to be so today. Part of the Guards' role in developing the SCIRI was to send Hakim's followers back inside Iraq with specific instructions to disrupt Saddam's army, using covert military operations, infiltrating his operations, and gathering much-needed intelligence.

My learning all of this provided a treasure trove of information for Carol.

[Letter #—]
[Date:———]

Dear Carol:
  1—Khomeini issued an order to the Revolutionary Guards to further help Ayatollah Hakim in strengthening the Supreme Council for Islamic Revolution in Iraq in recruiting

*and forming military units and performing cross-border
operations in conjunction with the Revolutionary Guards.*

*2—The chief commander, Mohsen Rezaei, has appointed
Esmaeil Daghayeghi as the Guards officer to coordinate
the recruitment of Iraqi Shiites and sympathizers from the
POWs.*

*3—Esmaeil Daghayeghi is fluent in Arabic and has been
working with the POWs. He has successfully recruited other
Iraqis trained under the Revolutionary Guards. He has
formed the Badr Brigade and is the commanding officer of
that brigade. They are being used for intelligence on Iraqi
army communications and on cross-border operations. They
are routinely sent into Iraq to carry Ayatollah Hakim's
messages, recruiting Shiite volunteers and inciting rebellion
by the Shiites in the southern cities of Iraq.*

*4—The order now is to expand the brigade into a division.
Mohsen Rezaei has promoted Esmaeil Daghayeghi to be the
commander of the new division.*

*5—Many of the Iraqis are being trained in the Revolutionary
Guards' bases in Tehran.*

Wish me luck!
Wally

The following Persian New Year, with the war pushed back at the
borders and peace in the sky of Tehran after a long conflict, Somaya's
doctor gave us the good news we'd been hoping to hear: she was
three months pregnant. I desperately wanted to believe that this was
a sign that my life was at last aligning with my dreams.

HOPE AND PERIL

UNFORTUNATELY, MY DREAM of a more peaceful homeland continued to be nothing more than a dream. The repressive atmosphere in Iran was becoming more and more pervasive. Arrests and executions escalated to the point where it seemed everyone knew someone caught in the nightmare. And the spread of Khomeini's version of Islam that was affecting every aspect of people's lives was extending beyond Iran's borders. Things had never been busier for the Guards, and these days my time was decidedly not my own.

This activity couldn't have come at a poorer stage in my home life. Somaya was pregnant and I wanted to be with her to share as much of this singular stage in our relationship as possible. Instead, I was spending most of my time at work and attending meetings and gatherings afterward with Kazem, which left me feeling terribly guilty.

For most of her pregnancy, Somaya didn't utter a word of complaint. In fact, she gave me so little trouble about my long hours that I thought she was fine with it. Until I came home late one night during her third trimester and found her sitting in the living room looking miserable.

"What is wrong, dear?" I asked as I sat next to her.

She immediately burst into uncontrollable tears. For a minute, she couldn't say anything and I simply held her. Then she pulled back angrily. "What is wrong? *Everything* is wrong. I barely get to see you. I am here all alone with my big belly and no one to talk to. I am tired of this." She wiped her nose with the end of her sleeve and I could see that it took a great deal out of her to say what she'd said.

My heart went out to her immediately. The last thing I wanted in the world was to see her upset. "I am sorry that you feel this way, honey. I wish I didn't have to spend so much time away from you, but I don't know what I can do. Why don't you get together with some of your friends and do some fun stuff?"

She shook her head and sniffled. "Like what? Everybody is busy with their own lives and I am stuck here all alone."

"Then maybe you should go to England and spend some time with your parents. That would be nice, wouldn't it?"

I actually thought I was making a productive suggestion, but Somaya saw this very differently. She threw her eyes heavenward and then looked at me in a way I had never seen before. "Your stupid solution to this problem is to get rid of me? You want to send me back to my parents so you can do your nasty Guards stuff with Kazem and those other awful friends of yours? Or maybe it's so you don't have to think about me while you do whatever you do during those nights in the den."

She'd chosen these words to sting me and she accomplished that task. I had no idea she felt this way about what I was doing. Why hadn't she said anything before this? It was almost as though some other woman now inhabited Somaya's body.

She stood up to go to bed and delivered another salvo. "Or maybe it isn't your work at all. Maybe you're in love with another woman—a woman without a big, ugly belly."

As much as I sympathized with how upset she was, I found this last comment to be a relief. I almost felt like laughing at the absurdity of the notion that I would seek another woman. I blew out a deep breath, happy to allay her interpretation of what I did at night.

"I would never, ever, *ever* cheat on you," I said, hugging her. She resisted at first, but soon leaned into my embrace. "You never have to doubt how much I love you. You are the best thing in my life.

And if your belly gets bigger and stays that way even after you give birth, I will adore you even more."

She let me kiss her and then she went to bed, seemingly worn out by the entire experience. I knew that what I'd just said to her didn't make her feel completely better, but at least I'd calmed some of her concerns. Still, she'd made it clear that she resented my work with the Guards and that she had some suspicions about what I was doing routinely in the middle of the night. She might believe now that I wasn't communicating with another lover, but she was smart enough to consider other possibilities. I would need to navigate this carefully with her.

Feeling shaky from this exchange, I probably should have gone to bed with Somaya. But first I needed to write Carol about all that I'd learned recently.

[Letter #——]
[Date:————]

Dear Carol,

1—The Guards are sending hundreds more fighters to Bekaa Valley in Lebanon through Syria.

2—The operations are being coordinated by:

The Revolutionary Guards Commander Mostafa Mohammad-Najjar, who is in charge of the forces in Lebanon;

Ali-Akbar Mohtashemi, the Iranian ambassador in Syria; and

Ahmad Vahidi, the Chief Intelligence Officer of the Guards in Iran, who is also charged with expanding the Guards' extraterritorial activities in Lebanon.

3—Rasool, who works out of the Intelligence Unit at our base, is constantly traveling to Syria. He tells me that the activity is picking up and Guards are transporting arms and ammunition to Syria.

4—Planes loaded with these munitions are regularly flying to Syria in the middle of the night.

5—Imam Khomeini issued an order to Mohsen Rezaei, the

Chief Commander of the Guards, that the Guards are to get more involved in Lebanon to fight the Israeli and American forces.

6—Somaya is doing fine. A little emotional, but that's normal. Thanks again for asking. The baby is due in a few months. They told us it is a boy! I am so excited!

Wally

Over the next few months, the Guards continued to dominate my time, though I tried where I could to get away early to be with Somaya. Then, while I was having lunch in my office, she called with information that pulled me delightedly from my work.

"I had some contractions after you left this morning. They've been coming and going. They started twenty minutes apart and now they are down to fifteen. I think it's time for us to go to the hospital."

I told Rahim what was going on, jumped into a taxi, and headed home. When I got there, Somaya was already at the door with her little duffel bag and we rushed to the hospital.

I wanted to go into the delivery room with her, but a nurse stopped me. "We will let you know when the baby is here. Then you can come inside."

"But is there any way I can come in, please? I want to be with her for this."

"I'm sorry," the nurse said firmly. "I cannot do anything. It's the hospital's policy." Then her expression softened and she offered me a little smile. "We will take good care of her."

There was another man sitting in the waiting room when I settled into a chair. He looked up at me when I sat. "Is this your first?" he asked.

I nodded.

"Prepare to be here for a long time. The first one takes the longest. My wife is having our third right now and I have been here for almost ten hours."

I did not care how long I needed to wait; I just prayed to God that Somaya and my son would be healthy. Thinking of the new baby as my *son* thrilled me. We'd been talking about names, and after juggling with many, we decided that Omid—which means "hope"—sounded perfect to us.

"I just love it because he will bring hope to our life and we will have big hopes for him," Somaya said when we agreed upon it.

I took my first glance at the clock fifteen minutes after I sat down. As much as I would have been willing to wait as long as necessary to ensure that everything went well, I also desperately wanted to see Omid. I wanted to touch his little fingers and feel what it was like to be a father. I found dreaming of him and the future he would have to be a welcome diversion as the time passed.

A few hours later, a nurse opened the double doors leading to the delivery room. Behind her was another nurse holding a baby. I looked at the man with me in the waiting room, assuming the child was his. He got up with a big smile and approached the nurse.

"It is not yours," the first nurse said to the man. Then she turned to me. "Mr. Kahlili, come see your son."

For the first time all day, I felt nervous. I was about to meet my little baby boy. The other man congratulated me and I just turned my head and smiled. I could not say a word. I stepped through the doors and saw the face that would change my life forever. Omid was beautiful, and magical, and mine.

The nurses allowed me to move to Somaya's room after they transferred her from the delivery room. They took Omid with them to bathe him and set him up in his little crib.

My wife was all smiles. "Did you see him, Reza? He is so cute. So little."

I kissed her wet forehead. I was still having trouble speaking.

"He was so good, Reza. He came so fast and I didn't even have to push hard. I just love him."

They brought Omid in shortly, and we both stared at him and laughed with every little sound or move he made. Later, after they took him back to the nursing room, I stayed by Somaya the whole night. Neither of us could sleep, so we talked about Omid and about what our lives would be like now that he was around. I felt a huge sense of completion, and I knew I needed to strive ever harder to make my home the center of my life.

But this goal would continue to elude me. On October 23, 1983, I woke up to the delightful sound of Omid giggling in Somaya's arms. I kissed them both and got ready to go to work. Just before leaving, I turned on the radio to catch what I could of the morning news when a breaking report announced that suicide bombers had attacked the U.S. Marine Corps headquarters and the French soldiers' barracks in Beirut, Lebanon. The bombers detonated twelve thousand pounds of TNT, reducing a four-story cinder-block building to rubble and killing 241 U.S. personnel and 58 French paratroopers.

(Four years after this suicide bombing, Iran's then–minister of the Revolutionary Guards, Mohsen Rafiqdoost, boasted that "Both the TNT and the ideology which in one blast sent to hell four hundred officers, NCOs, and soldiers at the Marines headquarters were provided by Iran.")

I'd written to Carol about the regime's flying munitions and arms to Syria and Lebanon, about the Guards and other fighters being inserted into those countries, and about the infusion of capital into these regions to fund Khomeini's expansion activities. The news of this bombing was shocking not only because of the enormity of the attack, but also because of its possibly devastating consequences. Would the U.S. retaliate? Would it start a war where American forces overwhelmingly outnumbered and outgunned us? If the U.S. didn't retaliate, would Khomeini feel even more emboldened and generate further attacks? As my wife and son played in the adjoining room, the sounds of their innocent entertainment served as heartbreaking counterpoint to the grim reports on the radio.

I left for work filled with apprehension. I intended to drop off another letter to Carol on the way, feeling a greater sense of urgency to communicate with her and ironically touching on some of the themes the new attack drew to the forefront. This new letter focused on the expansion of the intelligence arm of the Revolutionary Guards under the command of Ahmad Vahidi—a special force that would later be christened the Quds Force, whose mission was to organize, train, equip, and finance underground militant organizations throughout the world and conduct terrorist activities.

[Letter #—]

[Date:———]

Dear Carol,

1—*The Guards' Special Forces is in contact with several terrorist organizations, among them:*

The Islamic Front for the Liberation of Bahrain;

The militant Egyptian Islamist "Gamaat Islamiya";

The Japanese Red Army;

The ETA Basque nationalist terrorist group; and

The Armenian Secret Army.

2—*Kazem told me that Rafiqdoost, the Minister of the Revolutionary Guards, was personally involved in setting up a relationship with the Red Army Faction in Germany.*

3—*The Revolutionary Guards are recruiting and training candidates from Islamic countries for terrorist activities with training bases in Lebanon, Sudan, and Iran. I witnessed Palestinians helping with the training of those candidates operating out of the Guards' bases.*

4—*Through Akbar, a Guard in our unit, I learned that the Foreign Ministry has assigned members of the Revolutionary Guards' Special Forces to Iranian Consulates and Embassies. These are not political assignments; it is a diplomatic cover for their operations. Their task is to take control of all intelligence activities overseas, including assassinations, abductions, and the transfer of arms and explosives.*

5—*Akbar is in close contact with several of those agents and is in and out of the Foreign Ministry constantly. Akbar explained that the Special Forces communicate orders to the agents outside the country through the use of radio frequencies. He went as far as talking about the formula. Maybe he will elaborate more so we can break their codes.*

6—I have learned through several sources that the Guards' agents have been placed in and are now working out of Iranian banks and airlines, and in shipping line offices abroad.

7—Rafiqdoost is personally involved in buying arms through the black market. Some of these arms are then shipped to Hezbollah and Islamic Jihad through Syria—with their cooperation.

8—Rafiqdoost will be traveling to Syria soon with Ahmad Vahidi. I will update you when I find out more.

9—The situation here is tense with the war and the Mujahedin conducting assassinations. The Guards are on the lookout for infiltrators because of this.

10—Javad, who works out of the intelligence department in our base and who also knows Kazem, is constantly visiting me in my department trying to start up conversations, and asking questions. I sense he feels uneasy about me working there. However, it's not a major concern yet.

11—Rasool told me about the Special Forces unit setting up safe houses in many countries, successfully infiltrating the Muslim communities in Argentina, Brazil, and Paraguay, particularly those of Lebanese descent. He explained that the notorious Triangle there, with no police presence, makes it easy for transferring arms and explosives. Their operation is coordinated through the Iranian Consulates and Embassies.

Wally

(More than a decade later, the Guards' infiltration of the Muslim communities in Argentina paid off for them. In July 1994, with the assistance of Hezbollah, the Guards conducted a terrorist attack

166 | REZA KAHLILI

on a Jewish community center in Buenos Aires, killing eighty-five
and injuring hundreds more. After the attack, Argentinian intelligence services completed a comprehensive report specifying the
Iranian government's involvement. The report also concluded that
the Foreign Ministry of Iran provided diplomatic cover for the Iranian agents that perpetrated the attack with the help of a Hezbollah
terrorist mastermind known as Imad Mughniyeh. In late 2006, an
Argentinian federal judge issued arrest warrants for Hashemi Rafsanjani, the president of Iran at the time; Ali Fallahian, the head of the
Ministry of Intelligence at the time; Ali Velayati, the former foreign
minister; Mohsen Rezaei, the commander of the Guard at the time;
Ahmad Vahidi; and three other officials from the Iranian Embassy in
Buenos Aires. Interpol also issued red alerts for the arrest of Mohsen
Rezaei, Ahmad Vahidi, and several other Iranian officials for their
participation in that attack.)

As I dropped off the letter to Carol along with another to my aunt
Giti, I felt somebody watching me. I always dropped Carol's mail
with other letters to friends or family members in America or Europe to avoid suspicion. If somebody saw me dropping the mail off
and checked the mailbox, they would find the actual letters from me
to an actual person, but I was still nervous today. The news of the
Beirut suicide bombing had put me on edge.

I decided to go to see Kazem as soon as I got to the office. I
needed to maintain a close connection to him. I needed him to continue to be my friend.

"*Salam,* Baradar Kazem," I said as I entered his office. "I heard the
news on the radio this morning. God is with us."

"*Salam,* Reza," he said as he picked up his phone handset and dialed a number. "Come in. It is great news."

He gestured with his head for me to take a seat and then spoke
into the handset. "*Salam, Baradar.* It's Kazem. . . ."

I couldn't hear the conversation on the other end.

"This is *shahadat,*" he said, obviously speaking about the martyrdom of those who'd committed the suicide bombing. He then

nodded his agreement as the other party spoke. "Of course . . . both were successful . . . they were demolished."

His expression changed and became serious. "On that . . . I will explain the details to you tomorrow at our meeting. Congratulations one more time, Baradar. God save our *rahbar.*"

I needed to keep a bright expression on my face through this. Only God could know how sick I felt at this and every other moment when I had to pretend that I was enjoying the killings, betrayals, suicides bombings, and martyrdoms.

For several minutes after he hung up the phone, Kazem bragged about the Guards' power and about how soon we would defeat the enemies of Islam.

"Reza, you would be amazed at how much effort intelligence agencies like the CIA, MI6, and the wretched Mossad put into learning about our activities. They are obsessed with us. These evildoers don't even realize what we get away with right under their noses."

The mention of the CIA sent a chill up my spine. Then I remembered that he mentioned a meeting tomorrow to the person on the phone.

"Reza, I have to ask you something. It's very important. I am meeting with Haj Agha Golsari tomorrow. He has some questions about you and I want to be prepared when I meet with him."

That comment terrified me. What if they knew? I thought again about the feeling that someone had been watching me that morning.

Oh God, if they find out, what are they going to do to Somaya. What about Omid? I want to see him one more time. I want to hold Somaya and tell her I am sorry for everything.

Kazem's phone rang and he took the call, shifting away from me at the same time. "*Alo, salam aleikom.* . . . Good. . . . Thanks. . . . It was great news. . . . I am with Baradar Reza now."

He spun his chair around to look at me. That's when I noticed the wide smile on his face. "No, actually I was about to tell him. . . . We probably leave in about three weeks. . . . I told Haj Agha Golsari that I will go with Reza. . . . I know, I have the same respect for him, too. Reza is a gift to our base, Baradar Rahim."

Only then did I start to breathe normally again. For a few moments, Kazem's talking on the phone faded into the background as I tried to gather my thoughts. It finally dawned on me that they'd picked me for a special mission. As much as I'd experienced mortal dread just a minute ago, my first thought was *More news for Carol and the CIA.*

Kazem finished his phone conversation with Rahim and returned his attention to me. His tone turned confidential as he related the news about our traveling to Dubai to purchase equipment for the Intelligence Unit. He emphasized that I could not discuss the details with anyone and smiled while telling me about the special request he had placed with Haj Agha Golsari, the head of the Intelligence Unit at our base, to bring me along because of my knowledge about computers, the fact that I spoke English fluently, and, above all, because he trusted me.

Kazem was in an expansive mood. He proudly revealed several specific incidents in European and Middle Eastern countries involving the illegal transportation of arms and explosives through their seaports and airports. I made mental notes, trying to remember as many details as possible for the letter I planned to write to the CIA that night.

When I finally stood to leave, Kazem gazed up at me with fire and pride in his eyes. "Going on this mission is a great honor, Reza. I hope you are excited about it."

I smiled and tipped my chin forward. "You know, Kazem, that I would do anything for Islam and Imam Khomeini," I said with as much enthusiasm as I could muster.

THE NIGHT AFTER I learned about the Beirut bombing, I wrote Carol another letter.

[Letter #—]
[Date:———]

Dear Carol,

1—The bombing news in Lebanon caused a big commotion in the Guards today. Kazem was constantly on the phone congratulating other commanders. He talked proudly of the bravery of the martyrs involved in the suicide bombing. He was fully aware of the success of the bombing mission.

2—Kazem talked about transporting arms and explosives in Europe and the Middle East. On one occasion, they transferred arms and cash in the amount of $1 million through a high-ranking mullah and his entourage while on an official trip to Germany, where it was given to Iranian agents. In another incident, explosives and arms were transported by Iran Air to Spain then transferred from the Iran Air office to Iranian agents to be used against the Mujahedin. He told me an opposition member in Dubai named Ali was abducted and taken to the Iranian Consulate, interrogated and transferred by Consulate car to the airport, then to Iran Air and to Tehran and finally to Evin Prison. I don't know what became of him.

3—Kazem has asked me to travel to Dubai with him. He received authorization from Haj Agha Golsari, the head of the Intelligence Unit at our base. We are leaving three weeks from today.

4—The mission is to purchase computer equipment and software for networking and data processing for the Intelligence Unit.

5—Please advise if you can be available for a meeting in Dubai. I would appreciate a face-to-face meeting.

Wally

The following Friday, I received a message back from her.

Hello, Wally,

*   We received your letters.*

*   Very important information. Excellent effort.*

*   I will be in Dubai at Hotel X. Use———to contact me.*

*   Abort contact if any suspicion.*

*   Please update on Rafiqdoost travel to Syria, date, purpose, people with him.*

*   We are proud of you. Stay safe.*

*   Keep us informed on Javad.*

*   See you in Dubai.*

Carol

Somaya was not happy about my trip to Dubai. The whole situation in Iran had become so terrifying to her that she no longer felt safe going out by herself. This feeling intensified after her personal involvement in a frightening incident.

One night I volunteered to watch Omid so she could visit a friend. I was a little worried that she didn't come home when I expected her, but I brushed it off, figuring she was enjoying herself and had lost track of time. Somaya didn't go out often, so I could easily imagine her reveling in the rare opportunity. Given the state of our country, though, I should have been more apprehensive.

When she came home hours late, she was in shock, shivering, and crying. I had never seen her so scared and I immediately leapt to horrible conclusions.

"I was waiting to catch a cab," she said, hyperventilating. "There were two other girls standing a few feet in front of me also waiting for a ride. All of a sudden, a big SUV slammed on its brakes so hard that the car skidded forward a few yards before fully stopping. You could see the smoke and smell the burning tires. Then they backed up and got out of the car, yelling at us to get into their car." She burst into tears. "I was so frightened. All I could think was what they would do to me."

I quickly thought of Somaya's friend Farah. The Zeinab Sisters—the "Moral Police" in charge of monitoring the women's dress code—had arrested her for wearing makeup. The regime forbade polished nails, a peek of hair under a veil, a hint of lipstick, some rouge, and anything of that sort, and they would subject young women to lashings for attempting to look more attractive. Farah stood up to them, thinking she was defending her rights. They jailed her for four days, beating her and keeping her in a cell with criminal women. Farah was tough, but upon her release, she was so terrified that she never went out without a chador.

I put my arms around Somaya and pressed her into me, trying to calm her, and trying to find out exactly what had happened.

"Reza, they took me to the Komiteh. It was so scary. There were two other girls already in the car when they arrested us. The Zeinab Sisters were very rude, mean, and filthy. Every time any of us would ask why we were being arrested or where they were taking us, they would tell us to shut up and that they would beat us if we said another word. They took down our names and addresses.

"After they dropped us at the Komiteh, I saw another group of women lined up in the corridor behind a door. I could hear a lot of screaming and crying. While we waited, a guard came and said they were going to whip us fifty times for disrespecting and disobeying the Islamic rules."

My outrage exploded upon hearing this. If these bastards did what I was thinking they did at that point, I vowed I would kill every one of them.

But before my imagination incensed me further, Somaya told me they let her and some other women go without any physical harm. Apparently, the head of the Komiteh released them since they had the appropriate *hejab* and because the Zeinab Sisters had arrested them unfairly.

Though I desperately didn't want to leave Somaya at this point, I had to take the trip to Dubai. I tried to reassure my wife that I would be back quickly, but I was obligated to go. On the morning I left, Somaya cried so hard that I felt miserable. At the same time, though, her tears emboldened my mission. I needed to do everything I could to prevent the people who made her so fearful from maintaining control of our country.

Kazem booked two rooms at the Sheraton in Sharjah, not far from Dubai and definitely a poorer neighbor of the growing modern city. Fortunately, our rooms were located far away from each other. This made it so much easier for me to meet with Carol. Shortly after we checked in, I called her to let her know where I was staying, and to tell her that I would call her again to arrange our meeting as soon as I found out my schedule with Kazem.

The next day, Kazem and I met with an Iranian merchant Kazem knew well named Saeed. He owned an import/export business partnered with an Arab named Fahid. Saeed arranged an appointment with an Arab middleman named Abdul who was fluent in English. During this meeting, each of us had distinct roles: Kazem was the point man and did the talking and negotiating. Saeed was the co-ordinator and logistics man, and I was the computer expert. Since Abdul spoke only Arabic and English, and since none of the rest of us spoke Arabic, I also served as translator.

Abdul took us around to several companies that specialized in computer equipment, telling them we were opening a new business with headquarters in Tehran and expanding throughout Iran. We explained that we needed not only computers but the networking, data-processing, tracking, and communications software to support our business development plans. We needed to use this level of sub-terfuge with these companies to prevent U.S. intelligence from find-ing out what we were doing. If anyone learned that we were seeking to purchase equipment for the Guards, it was likely that the CIA or some other intelligence organization would have attempted to bug the equipment in some way to monitor our activities or perhaps even sabotage it.

Kazem made plans to visit the Iranian consulate in the morning and said we would continue our tour of Dubai in the afternoon. After we got back to the hotel, Kazem went to his room to do his prayers, giving me an opportunity to call Carol. Now that I knew Kazem's schedule, I could arrange to meet with her the following day. We discussed a variety of options and decided that it would be safest for us to get together after Kazem was asleep. Since it would be dangerous for me to be seen leaving the hotel on my own at that time, Carol told me she would meet me in my room at one in the morning.

I left the door to my room unlocked so she could enter when she felt it was safe. Then I waited for her, seemingly forever. I kept checking my watch and checking the door, while I tried to focus on the issues I wanted to address with Carol. Intermittently, I would gaze at a picture of my son that I planned to show to her.

It occurred to me that the CIA must have gained at least a modi-cum of trust in me to agree to such a risky meeting. I'd requested this appointment because I had no idea what impact my reports were having and I needed feedback. I was feeling isolated and vul-nerable, and I needed to know that the risks I'd been taking were serving some purpose.

Finally, the door opened and Carol stepped inside, locking the door behind her. Her disguise—a long, light blue coat and colorful veil sitting loosely on her head with her bangs peeking through— surprised me a little. She looked very Middle Eastern and I didn't recognize her at first. She actually reminded me of Somaya's aunt. Surprise registered on her face when she saw that I was clean-shaven. It was Kazem's idea to shave our beards to look more like the businessmen we were supposed to be.

Carol immediately assured me that she hadn't attracted any attention on the way to my room, but stressed that she couldn't stay too long because of the late hour. Even though Dubai was a more open city than most in the Middle East, it was not wise for a woman to be out by herself in the early hours of the morning. Carol took out a pad and we got down to business.

"This morning, we went to the consulate and I saw Revolutionary Guards members masquerading as political operatives. Kazem knew a few of them and introduced me to them, but he didn't mention their last names. There was Baradar Mehdi, Baradar Jafar, and Baradar Gholam. While we were there, two black stretch limos arrived displaying Iranian flags and consulate license plates. Later that day, Kazem leaned over and said, 'Do you remember those two limos that drove up today? That's how we do it. They were carrying explosives and firearms.' Then he smiled and told me that officials had even stopped the limos, but that no one dared search a consulate convoy."

"Did Kazem give you any specifics about what kind of explosives were involved?"

"No."

"Have you heard anything else about the bombing in Lebanon?"

"Kazem had a meeting with Haj Agha Golsari the day after the bombing. He did not discuss the details with me, but they were all calling and congratulating each other."

"What are Kazem's plans here in Dubai?"

"As I explained in my letter, we are purchasing computer equipment and software for the Guards' Intelligence Unit. Kazem said that the Guards are expanding their operations and have set up separate departments for each region of the world. Each department oversees special ops and the political situations of each region. They are going to be dealing with a lot of data processing and storage."

"What company are you dealing with, and how long will you stay in Dubai?"

"We've been negotiating with several companies and I think Kazem will finalize a deal with Computer Dynamics Unlimited tomorrow. If everything goes smoothly, we will fly back home in two days."

I filled her in about Saeed and Fahid's import/export business in Dubai, explaining that they exported exclusively to Iran and adding my strong suspicion that they were operating a front company for the Guards that handled transactions for equipment under one guise (industrial, for example) when the ultimate purpose of that equipment was military use. The Guards had been using front companies for requisitions since their formation. We then focused on the events back in Tehran, including an overview of the Guards' activities. Though she knew the arms blockade was working, Carol didn't know until I told her that it had caused an especially severe shortage of spare parts for Iran's air force. She took notes as I explained that Rafiqdoost had made several contacts in the black market for the purchase of necessary firepower. He had acquired a number of older, smaller ships for the Guards, using these to transfer black market munitions to the ports of Iran. These ships evaded suspicion because of their size and appearance.

"I heard from Kazem that Rafiqdoost will be traveling to Syria in the next few weeks along with Ahmad Vahidi; I have seen several of his directives to Rahim, our base commander. Vahidi is very active in organizing operations outside of Iran. Besides Lebanon, where Mostafa Najjar is running the Guards' operation in close coordination with Vahidi and the Guards Intelligence Unit, they are also focusing much of their effort on the countries in the Persian Gulf and Africa. I am still not aware of the exact date of their departure."

Carol kept writing and the details kept pouring out of me.

"A week before coming to Dubai, I had a long conversation with Rasool, whom I've mentioned in my reports. He is also in the Intelligence Unit out of our base. He told me that during the last international day of Quds, the annual event protesting Israeli control of Jerusalem, millions of dollars were handed out in cash to the Hezbollah and Islamic Jihad leaders who had participated. Rasool told me that he personally handed out some of this money in secret meetings that were held by the Guards. This upset him because he couldn't understand why we needed to pay these people if they were fighting for Islam. Apparently, the money was payment for terrorist activities against the U.S. and Israel."

Carol took in all of this. When I mentioned Rasool, she stopped writing and said, "Rasool sounds like an interesting man," without any further explanation.

We continued to talk at length. When she finished debriefing me, Carol gave me more of the supplies I used to communicate with her and a new codebook.

"Wally, I hope you know that the information you've been relaying is highly valuable to the U.S. government and that we are very grateful for your efforts," she said. "Now tell me more about Javad in your office. What does he do to make you so uncomfortable?"

"Javad works in the Intelligence Unit at our base. He comes to my office often and he has a very menacing way about him. He stares straight into my eyes while asking me questions. The questions themselves are innocuous enough: 'How is your aunt doing in America?' or 'Did you like it there when you were a student?' But the way he asks them makes me feel like he's probing. One day he asked me how a guy like me with the opportunity to live in America could live in Iran with so little pay when I could have it all with 'the Great Satan.' He said it jokingly, but I didn't get the impression he was joking at all."

"How would you react to his questions?"

"I usually handle his questions okay, but I'm worried that he is up to something and that he is having someone follow me. He's a hard-core zealot and suspicious of anyone who's traveled to America. I think he's just testing me, but it makes me very uneasy."

Carol was supportive, telling me that it was going to be the case that some people would make me nervous and that I just needed to stay on guard. She reiterated how grateful everyone in the CIA was and stressed, as she had on other occasions, that the agency would never pressure me to do anything I didn't want to do or felt uncomfortable doing. If I decided to stop at any time, they would back me completely. I appreciated this. In fact, I'd been looking for precisely this kind of pep talk.

"Don't do anything to compromise yourself or your family," she said. "I want to see you back in the U.S. with your wife and son someday."

That prompted me to show her the picture of Omid, and we talked about him and Somaya for a while. She genuinely seemed to care about my family. Then she reached into her purse and handed me an envelope.

"This is a bonus for all the hard work you have done. We consider you our best contact in Iran. We've come to trust all the information you've given us."

There were about fifty one-hundred-dollar bills in the envelope. That was a great deal of money in my country. A middle-class Iranian could easily live a prosperous life on five hundred dollars a month, given the exchange rate on the black market. As tempting as those bills looked to me, and as much as the money would have made a difference to my family, I did not feel right about accepting it. It made what I was doing feel like a business transaction, and it was anything but that for me.

Carol seemed to understand my sense of conflict. "You deserve it. Take it," she said.

My eyes went to Omid's picture one more time, and then I thought about how this money would help him and Somaya if something should happen to me. "Why don't you wire it to the same account where you deposit my salary?" I said, as I handed back the envelope.

Carol smiled at me gently and agreed to do so. Now we had to figure out the best way for her to get out of my room. It was nearly 3:00 a.m. I grabbed the ice bucket, opened the door, and walked out toward the ice machine, leaving the door half open for Carol. I told her I would drop the ice bucket if I saw something suspicious. She slipped out while I went down the hall.

Back in my room, I immediately hid the supplies in the bottom layer of my suitcase among my notebooks and the magazines I had purchased that morning. Then I put the codebooks in the frame that held Omid's picture. The thought of the image of his innocent face serving as cover for my dangerous activity jarred me. I kissed the picture and whispered, "I am so sorry, Omid *jon.*"

THE TORCH IS PASSED

Inside Mehrabad Airport's terminal, echoing voices competed with loudspeaker flight arrival and departure announcements. Somaya and Omid were waiting at the gate outside customs. I rushed toward them, eagerly anticipating a hug and leaving Kazem behind. My wife and son had become my refuge, my one safe place where I could be who I wanted to be.

But Somaya's usual smile was missing that day. As I got closer, I could see tears in her eyes. We embraced briefly, and then she buried her head in my shoulder and started crying.

I cradled her and took Omid from her arms, pulling him close to me. "What's wrong?" I said to her.

Somaya looked up at me sadly. "Reza, Nima was killed in *jebheh*. We just got the news this morning."

The army had conscripted Nima, her eighteen-year-old cousin, four months earlier. They gave him only rudimentary training and sent him to the front. The revolution had now claimed another one of us.

Kazem had given me a little space to greet Somaya. Now, having witnessed our drama, he came over and asked what was wrong.

"Baradar Kazem, I just heard that my cousin was killed at the front," Somaya said.

Her calling Kazem "brother" touched me. It warmed me that she would make the effort to show respect for my position, even though she detested my being in the Guards, and even while she was contending with a tragedy.

"I am so sorry for your loss, *khahar*," Kazem said, calling Somaya "sister," "but he is a *shahid* now and he paid his share of sacrifice for Islam."

For reasons that I can't comprehend in retrospect, I felt it was important for me to support this point. "Baradar Kazem, you are right. We should be proud that now our family has a God's warrior, a martyr."

The words felt artificial to me the moment they left my mouth. And, more important, I knew that by saying them I had crossed the line with Somaya. While she might grudgingly accept my role in the Guards, she would never accept my trivializing the death of a loved one in this way. I felt miserable instantly.

Somaya reacted as I knew she would—and should. As soon as Kazem turned his head to a voice calling his name, she pushed my arm away. Glaring at me angrily, she said, "Let's get out of here."

On the plane, Kazem had told me that he'd learned from Rahim that the Iraqi army was using chemical weapons on our forces in the offensive dubbed Operation Kheibar, which took place on Majnoon Island in Iraq. These weapons, a combination of sarin and mustard gas, had killed or injured thousands. Because we lacked treatment facilities, the Guards were seeking help throughout Europe. With no cure or antidote available and nothing to alleviate their suffering, our soldiers experienced convulsions, nose and mouth bleeding, and finally suffocation. Picturing Nima dying a slow, painful death made me feel all the more guilty for what I had blurted out.

Our reunion destroyed by my callousness, Somaya had turned away from me and was walking quickly toward the exit. I rushed a good-bye to Kazem, saying I'd see him in the office next week, and ran to catch up with her.

Somaya did not speak on the way home, keeping her head turned out the window. I knew I should have said something to her, but I couldn't think of anything. Should I apologize for being a devoted

Guardsman and believing in martyrdom? Should I tell her that I didn't believe what I'd said, and did it only to impress Kazem? Both explanations seemed empty to me, and I knew that neither would comfort her. For the thousandth time since I contacted the CIA, I wanted to tell Somaya exactly what was going on, and the fact that I couldn't do so frustrated me and left me feeling like a miserable husband.

When we got home, Somaya put Omid in his bed while I went to my study. Minutes later, she stood in my doorway and broke her silence.

"You are a very insensitive person, Reza. You are not stupid, I know that. But sometimes you do things and say things that make you unrecognizable to me. How could you possibly say what you said at the airport? My aunt losing her son makes you a proud Muslim? You are becoming blind, Reza. You are not seeing things the way they are. I am so tired of this." She paused and her eyes narrowed. "And I am tired of you."

She slammed the door as she left the room, leaving me with my head in my hands and fighting back tears. I'd been so excited about coming back home to her. This was the last thing I wanted when I saw her. I rested my arms and forehead on my desk. Trying to be both Reza and Wally was causing me to make mistakes and leading me to be inconsiderate to the ones who mattered most in my life.

My head was still down when I awoke with a stiff neck in the middle of the night. It was now Friday, which meant that I'd soon be receiving a message from Carol, but I still had some time before that. I left my study and tiptoed down the hall to check on Somaya and Omid, opening the bedroom door quietly. Somaya was cuddling with Omid in our bed. I watched them for a while, wishing I were there with them, longing for the simple pleasure they shared with each other. Then I reached for the end of the blanket and covered Somaya's feet, blew a kiss to them, and left, closing the door softly.

Before turning on the radio, I wrote a short letter to Carol.

[Letter #—]
[Date:———]

Dear Carol,

1—I got back from Dubai to learn Somaya's cousin was killed in the war.

2—The Iraqi army used chemical weapons against the Iranian forces in Operation Kheibar. The casualties are high. The Guards are trying to transfer some of the casualties to European countries for medical help.

3—Mustard and sarin gas was used in the attack.

4—We placed the order with Computer Dynamics Unlimited.

5—We expect to receive the first shipment of the computer equipment within four weeks.

Wally

That night, I received no message from Carol. She knew I was just getting home and she might have assumed that I'd be too tired to check the radio. However, a modicum of worry crept into my thoughts. The last time I saw her was when we were preparing for her departure from my room in Dubai. What if something had happened to her on the way back from the hotel?

A week passed, Somaya was still not talking to me, and I still couldn't think of anything to say to make things better. Somaya spent time with her family and was involved in making funeral arrangements for Nima. Fortunately, work kept me distracted, as I needed to visit two bases with Kazem and Rahim, where the Guards were conducting missile tests.

Finally, on Thursday morning, Somaya opened the door to my study. I was sleeping on the floor on a tiny blanket, squeezed between the wall and my desk, which filled most of the room.

"I'm wondering if you would come with me to go shopping for Eid-e Norouz," she said softly, referring to the upcoming celebration of our New Year. Unlike the last time she'd spoken to me, there was no sign of hostility in her voice now. I told her I would be happy to take her shopping. She nodded and then said nothing for several long seconds. Finally, she pointed to where I was lying.

"You should have more blankets to sleep on. I put them all in the storage downstairs." Then she offered me a smile that went right to my soul. "But you can sleep in the bedroom with us tonight."

I wished that I could have found the words to bridge the gap between us before she had to do it. And once more, I wished I could explain to her why I'd created that gap in the first place.

I smiled back at her and said, "I'd like that."

As glad as I was to return to our bed, the next day was a Friday, and I'd need to get up for Carol's messages. I would have to take extra care that night to leave our room without Somaya's even knowing I was gone. I couldn't let Somaya think that anything—especially something that we'd mysteriously never spoken about—was more important to me than she was at this point.

As always, my body awoke me with time to spare. I decided to use this time to begin a letter to Carol. Rasool, the Guards member from the Intelligence Unit whom I'd mentioned to her in Dubai, told me about arms sales and Guards training provided by China and North Korea. Inadvertently, Rasool had become one of my better sources because his travels brought him in contact with dealings that I ordinarily wouldn't hear about. Rasool liked to impress his friends with who he was and with the importance of his job. It took only a little encouragement to get him to start bragging about the extent of his insider knowledge and to get him to offer details.

Rasool had joined the Intelligence Unit directly after graduating from Amir Kabir University of Technology with a degree in electrical engineering. His father and Rahim's father belonged to the same mosque and had been friends for many years. His job interview was perfunctory because his credentials met all the criteria required to work in the IU, he was deeply devoted to Islam, and he had a family connection to the Guards. The Guards preferred people who came with strong recommendations and who they could background-check easily. Rasool's colleagues called him *gondeh bak,* the big guy, because of his six-foot height and heavy build.

In the midst of my letter to Carol that included new information from Rasool, the time came for me to listen to messages. I put on my headphones and listened carefully.

> *Hello, Wally,*
>
>   *Urgent. Have you heard anything about a CIA operative in Beirut named William Buckley? We believe he was kidnapped by Hezbollah. Any info appreciated. Let us know if you hear anything.*
> *Carol*

This was the first time the CIA had asked me for specific information on one of its operatives. To me, this suggested a new level of trust in the details I'd been providing them. The fact that Carol didn't mention my last letter probably meant that she didn't receive it yet, but I was glad, after not hearing from her the week before, to know that she had arrived back in England safely.

After the message, I completed my letter.

[Letter #—]
[Date: ———]

Dear Carol,
  1—The Guards last week successfully tested their first remote-controlled drone. The test was done at a base outside of Tehran in the vicinity of the city of Karaj.
  2—The Guards also successfully conducted a surface-to-surface missile test.
  3—North Koreans are here in Iran helping the Guards in the development of surface-to-surface missiles.
  4—Revolutionary Guards are being trained in fighter pilot programs in North Korea.

5—*The Guards Intelligence Unit sent members for counterintelligence training to North Korea.*

6—*Revolutionary Guards naval forces are being trained by the Chinese at a naval base in China.*

7—*Guards have purchased Chinese Silkworm missiles and have received the first delivery.*

8—*The Swedes are selling the Guards small attack boats equipped with small missiles.*

9—*Have heard nothing about W.B., but will listen for any info.*

Wally

At the time, I'd heard no mention of William Buckley on the news or in my offices. Because of this, I knew it wouldn't be wise to ask. My poking around about an individual whose name should mean nothing to me would certainly have generated suspicion. The implications of Carol's message concerned me, though. Kidnapping of Americans and other foreigners by the Guards and their proxies to use as bargaining chips was becoming commonplace throughout the Middle East. But kidnapping a CIA operative was not. In all probability, the kidnappers would not release Buckley alive—and this meant that the CIA would likely react disproportionately and that tensions would continue to ratchet up. I kept my ears open for any mention of Buckley, but heard nothing about this for the longest time.

Just before Norouz, the Persian New Year, I received a message from Carol requesting some additional details regarding my previous letter.

[Letter #—]
[Date: ———]

Dear Carol,

1—*The Guards are looking into purchase of protective gear and equipment for defending against chemical attacks.*

2—I heard from Rahim that Mohsen Rezaei has given the Guards the go-ahead for research and development of chemical weapons.

3—China is very active in the sales of military armaments to Iran. They are providing long-range artillery guns along with ammunition. Kazem told me that due to heavy usage of artillery guns at the front, the barrels fail and blow up, but China is keeping a steady flow of new guns into Iran.

4—The Swedish boats are 30–40 feet in length with missile launchers on the side of the bow. The missiles I saw were 4 to 6 feet long. Each boat carries two missile launchers along with a heavy machine gun.

5—The Guards plan to use drones both for reconnaissance and as means of attack by arming them.

6—There are Guards commanders that routinely travel to North Korea and there is a close relationship between the Revolutionary Guards and the North Korean military.

Wally

With a few days off for Norouz, I had a chance to relax and pay attention to my family, something I welcomed and relished. Moheb Khan and Zari Khanoom, Somaya's parents, arrived from England to help us celebrate and to meet their new grandson, who was now crawling and displaying two bottom teeth. Somaya was exuberant to have her parents be part of Omid's life. She busied herself with the preparations of the Norouz *haft sin sofreh,* the traditional New Year table, and the scent of the purple and white hyacinth, the center-piece of that table, filled the room.

Earlier that day, I had gone to Agha Joon's house to pick him up for our dinner. He was too old to be able do things on his own now. In fact, he would be moving into the house of my uncle (Haleh and Mina's father) the next week. Agha Joon could no longer host No-rouz, though he'd done so for so many years. As I drove over to get him, I realized that the torch had been passed from his generation to mine to continue the family traditions.

Entering the front yard of his house and going down that familiar path of geranium pots, I experienced a rush of fond memories. I closed my eyes for a moment and let out a deep breath, savoring the simplicity those memories evoked. I could hear Khanoom Bozorg calling me a lifetime ago: *"Reza* jon, *get inside and bring your friends. It is New Year and I want to give you your* eidis.*"* When we went to her, she handed Naser, Kazem, and me each a brand-new thousand-rial bill (worth about fifteen U.S. dollars then), which she had kept inside the Quran. Kazem kissed the Quran and thanked Grandma for her generosity. Naser saluted the shah's picture on the bill, put it in his pocket with all of the other gift money he'd collected, and we all went back to the yard to happily discuss how we were going to spend all our *eidi* money.

It was in this same yard that we gathered with Naser and Davood and where Naser fell in love with Haleh. It was in this same yard that we celebrated every day of life without worrying about tomorrow.

As I stood there, I wished Davood was the one giving Agha Joon a lift to our house and that Naser, Soheil, and Parvaneh would be joining them.

Norouz means "new day" and always begins on the first day of spring. It represents two ancient symbolic concepts: End and Re-birth, or, more specifically, the end of evil and rebirth of good. One of our traditions involved an older family member, usually Agha Joon or Khanoom Bozorg, telling stories about Norouz and the meaning of the New Year while we waited for its arrival.

Khanoom Bozorg would tell us about the *haft sin,* or the seven S's. She would explain that the *haft sin sofreh* included seven items that started with the letter S: *sabzeh,* sprouts, which symbolize rebirth; *samanu:* a sweet pudding made from wheat germ, symbolizing afflu-ence; *senjed:* the dried fruit of the oleaster tree, symbolizing love; *siib:* apple, which symbolizes beauty; *somaq:* sumac, symbolizing sunrise;

serkeh: vinegar, symbolizing age and patience; and *sonbol:* hyacinth, to denote the coming of spring. When we were kids, we were more excited about the gift money than learning about the traditions, but we patiently sat through Khanoom Bozorg's explanations.

For the remaining thirteen days of our New Year celebration, we would gather and party incessantly. Relatives would come and visit the older members of the family, and then in return, the elders would pay their respects by visiting them back. All of this meant more gift money for the children. On the last day, as was the tradition, we all went picnicking in the suburbs area, dancing, singing, and playing outside until the night forced us back to our homes.

Somaya's table was as colorful and delightful as what I remembered of my grandmother's, and as is the custom, it included a mirror and lit candles for enlightenment and happiness.

As the New Year approached, we gathered around the table—Somaya and her parents, Agha Joon, my mother, and me holding Omid. My mother and I had not resolved our differences, and I still saw scorn in her eyes whenever she looked at me. But Omid's birth had softened her, and she visited us fairly regularly to see him. She loved her grandson very much and she would endure my presence if necessary to spend time with him.

Moheb Khan started to read verses from the Quran. We all closed our eyes and prayed in silence. Shortly after our prayer, the room suddenly got dark—a power outage, a common occurrence during the war.

"I know they did this on purpose today," my mother said, shaking her head. "They don't want us to have power for the New Year. They don't want us to celebrate the Norouz and have a happy life."

Although the power outages happened nearly every day, I knew my mother was making a point here: that the mullahs were trying as hard as they could to ruin our culture. I suppose she was also reminding me how much she disapproved of my association with the regime. As far as the mullahs' aims were concerned, she was right. They tried very hard to take away our Persian heritage and force

Arab/Islamic tradition down our throats. They had gone so far as to try to ban the New Year celebration, calling it un-Islamic.

There was a pregnant silence in the room when the lights went out. Then Agha Joon patted my mom's back and said, "You are right. It is not going to be the same as long as our country is being ruled by these long-bearded, motherless donkeys. But, Fataneh *jon,* this is the only thing we have left. Norouz is the only part of Persian heritage that has kept our identity intact besides our family." Agha Joon moved a candleholder closer to him. "We've been celebrating Norouz for three thousand years and they can't prevent us from doing so now or ever."

Then he got up with the help of his cane and kissed my mom's forehead. He took an envelope from his pocket and handed it to Somaya. "Somaya *jon,* this is Omid's *eidi.* I hope to God that next year we have Shahanshah's son, back from exile in America. Then Norouz would be the same as it used to be and happiness will be back to our homes."

Agha Joon then walked around and kissed every one of us to mark the coming of the New Year. It was usually the job of younger ones to get up and kiss the elders to show their respect and love for the family. But that had changed, too.

I looked over at my mother and whispered, "Happy New Year." I wished so much that I could tell her I was sorry, but, as always, I choked this back.

The candles on our table, which had been there to symbolize happiness and enlightenment, now served as beacons through government-imposed darkness. The mirror, which should have reflected the light for a brighter future, instead reflected the disappointment in my mother's eyes for me.

THE RADICAL

OVER THE NEXT few months, I watched Kazem rise meteorically in the Intelligence Unit. He worked incredibly hard and never took days off. When the Guards offered the opportunity to acquire land and a car, he demurred, making it clear that he was in this job for the contribution he could make to the revolution rather than any wealth he could accumulate. Meanwhile, he laced his conversation with religious references and urgings, becoming in his actions and words the model radical Islamist. As much as this behavior disturbed me, and even frightened me at some levels, I recognized that it insulated Kazem completely from suspicion. He had become beyond reproach. Realizing that I needed to create the same kind of protection for Wally, I started to emulate Kazem's behavior. Instead of going home after work, I would follow him to the mosque to attend the sermons of mourning in support of our troops heading to the front to become martyrs. I would also accompany him to Namaz Jomeh, the Friday prayers.

During one of these times, the mullah conducting the sermon was Hashemi Rafsanjani. He was then the speaker of the parliament and would eventually become president and then a pivotal "moderate" figure in the uproar surrounding the 2009 elections.

"The West and the Zionist media accuse us of torturing our prisoners in Evin Prison," he said to the gathered thousands. "They say we torture the members of the opposition and force them into confession." At this, he smirked. I peeked at Kazem, who was listening enthusiastically and responding to Rafsanjani's every gesture. "The West does not understand that the prisoners are introduced to Quran and the Islamic values by our committed Guards. It is the power of Islam that helps these people to understand their mistakes. They repent and ask God for forgiveness—and that's how they confess."

The crowd responded exuberantly, shouting, "*Allaho Akbar.* . . . Khomeini *Rahbar.* . . . Death to America. . . . Death to Israel. . . ."

Rafsanjani continued to offer preposterous disinformation to the masses—who applauded it feverishly—while I stewed. Radical rhetoric always disturbed me, but what Rafsanjani was suggesting about Evin Prison after what I knew happened to Naser, Soheil, Parvaneh, Roya, and so many others inflamed me, though I couldn't show any sign of this. I wondered how Kazem could raise his fist in the air in support of these words with so little regard for the memories of people he once loved. It shamed me to watch this blind display of loyalty, this damning of the media of the West for telling the truth. Though I pretended to participate in this mass hysteria, the experience brought me to tears.

Kazem peeked at me and handed me his handkerchief to wipe my eyes. He had once known me so well, but now his fanaticism had overwhelmed him so completely that he had utterly misinterpreted my emotions. "We are so alone in this world, Reza," he said, touching me on the shoulder. "But God is on our side. The West can lie all it wants about our revolution to the rest of the world, but victory will be ours. It is all in Allah's hands."

I nodded at him earnestly. Though it was critical to my mission that I maintain his trust, there were times when I just wanted to scream at him, shake him, or smash him against a wall while telling him how stupid and blind he was.

A few weeks after the Rafsanjani sermon, Kazem came to my office.

"Reza, get your bags packed," he said. "We're leaving in two days for Bandar 'Abbas. We have to set up the new computer system for our command and control centers in the Persian Gulf area."

Bandar 'Abbas, a Persian Gulf port city on the southern coast of Iran, is in the most strategic position on the Strait of Hormuz, through which all shipping in the area must pass. Deployed at the mouth of the Gulf, the Guards were in place to control or disrupt the flow of oil to the world. The idea of going on this trip with Kazem excited me because it presented an excellent opportunity to gather intelligence for the CIA.

Bandar 'Abbas also served as the hub from which personnel and military equipment were secretly transferred in large old fishing boats to the Guards' naval bases on the islands in the Strait of Hormuz. They also used other old ships to transfer arms from international waters into Iran.

During the course of our stay there, we witnessed large-scale training of the forces and talked to many commanders about the buildup. Guards were training thousands of smaller units as divers and missile launchers along with the regular forces, who were trained on smaller boats designed for maneuverability in the Persian Gulf. As we moved from one base to another along the coast, we saw that the Guards' surveillance units kept an eye on every ship from the time it entered the Gulf through the Strait of Hormuz all the way up to the ports of Iraq.

We also witnessed the training of Guards naval forces. They attacked dummy enemy ships with hundreds of smaller boats. It became clear to me that the intention was to build an unconventional navy. The Guards knew their current ships could be destroyed in a matter of hours in any conflict with the U.S., but hundreds of smaller units armed with missiles could pose a serious problem for any entity on the water.

After a tiring day-trip to the Qeshm and Abu Musa islands, Kazem and I fell into our beds at the base. Kazem was on the top bunk bed and I was on the bottom. Though I was exhausted, I had trouble sleeping because of the heat and humidity. A soggy breeze wafted through the torn drapes of the barracks, carrying the salty scent of the ocean and the soothing slapping of the waves. The sounds and smells of nature at peace might have lulled me at another time in my life, but this was not nearly enough now. Instead, this evidence of nature's purity reminded me how far from pure our ambitions were in my country. I wondered if my reports to the CIA would change any of this, though I was less than certain. I blew out a deep breath as I sank into my thoughts.

As I did, Kazem bent over my bed. "Reza, are you awake? Are you okay?"

I hated that I couldn't express despair in private when I was at work—even in the middle of the night. "It is so hot, Kazem. I can't sleep. How can you sleep with this humidity?"

"I am not sleepy. I was just thinking and wondering about where life is going to take us. You know, Reza, sometimes I wonder how we could defeat America. I believe that our Imam Mahdi will reappear and bring justice to the world and put an end to these sinful evildoers. But I wonder if I will be there when it happens. Could I have the honor of serving under his leadership and witnessing this victory?"

The belief in the eventual reappearance of the Shiite's twelfth Imam, Mahdi, brings much excitement to Shiites. I always thought we were meant to interpret the promise of Mahdi's reappearance as an allegory. However, Kazem—and the many others who thought like him—believed that a human being, even a holy one like the last Shiite Imam, could hide in a hole for hundreds of years and then come back to lead Khomeini's movement, bring justice and fairness to the entire world, and provide hope for divine change.

"Do you know this hadith about Imam Mahdi by the prophet Mohammad?" Kazem asked. "It says: 'During the last times, my people will be afflicted with terrible and unprecedented calamities and misfortunes from their rulers, so much so that this vast earth will appear small to them. Persecution and injustice will engulf the earth. The believers will find no shelter to seek refuge from these tortures and injustices. At such a time, God will raise from my progeny a man who will establish peace and justice on this earth in the same way as it had been filled with injustice and distress.'"

"Of course I know the hadith!" I lied. "You know, Kazem, I some-times wonder myself. But then I think about how you and I ended up being here, sharing a belief, our commitment to Islam, and about how our destiny and faith kept us so close together. We are achieving a lot under Imam Khomeini's guidance and leadership. I strongly believe we both will be honored to serve under Imam Mahdi's lead-ership, *inshallah*."

I was thankful for the darkness because it was difficult to believe that my expression wouldn't have betrayed me as an impostor when those words came from my mouth.

"Reza, you are an asset to this nation and you should know how much respect I have for you. I've wanted to say something to you for a long time; I wish that Naser had chosen another path. I wish he had been more like you. I pray for him often, you know. I pray that God forgives his sins."

I wondered why Kazem was bringing up Naser's name now, since he hadn't said a word about him since he told me about our friend's execution. It made me cringe to think that Kazem wished Naser had been more like me. Did that mean he wished that Naser were a liar and someone who needed to hide behind his own shadow?

"We all suffer for our ignorance," Kazem continued. "God is divine and Islam is our guidance. If we ignore the truth, *Jahanam* is where we end up. Now you better get to sleep. We've had a very long day today."

There was Kazem's philosophy in a nutshell: true believers like radical Muslims who kill in God's name go to heaven, and people who question the authority of the mullahs and fight for their rights go to hell. If Kazem thought I could sleep with that concept in my head, he was even more deluded than I realized.

The night was long and sleep completely eluded me. A warm breeze forced itself through the drapes, reminding me of the drapes in my room at Grandma's house. She used to push them away in the morning, asking me if I had done my morning prayer. "Grandma, I will do it later," I would say, to which she would respond, "My dear, if you skip your prayers you go to *Jahanam*. You don't want to end up in the fire of hell with snakes and scorpions around you. Do your *namaz* and be good and you will go to heaven." The path to heaven she described seemed as much of a fantasy as the one Kazem envisioned. In either case, the question for me remained the same: Was there a place in heaven for those who betrayed?

After two weeks in the Gulf, we returned home to a life that had the veneer of normalcy even at a time of war. I felt the trip had been successful for two reasons. First, I'd gathered a wealth of information. And second, though I felt more like an impostor than ever, spending so much time with Kazem had created the illusion of closeness. I'm sure in his clouded eyes he saw this as a stretch that equaled the true brotherhood of our youth.

In my study, before listening for my next message from Carol, I wrote another letter. Then I started to decode the latest signals.

Hello, Wally,
   We need to change the mailing address for your letters.
   No concern; just routine procedure.
   From now on mail to:

   51 X Street, Apt. 112
   London
Be safe,
Carol

I could not understand why they needed to change this address. Had there been a security breach or was this as routine as Carol suggested in her message? If there had been a breach, would they hide it from me so I would continue to work? Would they try to help me and my family get out if I'd been exposed? My thoughts became frantic for several long minutes until I calmed myself. I had to trust them or I would drive myself crazy and make unfixable mistakes. There were good reasons for them to take the precautions they were taking. Using one location for a long period made our correspondence easier to discover. I had to believe this.

The next day, Rahim summoned me to his office. When I arrived, he rushed in behind me, closed the door, and sat behind his desk.

"Beshin, Baradar," he said, commanding me to sit down.

I did as ordered. He opened a drawer, grabbed a folder, and slid it toward me. Before I could read the bold words on it, he covered them with his chubby hands and slid the folder back toward himself. He tapped his fingers on the folder with his left hand while he reached into his breast pocket with the other for his reading glasses.

"I have some documents here that I need you to translate for me."

He pushed the folder toward me again. The bold letters, N-A-T-O, did not register with me right away, but when I opened the folder and saw pictures and descriptions of heavy military machinery, I realized the folder contained secret documents. I could not believe that NATO members were offering various types of military equipment to the Revolutionary Guards, turning their backs on the U.S. arms embargo on Iran.

"Do you want me to translate the whole thing for you, Baradar Rahim?" I asked.

"No, no. That has been taken care of. I am just interested in certain equipment."

Apparently, the Guards had already arranged for a sizeable purchase. We went over details for an hour or so with Rahim growing increasingly excited about the machinery we'd been able to acquire. Rahim took notes. I did as well, in my head.

[Letter #—]
[Date: ———]

Dear Carol,
1—Got your message. Please confirm receipt. I hope I have the new address right.
2—Today, in Rahim's office, I was asked to translate documents from a folder containing pictures and descriptions of heavy

machinery to be used at the front. "NATO" was written on top
of the folder. Some of the machinery is used to make bunkers and
others are to carry heavy equipment and tanks.
3—Rahim said the Revolutionary Guards were going to place an
order and some of the equipment will originate from England and
Germany.
4—Kazem told me that the Guards have set up R & D to produce
chemical weapons and are making progress on weaponizing
mustard gas. This effort has been cleared by the leadership to
counter Saddam's use of chemical weapons.
5—I am to be sent back to the front in a few weeks. I will keep
you informed on the date.

Wally

I was nervous about the prospect of making another trip to the front. So many people were dying there and I felt that the risks increased for me every time I went. Little did I know that I would face an even greater risk before then.

19

SUSPICIONS

THE NEXT DAY, I took the report I wrote for Carol along with several other pieces of mail to the mailbox. On my way to make my drop, I felt sure someone was watching. I rechecked the mail before inserting it through the slot, allowing me time to take in my environment. A man dressed in khakis and a long-sleeve shirt was eyeing me from the other side of the street. I caught his gaze for an instant, and he didn't acknowledge my presence in any way. For some reason, this made me more nervous than if he'd started chasing after me. My heart was beating fast, so I took a deep breath and walked a couple of blocks as I usually did before catching a cab. I watched vigilantly to see if the man would follow me. He crossed the street near the mailbox, but then just stayed there. Wanting to get away as quickly as I could, I hailed a passing cab, getting off a few blocks from my office to see if anyone else was following.

Fortunately, I didn't notice anyone. I spent an extra minute surveying the area, then rushed inside our office building. A few *pasdar* were waiting to catch the elevator in the hallway. I didn't feel like engaging anyone at that moment, so I kept my head down and hurried to the end of the corridor to the stairs. I took two steps at a time up to my fourth-floor office, and when I got there, I was short of breath. I shut the office door and held my face in my hands, rubbing my eyes. The experience had unnerved me. The fact that the man in khakis stopped by the mailbox was scary. If he found my letter to Carol and knew how to decode it, he would find out that

I'd written it. The level of detail in that report would verify that I was Wally. I realized that it had been ridiculous of me to continue the mail drop when I knew I was being watched, and I beat myself up over this.

What was done was done, though. I tried to calm down and reassure myself that I was being paranoid. No one would be able to decode my letter. Only the CIA could do that.

I blew a deep breath and opened my eyes.

And the sight of Javad—sitting in my chair behind my desk—jolted me.

"*Salam,* Baradar," he said, snickering and getting up from my desk. "You look exhausted. Did you jog to work today?"

I tried to maintain my composure and stay grounded. "What are you doing in my office?" I didn't want to sound confrontational, so I softened my tone. "Is everything okay, Baradar Javad?"

"Yes, everything is okay. But you seem upset," he said sarcastically.

He clearly had a purpose for being here, but he was not forthcoming about it. Scanning the room, he selected a new chair while motioning me to sit. He leaned forward, stared at me, and didn't move.

I knew he was up to something; he usually was. His body language was aggressive and his gaze was intimidating, even though he wasn't doing anything outwardly confrontational. Despite his sitting, he managed to use his size—more chubby than imposing—to menace.

Akbar, a friend of his, a member of our department and someone who was a good source of mine with a number of contacts in the Foreign Ministry, had told me that Javad was meddling in everyone's business and that he kept a file on everyone, even though this was beyond his job assignment. I had already experienced his intrusions several times and I had written Carol over my concerns about him. Akbar told me that Javad used the information he gathered to ingratiate himself with his superiors and to gain more power.

Javad was the youngest of three brothers. The oldest brother had been martyred in the war fighting the Iraqis. The middle brother was paralyzed from a childhood disease. Javad took care of his surviving brother and helped his parents, who were still living in poverty. He'd been rising quickly through the ranks in the Intelligence Unit, primarily because of his devotion to the Islamic government and his willingness to sell out his family members and neighbors. He'd recently arranged for the arrest of a man who lived in his neighborhood whose only crime was whispering to a neighbor about the lack of freedom for his daughters while waiting in a line at a grocery store to exchange his food coupons for some sugar and rice.

"What brings you here, *Baradar*?" I asked again.

"I am planning on visiting an old friend, Abbass, at the Intelligence Headquarters. He studied abroad, just like you. I think he also lived in California for some time. I told him I would bring you along to meet him. Maybe you know each other."

"Today?"

"Yeah. I checked your schedule with Rahim and he said you are pretty open."

This caught me off guard and ratcheted up my sense of apprehension. Javad was definitely up to something. Was the man I saw this morning somehow connected to this? I did not know what to say or how to react.

"Is that a problem?" Javad's voice had turned threatening. He still hadn't moved.

I scrambled for an explanation. "Omid, my son, is sick. My wife wants me to go to the doctor with her." I felt a little relief as I came up with this story. "Do we need to go today?"

"Yes, we do," he said tersely. "Abbass is a very busy man. This is the only time he can see us. I hope your son feels better soon, *inshallah*. I'll be in my office. Meet me there in half an hour."

Javad stood up slowly, uncoiling, looking as though he were considering devouring me. I felt naked and vulnerable.

Without another word, he left.

I went immediately to Kazem's office. As complicated as our relationship had become, at least in my eyes, and as much as I felt he'd turned into someone very different from the boy I grew up with, I still saw him as a safe harbor. We had a long and deep history together, and that had to mean something. I felt in desperate need of that safe harbor now, so I needed to talk to him. I also wanted him to know that if I didn't come back, I'd left the grounds with Javad.

Kazem was on the phone, as usual. I didn't hear what he was saying, nor was it my intention to eavesdrop this time.

"What's up, Reza?" he asked as soon as he hung up.

"Not much. I just came to say hi. I am going with Javad to the Intelligence Headquarters. He wants me to meet somebody there."

"He does? Who does he want you to meet?"

"I don't know, some friend of his named Abbass, who apparently went to school in California."

"Hmm."

Kazem's expression showed that this was new information to him. I realized quickly that I wasn't going to accomplish much with this conversation. Kazem couldn't offer me any kind of security this time. By all indications, he knew nothing of what was going on.

"I should be going," I said. "He's waiting for me. By the way, Baradar Rahim said he would give you the details for our trip to *jebheh*. Let me know when you have them."

In the hallway, I ran into Rahim myself. "*Salam*, Baradar Rahim."

"*Salam*, Baradar Reza. Javad was looking for you this morning. Did you talk to him?"

"Yes."

"He checked to see how busy you were today, saying he wanted to take you out for lunch or something. Could you come to my office when you get back? I need your help with my computer. It's acting up again."

It appeared to me that whatever Javad's plan was, it was not coming from my department, as neither Rahim nor Kazem seemed aware of it. That offered me no solace. Regardless of who knew what was going on, Javad could be ushering me to my doom within the hour.

I needed to talk to Somaya. If Javad's intentions were as sinister as I suspected, I wanted to hear her voice one more time. As soon as I got back to my office, I hesitantly dialed our home number, not sure how I could explain a call like this. Realizing I was only going to make Somaya worried, I decided to hang up. But before I could, Somaya answered.

"Somaya *jon*, it's me," I said as I tried to work my way through a lie. "I just ran into my commander and he said there might be a need for several of us to be sent to the fronts right away."

Somaya gasped. "Is there going to be a major offensive or something?" She sounded frightened and I felt horrible that I was doing that to her. I didn't intend to scare her, but I had to give her something to hold on to in case the worst happened to me.

"Oh, no. Rahim just wants me and a few other guards to be ready for . . . Hold on a moment. . . ." I felt somebody was lurking outside of my office. I slowly put the handset on the desk and opened the door. But I did not see anybody. I looked down the hallway, and when I was certain that nobody was around, I shut the door and picked up the phone.

"I love you, Somaya," I said, still not knowing what to tell her. I'd called her so impulsively that I didn't think things through.

"Reza, you are making me so worried. Is everything okay? You are being very strange. You never call me in the middle of the day. What's wrong?"

What if this were the last time I heard her voice? What if Javad and the guy in the khaki pants I saw this morning were decoding my letter at this moment? What if I never saw my son again? These thoughts consumed me and I couldn't speak.

"And I love you, too," she said after a long pause from me.

In that moment, I realized that all of my strength came from her love. Even as worried as I was now, having such a pure, innocent being in my life brought me joy. "Would you promise me something?" I asked.

"If you insist," she responded with a hint of irony in her voice.

I looked up at the door again and sharpened my ear to see if I could hear anybody. Then I continued. "Should something happen to me, promise me you'll go to London with Omid and stay with your parents." She did not say anything, so I continued again. "As I said, I might go to the front today. If you don't hear from me in a few days, I want you to pack your bags and go to London. Do you promise me?"

"Reza, you don't need to remind me how dangerous your work is," she said with confusion in her voice. "But I don't understand why they need a computer guy at the front. I am just . . ." She did not finish and just stayed quiet while I told her one more time how much I loved her.

Then, as much as I wanted to continue to hear her voice, I realized that I needed to hang up. The Guards could have been listening to this call, further fueling their suspicion about me.

I met Javad at his office and from there we headed toward his car. I resolved to maintain my composure, trying to convince myself that Javad was acting the way he was simply to test me. After all, according to Akbar, he'd made a profession out of testing people. Meanwhile, my thoughts raced between wondering if the Guards knew about Wally and persuading myself that they couldn't possibly know.

We'd barely started driving when Javad raised my anxieties to new levels.

"Baradar Reza, we are going to Evin Prison instead of Abbass's office," he said. "Abbass is at Evin today."

The mere suggestion of Evin set my mind reeling. Images immediately flashed of the last time I was there. The sounds of terror, torture, wailing, and gunshots rang in my ears simultaneously. I thought of Parvaneh, Naser, and Soheil. Unbidden, the thought came of myself as a prisoner there, and I came very close to losing the façade of calm I'd managed to erect provisionally.

"I am looking forward to meeting this friend of yours," I said as I straightened my back in my seat. "It's Baradar Abbass, right?"

"Yeah, Abbass. God bless him. This morning he told me they had just arrested two *pasdar* who were working as spies for other countries. It's hard to believe those bastards thought they could infiltrate us, steal our secrets, and get away with their treacherous acts. We lose our brothers in war, and these sons of dogs sell us out for money to America, Israel, or the Mujahedin. They are going to pay and then pay again."

He looked over at me, narrowing his eyes. I could feel the hatred in his voice, the insane need to avenge his brother by bringing down anyone who opposed the regime, and therefore the cause for which his brother had died.

His mention of the arrest of the Guards sent the pendulum of my thoughts back to the belief that Javad was driving me toward my imprisonment. For the first time since I became Wally, I felt I had reached the end. I was caught. My mind raced to think of a way out. In this frantic condition, I remembered a spy movie I watched with Naser when we were teenagers. In the movie, a spy took cyanide just before he was captured to avoid certain torture. If I had a cyanide capsule on me at that moment, I might have done the same. But such a thing hadn't come in the "spy kit" provided by the CIA. In this moment, in this car that I believed was delivering me to a future of agony, I felt very alone. I looked out the window, as if something there would provide me with an option.

"They go to America, and instead of helping their country, they betray us. One of these *jasoosa* gave away a secret plan about the war and a lot of Basijis lost their lives."

Javad's resentment for me was very personal. If, in fact, he did know that I was a spy, he was equating me with the death of our soldiers and, by extension, the death of his brother.

I continued to play the role of the faithful Guard. "Baradar Javad, we are fortunate that we have people like Abbass, whose knowledge is building a strong coalition for our Islamic movement. His American education is an asset for us. He knows the Americans better than they know us. He is not a betrayer."

Javad glanced at me quickly before returning his eyes to the road.

He didn't respond, and I stayed quiet as well, hoping that doing so would allow my words to sink in with him. If Javad and his cohorts had evidence against me, I knew I was already lost. But that didn't prevent me from trying everything at my disposal to convince them that they'd misjudged me.

A short while later, we entered through the main gate of Evin and headed toward the prosecution wing, southwest of the main prison building. Javad knew exactly where to go, probably because he'd spent a great deal of time here. I followed behind him in the long hallway lined with doors on both sides. He then made a left turn to another smaller hallway, stopped on the right side, and knocked on a door. Before anybody could answer, he opened the door.

Two Guards sat facing each other at desks piled with files and stacks of paper. One Guard gestured for the other to leave the room. Then he got up and approached Javad.

"*Salam aleikom,* Baradar Javad," he said, giving Javad a hug and kiss on each cheek. He reached his hand to me. "You must be Reza. I'm Abbass."

I nodded as I shook his hand.

Tall with broad shoulders, Abbass cut the image of a handsome *pasdar* in his tailored uniform. Despite his full beard and trimmed mustache, he looked neat and clean, unlike so many of his brethren who cared little for their appearance.

Abbass's manner could not have been more different from Javad's. He casually asked me about my life in Southern California and his manner was affable and gracious. He opened the conversation by saying that he went to school in Los Angeles around the same time I was there. I responded by telling him of my association with Islamic students in LA.

"Oh, did you know *Shahid* Baradar Hassan?" he asked.

"No. I knew a lot of people in the association, but I mostly hung around with Farzin and Mani, who were in charge of most of the meetings. Perhaps you knew them?"

"Yes, I knew them," he said, smiling. "They were a mainstay of the association in those days. Did you know that both Mani and Hassan came back and were martyred on the front? Two great *shahid*. But I never heard anything more of Farzin. Do you know where he is?"

"No, I've lost contact with him. I'm sorry to hear about Mani and Hassan. We're fortunate to have such devoted *baradaran*."

Abbass seemed to consider this for a moment. "Javad said you took a trip back to America a few years ago. You didn't see Farzin or contact him then?"

I told him about the nature of my trip and that I had only a short amount of time to spend with my aunt and help her transition to the assisted-living facility. I mentioned that I'd met with my old roommates, assuming he already knew that.

We talked about the student association for a while and I learned that Abbass was a committee head of the association and attended some of the meetings on the same days I was there. There was a surreal feeling to this conversation. I'd entered the office believing that they were about to ship me to hell, yet we spoke in a relaxed manner, like nothing more than two people with common acquaintances.

Javad, however, had a point to press. "Some of those students joined the Mujahedin, and the rest of them are working for Zionist America," he said sharply.

As he said that, I remembered that Johnny, my college roommate, had mentioned something about someone named Farhad—I didn't know anyone named Farhad—who'd joined the Mujahedin with his sister. I now realized that Johnny was talking about Farzin. Johnny told me that Farhad/Farzin had been arrested and killed in Iran.

So that's what this is all about. They're trying to connect me to Farzin with trick questions.

Javad continued, insisting that all Iranians who studied abroad were criminals and had no decency.

Impatiently, Abbass turned and said, "Javad, we have many Guards who have been educated all over the world and are serving our country well and with pure belief." He was obviously offended.

This exchange only increased the tension in the room from

my perspective. I still didn't know what was going on. Had Javad brought me here to set me up, hoping I'd say something out of nervousness that would indict me? If so, had I already said something to compromise myself? Or did Abbass know more than he was letting on, in which case his friendliness was just a sham before they destroyed me.

Just as Abbass started to ask another question, a loud knock at the door interrupted us and two tall and well-built *pasdar* entered the room. Their machine guns were hanging on their backs, and they had small guns at their waists. Their arrival immediately led me to believe that my time of reckoning had come. I felt all my resolve leave me; I was suddenly ready to surrender, to admit anything they wanted to know or confirm everything they already believed.

Long moments passed with the gaze of these *pasdar* seemingly boring a hole into me. Then Abbass approached them, handed over a folder, and whispered something to one of them. I had never felt so vulnerable in my life. I was certain that I had failed to meet Abbass's scrutiny. I stared at the floor, feeling numb; my ears, mouth, eyes—my whole body was senseless. I couldn't think of anything, not even my son. The image of Somaya's smile didn't bring back my strength. Naser's unjust death meant nothing at that moment. I couldn't think of any ifs—if I survived this, if I got to go home, if I could just see my family one more time . . .

"Okay, then. Come on, we're going now," Javad said, tapping my shoulder.

Resigned to my fate, I got up, thinking I was leaving with the two Guards. That's when I saw that they were no longer in the room. I had missed their departure in my panicked reverie. Then Abbass got up and rearranged the papers on his desk, grabbed a folder, put it under his arm, and shook my hand.

"I should be leaving as I have to be in my office soon," he said. He then patted Javad's shoulder and told him that he would be in touch.

Still feeling numb, I said good-bye to Abbass, and Javad and I left.

Back in the car, my senses started to return. "Are we going back to the base?" I asked, still wondering if Javad might be taking me elsewhere.

Javad threw me an arched eyebrow. "Where else do you want to go?"

"Nowhere," I said quickly. "I promised Rahim that I'd fix his computer sometime today. I just didn't know if you needed to go somewhere first."

Javad scratched his mustache with his bottom teeth, rolled his eyes, and kept driving. We returned to the base and I got on with the rest of my day.

As much as I tried, I couldn't begin to understand what this experience was all about.

That night at home I told Somaya that I would be staying in my study to take care of some unfinished work and that I would not be coming to the bedroom at all. I could see that she wasn't sure what to make of this. I'd rattled her with the phone call earlier in the day, and my explanation when I got home about a delay in our mission to the front hardly seemed to mollify her. But she simply nodded her understanding. I promised myself that I would explain things to her better later, but I didn't have the strength to do so tonight.

Alone in my study, I pondered for hours. I'd made any number of monumental decisions over the past few years and it was time for me to make another one—maybe the toughest of my life. I chain-smoked an entire pack of cigarettes, and when I lit my last one, I realized that I knew what I had to do.

[Letter #—]
[Date: ———]

Dear Carol,

You might be surprised to see that the format of this letter is different—no numbering and no outlines. I was at Evin Prison today. I am not certain as to what happened or what is about to happen.

I have told you about Javad, the guy who constantly asks me questions. He has connections in the Intelligence Unit and he took me to Evin Prison today. I thought that I would never come out again. He introduced me to a guy named Abbass Karmani. I don't know who he is or what his exact position is, but he was a member of the Islamic Students' Association in Los Angeles while I was studying there. He works at the Intelligence Headquarters now. While I was there, two other Guards came in to check me out. I am not sure whether they think of me as a member of the Mujahedin or if they suspect me of spying. But as much as I want to believe the whole thing is a game that Javad is playing to shake me up, I have to be careful.

I am especially worried about my family. I am going to talk to my wife and try to convince her to move to London. I will be transferring the codebook out of my house, and will not be sending any mail or listening for any messages. If things get worse, I will destroy the codes. Please remember that I will need one favor and one favor only. Should anything happen to me, I beg of you to look after my wife and son.

I will continue my daily life here, as I have no other choice. I am being sent to the front again soon. You will hear from me if I verify this was a one-time incident and I feel I am safe.

God bless,
Wally

20

ANOTHER MARTYR

THE INCIDENT AT Evin Prison left me stunned. Javad had drawn a bull's-eye on my back and I felt more unsafe than I'd ever felt in my life. The comfortable routine I'd settled into of collecting information and passing it on to Carol was no longer an option. I'd been aware of the consequences before, but now they seemed so much more real. I had to think of something to do to protect my family in case the Guards arrested me. When they caught people doing what I was doing, they tortured them in unimaginable ways. They would subject my wife and son to the same treatment, and I would be forced to watch until I confessed. The idea of that caused me levels of emotional pain I didn't think I was capable of feeling. How could I have ever put them in this position?

I remembered Steve's warning at the outset of my engagement with the CIA: "I want you to be completely aware of the consequences if things go wrong, Wally. The United States government will deny any relationship with you. There won't be a navy fleet coming to your rescue."

In other words, no one would save me from a horrific fate.

There was one thing—perhaps the only thing—I could do: commit suicide. Sometimes defeat is not a man's choice, but to die with pride and dignity is. The only way I could protect my family in the event I was arrested was to kill myself. The Guards wouldn't torture Somaya and Omid to force a confession out of me if I were already dead. So I drove to a local drugstore and purchased rat poison. I filled four gel capsules with the powder and carried them with me from then on.

Next I had to hide the codebooks. If the Guards were on to me or had any suspicions about me, they would ransack my home looking for evidence. I needed to get the books to a place where they'd be less likely to look, and I decided that my mother's condo was the most secure place available to me. I asked Somaya to get Omid ready to visit my mother.

I spent the entire drive to my mother's contemplating my life decisions and the path on which I'd placed those I loved. Because of me, Omid's future was like a dangling leaf on a bare tree with a storm fast approaching. As though to underscore the role I played in putting him in harm's way, I was using his diaper bag to transfer the codebooks, the very vouchers of my betrayal.

My mind was racing, and I must have exhibited this outwardly, because Somaya touched me on the arm and said, "Is something wrong, Reza? You don't seem to be yourself."

"It's nothing. I'm just concerned about going to the front again. I'm not sure when I'm going and there's so much to do before I leave. I'm a little stressed trying to figure out how to get it all done. It's nothing for you to worry about."

She gave me an understanding pat and let it go.

When we arrived, Somaya and Mom quickly started fussing over Omid. I took the codebooks up to the closet in what had been my room before I got married. I had other items stored there—schoolbooks, letters, photos—things I wanted to keep but didn't have the room for at my place. Before I stored the codebooks, I labeled the package "Ideas for Computer Programs" just in case my mother should find it. Then I went back to my family and tried to enjoy the simplicity of playing with a child.

In the following weeks, I took extra precautions. I made sure my daily routine of getting to and from work remained the same. This included dropping off letters to my aunt, though I was no longer using them to obscure the letters I was sending to Carol. At work, I stayed focused on my assignments. Not knowing what Javad was up to, I needed to appear to be the model Guard. I had barely seen him since we returned from Evin, but I still felt his presence.

During this silent period, many things happened that I'd been unable to report to Carol. One was the formation of the Ministry of Intelligence and Security (MOIS) in August 1984. The regime was consolidating most of their intelligence work into the ministry, which was to become the center of all that activity, though the Guards would continue to have an intelligence presence at every base. With the formation of MOIS, Javad and Rasool, along with a few others from our base, were transferred to the ministry. The fact that Javad was now working in the Ministry of Intelligence gave me chills because it meant he had more authority and autonomy. Kazem remained at our base as part of the Guards' Intelligence Unit.

Though it took longer than expected, Kazem informed me that Rahim had finally issued the order for us to go to the front. There was no particular reason why he chose us for this mission other than that he wanted all of the Guards under his command to be in close contact with martyrdom regularly. He felt that "getting close to heaven purifies the soul. Should you be worthy enough, you will become a martyr and join our great prophet Mohammad, Imam Ali, Imam Hussein, and all God's martyrs in heaven. But only if you are worthy enough."

When Kazem told me that Javad had volunteered to join us on this trip, it did not shock me, even though he was no longer in our unit. It simply confirmed that he was still watching me, and that he would continue to do so until he found something.

The night before I left, I was packing my bag. Somaya had put Omid in his crib for the night and now she sat quietly on our bed, watching me. She seemed terribly sad, her fingers playing with the end of her shirt, rolling it up and down. I knew she wanted to say something, perhaps something she'd wanted to say for a long time. I stopped packing and sat next to her. She bent her head and looked at her hands, but she remained quiet. I wrapped my arm around her and kissed her head. I couldn't think of what to say and ended up saying nothing. But I sat next to her for a long while. Finally, she broke the silence.

"You come back home in one piece, Reza," she whispered.

Her lower lip curled, her eyelids turned red, and a tear rolled down her cheek. I wiped the tear away, leaned my head on her forehead, held on to her hands, and then let her cry on my shoulder, too overwhelmed by a suite of emotions to do anything other than embrace her.

I reported directly to Kazem's office early the next morning. When I arrived, his expression was unlike any I'd seen on his face in a long time. His eyes were gleaming, and he seemed happy in a very different way from how he appeared after the regime scored a great victory.

"What's gotten into you?" I asked as I put down my bag.

Kazem got up from his chair. "My parents went *khastegari* for me a couple of weeks ago. I did not tell you before because I was not sure if they would be successful."

The chance to talk to Kazem about something as human as marriage warmed me. "Why would anybody reject a great man like you?" I said with a huge smile. "Who is the lucky bride?"

"Her name is Zohreh," he said excitedly. "She was introduced to my mom at a Quran reading. Mom thinks she is a very devoted Muslim and would make a great housewife. We are getting married after I come back from *jebheh*."

I reached out and gave him a hug, genuinely happy for him. When we were kids, we'd talked many times about getting married. It felt so good to bring those memories back now. He told me a little more about Zohreh, and we were both still smiling as we put our baggage in the back of the Toyota SUV supplied by the Guards. My good mood faded when Javad arrived, acknowledged me with a stiff hello, and climbed into the backseat.

Throughout the long drive to Ahwaz, a city in the southwest of Iran close to the border with Iraq, I worried about what Javad might bring up. Though we were going to the front, Javad's presence was the greatest source of my anxiety. He was mysteriously quiet, though. Kazem, who drove, listened to the news on the radio, and I pretended to be asleep most of the way, inventing the excuse that Omid had been up all night crying.

We made a few stops along the way in Hamadan, Khorramabad, and Dezful. The entire trip took more than twelve hours and darkness was upon us when we arrived at a garrison in Ahwaz. From there, we headed to the base behind the front lines. Our forces had no offensives planned the next day, so there was no sermon that night. It was already late, so shortly after our group *namaz,* we went to sleep. I was relieved that Javad had not challenged me on the trip, but I was still wary of him. I had to find a way to show him that I was devoted to my mission in *jebheh* and that I would fight for my country just like any other Guard or Basiji. If I could win his confidence, perhaps he would leave me alone.

The next morning, we drove on a narrow dirt road bookended by hills on either side. Several times, ambulances rushing back with wounded forced us to pull over, a stark reminder of what we were facing. The sound of artillery guns firing behind us was deafening. A loud boom shook the ground with such force it felt like an earthquake.

As we got closer, I could see the incoming artillery rounds from enemy fire blasting the surrounding areas. We felt a thump followed by a loud explosion as a round hit a small hill on our right, shaking our car and showering us with dirt and stones. Another one roared over our car, whistling as it went by. Kazem pressed harder on the gas. Javad ducked. Another shell seemed targeted for the roof of our car, but it hit a couple of hundred feet behind us. A hissing, screeching sound filled the air. It felt as if the sky were falling.

Kazem sped behind a hill close to the command post and slammed on the brakes. We got out, keeping our heads down as we made our way toward the commanding officer.

Kazem presented him with our orders from Rahim, saying,

"*Baradar,* how can we be of assistance?" Transferring ammo, distributing food, or helping with the injured had been our assignments on previous trips.

"For right now," the commander responded, "it would be best if you just take cover. The Iraqi forces are attacking our positions aggressively. Many tanks are approaching, using artillery and aerial support."

We took shelter in a shallow hole reinforced with sandbags. We could see flashes of light all around as explosions shook the ground. This was the closest we had come to war. We could hear the commander barking orders. Bullets whizzed overhead. A shell burst about twenty yards away. Someone screamed for a medic. It was chaos.

And then the fighting intensified.

The three of us squatted in that hole. Javad and Kazem seemed nervous, both mumbling verses from the Quran. To my surprise, I was the least flustered of the group. Even though I knew I might not escape this insanity alive, I felt strangely calm. *If I die here,* I thought, *Wally and the attendant burdens will die with me. Maybe that would be the easiest way out.*

Javad looked at me constantly. He tried to give the impression that he was not afraid, but I could see that he was. Remembering that his brother had died in the war, I felt a surge of compassion. Had he been thinking about that since we embarked on this trip?

"Kazem, tell me more about your new bride," I said to change the mood. "By the way, I agree to be your best man, even though you have not asked me."

Kazem smiled nervously. "I think the timing of *khastegari* was not right. It should have been done sooner."

"Don't worry, the wedding will go on as scheduled with or without you."

He chuckled, and just then a Guard approached our bunker, clearly in distress.

"You have to leave now and get back to the base behind the front lines. We are changing position and moving back. Get out now! Move!"

We ran toward our SUV. I was in front, with Kazem and Javad following. The sound of explosions mingled with the screams of the injured and shouts of *"Allaho Akbar!"* Billows of smoke surrounded us, making breathing difficult. As we neared the hill, I could hear the hissing sound of incoming rounds. I was running as fast as I could, but I felt heavy and slow.

Then I heard a short whistling sound. A shell hit close to us with a loud percussion followed by the buzzing noise of shrapnel splaying out into the air. We scattered and took cover. I couldn't hear anything but the ringing in my ears. I felt something hit my leg. Lying on the ground, I turned my head and saw some blood on my left ankle. I could still move the ankle and feel it, though, and it didn't hurt that much.

I looked around for Kazem and Javad, but they weren't behind me anymore.

"Kazem, Kazem!" I shouted. No answer.

"Javad, Javad." My voice was lost in the sound of explosions.

Another Guard, who was running for cover, reached me. "Just keep moving—run!" he said. But I could not. I had to find Kazem and Javad. I headed back in the other direction, and amid the dust and the smoke, I saw two Guards lying on the ground facedown, one covered with blood.

"Kazem, are you okay?" I called. No answer.

I broke into a run. *Please, God, not Kazem.*

As I got close, I saw that one of the two fallen Guards was trying to get up. I could now clearly see that it was Kazem. He noticed me and said, "I am okay, Reza. It's just my arm. Go check on Javad."

I blew out a deep breath and continued toward the second Guard. It was indeed Javad, and he was bleeding heavily. He had been hit by a large piece of shrapnel. It had torn into his back right under his left shoulder, taking out a chunk of tissue. He was not moving or making any sound. I took off my jacket and wrapped it around him, grabbed his upper body, put him over my shoulder, and bent over from the weight, started running. Kazem followed us, holding his arm. When we reached the car, I laid Javad in the backseat and drove back to the base. He didn't respond when we asked him questions, but his eyes were wide open and he was moaning.

Once at the base, we got out and called for help. The medics rushed Javad inside.

Kazem and I were both in shock. I have no idea how long we sat in one place before Kazem looked at me and said, "Are you okay, Reza? There is blood on your ankle."

I had forgotten about that. I looked down and saw that my ankle had been cut open by shrapnel. Medics soon came and closed the wound with seven stitches. They dressed the wound on Kazem's arm, assuring him he'd taken only a small hit.

While waiting to hear about Javad's condition, Kazem placed his jacket on the ground, took his holy stone and prayer beads from his pocket, and prayed. I walked back and forth gingerly on my repaired ankle, trying to process what we'd been through. We stayed like this until a medic walked up to us.

"Javad is now a martyr," he said flatly. He rubbed his forehead with the back of a blood-covered hand and went back in.

Kazem and I looked at each other in disbelief. I leaned against the wall, slid down to the ground, and sat there trying to compose myself.

Kazem handed me a cup. "Here, Reza, drink some water. You look pale."

"I am all right, Kazem. I am all right."

But I could not stop thinking about Javad. I felt responsible for his death. Had he chosen to come to *jebheh* because of me?

That night, while the Guards and Basijis gathered inside the base, thankful for the shelter and hot food, I walked outside and sat on a small hill nearby. The curtain of stars on an infinite sky provided a backdrop for the lights of Iraqi jets flying above, trying to find their targets. I stared at this dreadful portrait drawn by two madmen— Saddam and Khomeini—for untold minutes.

The sound of artillery rounds coming in and going out filled the air. I thought about God looking down and watching mankind once again killing one another for land, power, and other meaningless things. I maintained this tortured meditation for some time and then at last went back inside.

The light was dim. There were more than a hundred combatants in the room. Some were doing their prayers, some were lying down on blankets, and others were engaged in conversation. Looking around, I spotted Kazem sitting with a group of fighters. I joined them, listening to their war stories.

". . . He was in charge of bringing back three Iraqi POWs," one Guard was saying, "but he shot them instead, taking revenge for his brother who was captured and killed by the Iraqis. He said one of the Iraqis begged for his life and took out a picture of his wife and children. But he pulled the trigger anyway."

Another Guard added, "One of our buddies survived an offensive that turned against us. He told us that the Iraqis were going over to the injured Guards and Basijis, shooting them in the head to finish them off. He and a few others, who were also injured, played dead. At night, when no one was around, they crept on their bellies to get back behind friendly lines. In the morning, the Iraqi choppers swooped down, hunting for any Iranians they could find. He was lucky he managed to make it back after a couple of days without much food or water. He survived by chewing on grass and sipping the early-morning frost. He said he saw a light that guided him in the right direction."

It amazed me how sometimes one's faith brings extraordinary strength to accomplish impossible tasks. I felt compelled to contribute something, so I told them about Javad's fate—how he had come here to be of help at the front and became a martyr instead. They shook their heads, acknowledging his sacrifice. That story was nothing new for them, just a daily reality of war.

Javad's death left me with a strong sense of contradiction. I knew

I should have been relieved that he would no longer be pursuing me. The very real fact was that his loss was my family's gain. But at the same time, I couldn't stop feeling guilty. His pursuit of me was what killed him in the end, so if I hadn't made the decisions I'd made, he'd still be alive.

Since both Kazem and I were wounded, the Guards sent us back home the next morning. Kazem spent a great deal of time talking about Javad on the way back.

"He was only twenty-four, not even married yet," he said as he choked back tears. "He was not armed or fighting the enemy; he was just trying to help. He dedicated his life to Islam, and took care of his poor family and his disabled brother. God loves him and honored him with martyrdom. He will receive his proper rewards now." He attempted to say this last line with pride, but I heard the resignation in his voice.

Upon our return, we headed straight to Rahim's office to inform him about Javad. The news saddened our commander and he pledged to arrange the funeral and take care of Javad's family. A martyr's funeral was a special one, and as Rahim promised, Javad's was one worthy of a martyr. We held it the following Friday at Javad's house.

People throughout his neighborhood displayed pictures of him. They placed black-and-green banners reading YA HUSSEIN and SHAHID-E-RAH-E-HAGH (the martyr of God's path) along the roadside. Hundreds of Guards members in uniform gathered in the street. Several Guards, including Kazem and me, carried the coffin on our shoulders for a few blocks around the neighborhood while the rest followed us, some beating their chests with the palms of their hands while singing sorrowful songs of martyrdom. A ceremony of mourning then took place inside Javad's house with a mullah preaching and paying tribute to Javad and other martyrs.

After the ceremony, we headed to Behesht-e-Zahra cemetery for the burial. Inside the burial ground was a vast area dedicated to all martyrs. Thousands of young people who had given their lives were resting in peace in that section. Rahim had chosen a special place for Javad next to his older brother. On a stand on Javad's grave was a huge picture of him covered with flowers and flags. Javad's mother wailed while his father, an old man, was reading verses from the Quran. After the burial, we approached Javad's father.

"Congratulations to you for your son's martyrdom," Rahim said as he hugged the man. "Javad sacrificed his life for Islam. He is a great *shahid* and is now in heaven with Prophet Mohammad, Imam Ali, and Imam Hussein. You are very lucky to have given two sons to God."

Javad's father looked at us with tears in his eyes and said, "I wish I had more sons to dedicate to Islam."

The power this religion had on its most fundamentalist followers continued to astound me. As much as I believed many of the tenets of Islam, I didn't think I could ever accept congratulations on a death rather than condolences. Iranians have been practicing Islam for many centuries. For some, it offers guidance, a light that illuminates the darkness on the path of life. To others, it is a set of written rules from God through his Prophet Mohammad, and no one should ever amend these under any circumstances. During the shah's regime, people had the freedom to follow their interpretation of their religion. Not now, though. Now, not following it as the mullahs demanded you follow it carried serious consequences. Therefore, as always, I kept my thoughts to myself when in the presence of Kazem and others who thought as he did.

Kazem believed that the Islamic Revolution would lead to worldwide salvation. He talked about this as we drove back from the cemetery. He believed that the war with Iraq was not only to defeat Saddam, but also to ultimately defeat imperialism and Zionism.

"Can't you see, Reza? Saddam attacked Iran with the encouragement of America. They want to destroy our movement, as it is the first of its kind to confront the West. America is only interested in

Middle Eastern oil and not the progress of its people. And other Islamic countries like Egypt and Saudi Arabia are nothing more than
servants of the West. We are not like them. We are defending Islam
and will fight with the last drop of our blood."

Kazem did not see the crimes being committed by the mullahs as
unjust. He thought those who did not believe in Imam Khomeini
and the clergy were enemies of Islam. He believed Prophet Mohammad and his army fought and killed thousands of nonbelievers to
raise the flag of Islam. He thought that now we would raise that flag
at all corners of the world and that we would defeat the greedy, corrupt West once and for all.

I could see that religion had stripped Kazem and others like him
of perspective, common sense, and independent thinking. They did
not question what the mullahs decreed because they believed the
mullahs spoke the rules of God.

Not all of Kazem's animosity toward the West lacked validity.
England once wielded enormous power in the Middle East. It went
so far as to divide countries, draw new borders, choose sheiks to run
these oil-rich nations, and coordinate coups (in Iran, among others).
England chose to divide and conquer, and its most divisive action
was to enflame sectarian violence and to promote division within
ethnicities and religions such as the Shiites and Sunnis.

America had its own culpability in sending mixed signals and
promoting a confusing foreign policy. For example, it supported dic-
tators to the detriment of the citizens of those nations—Suharto in
Indonesia, Augusto Pinochet in Chile, Manuel Noriega in Panama,
Hosni Mubarak in Egypt, the shah in Iran, Saddam Hussein in Iraq,
and many others in Africa, Asia, and Latin America. American policies were also to blame for helping the Mujahedin in Afghanistan,
which then led to the creation of the Taliban and Al Qaeda. Thousands (probably hundreds of thousands) of people lost their lives
because of these policies.

However, many Iranians still saw America as a friend, a

superpower that respected and defended democracy, where people of different ethnicities and different ideologies lived in peace together. They hoped that somehow, some way, America would help rid Iran of the mullahs and end our long nightmare.

I was one of those Iranians.

21

TOO CLOSE TO HOME

SHORTLY AFTER RETURNING home from the front, I went over to my mother's condo to retrieve the hidden documents. No one had approached me since the Evin Prison incident, so I'd begun to believe that the entire thing had been less menacing than I'd originally perceived. And now that Javad was no longer a threat, I felt somewhat safer.

Even though I knew I had to be ever vigilant and prepared to deal with dangers even greater than any posed by Javad, I thought it was essential that I start writing to Carol again. Since I'd completely cut off communications, she might have assumed the worst about me and I needed to ease her mind. Most important, though, I had a great deal of information to convey. In a short letter, I told her what had happened to Javad and shared my belief that the threat was over. I also let her know that I would resume filing my reports. I promised not to let my guard down.

It was now important to focus on my family, whom I had neglected since the chilling experience at Evin. I'd been so fearful of what might happen to them if I were caught that I'd managed to push them away. I was physically there, but I'd retreated into myself. What they saw was a tense man with little ability to engage with them and share his soul with them. I needed now to show them how lucky I felt to be alive and to have them in my life. Somaya seemed happy to have my full attention again. How happy could we be if I were not living two lives and if we weren't under constant threat of having our world turned upside down?

I sent another letter to Carol a few days after I reopened communications, updating her about everything that had happened in the past several weeks, including the formation of the MOIS, and the transfer of Rasool and many other Guards to the ministry. I'd actually heard a rumor that Rasool was going to be on the move yet again. Someone told me that he was leaving the country to pursue his education, which surprised me a little. I bumped into him one day leaving Rahim's office, and I almost didn't recognize him. He was nicely groomed, he'd shaved his beard, and he was dressed in a business suit. Something was going on.

"*Salam,* Baradar Reza," he said brightly. "I'm glad I saw you. I wanted to say good-bye to you." He shook my hand and reached to give me a hug, overwhelming me with his size.

I tried not to look too surprised by his new appearance. "*Salam,* big guy. I heard you were going to England to continue your education. When are you leaving?"

"*Inshallah,* this afternoon."

Kazem validated my suspicion when he told me the same day that Rasool had been prepped to become an agent in England. This would be valuable news to pass on to Carol, and I needed to find a way to uncover more details about Rasool's mission. Getting Kazem to talk would not be difficult, but he seemed very busy at the time. As it turned out, Rahim was also traveling to England, which meant Kazem had extra work preparing to fill in, which he did whenever the commander was away.

When I finally got Kazem alone in his office, he told me that Rasool's new assignment was to infiltrate the Iranian opposition groups in England to learn about their activities. He also said that the reason for Rahim's travel was to meet with the Guards' agents in London. The Guards had gone abroad to confront the Mujahedin and others challenging the Iranian government. The Mujahedin were active in Europe, conducting a campaign aimed at toppling the

Islamic regime. They were also busy helping to coordinate assassinations of Islamic officials in Iran.

"Reza, we have the approval of several European governments to go after the opposition," Kazem told me.

"You mean we can take them out at will?"

"As long as we do not jeopardize the security of those countries or their citizens, we can."

This seemed incredible to me. I wondered how the West justified helping fanatics who could just as easily turn on them. As I thought this, I flashed on something Naser had said during the early days of the revolution: "Why would the West—or even the East, for that matter—want Iran to progress when they can take advantage of our oil while having stupid people rule the country?" If his observation were true, it seemed that the West was being incredibly shortsighted.

Kazem maintained that the Europeans raised no objection to Iranian agents' murdering the opposition—members of the Mujahedin as well as former officers and monarchists—inside their countries. This would result in the Guards' killing hundreds in Europe and around the globe, with bombs planted in their cars, by attacking them in their homes, by beheading them, or by shooting them execution-style. Some they abducted, tortured, and killed, dumping their bodies in remote areas. Among the many they assassinated was General Gholam Oveissi, the former commander of the shah's army, along with his brother, on the streets of Paris. But there would be many, many more. The most notable figure, assassinated some years later, was the last prime minister under the shah, Shahpour Bakhtiar. He'd escaped the country after the revolution and stayed active in Paris promoting opposition to the mullahs. The Guards finally caught up to him, stabbing him thirteen times in the neck and shoulder, and cutting his throat with a kitchen knife.

While we were talking, two Guards entered the room. Kazem got up excitedly and welcomed them. They shook hands and then hugged.

"Reza, these brothers are from the Central Command," Kazem

said as he introduced them to me. He then went on to brag about how my contributions helped set up the computer infrastructure that facilitated the Guards' activities throughout the country. At first I was worried that this might be another trick, but when they continued with their unfiltered conversation, I was relieved and felt they regarded me as one of them.

One of the Guards mentioned that Iraq was receiving military aid from the West, especially France. This included new fighter jets to target Iranian naval ships and oil tankers in the Persian Gulf. The Iraqis had also purchased jets that could drop bombs from high altitude, therefore remaining immune to antiaircraft guns. What he said next stunned me:

"Baradar Kazem, our intelligence has learned through arms dealers in the black market that Saddam is desperately looking for the technology to build an atomic bomb. We have verified this with our sources in Iraq."

"An atomic bomb in the hands of a madman," Kazem said, shaking his head.

"We won't let it go unanswered," the Guard continued. "We already have approval from the Supreme Leader, Imam Khomeini, to strengthen our capabilities with such technology. Don't worry, *Baradar,* Islam will conquer the evil forces. Saddam and his boss, *Amrika,* will be defeated, *inshallah.*"

Later that night, I wrote Carol again. This was the third letter in as many days, but with significant news I felt could not wait.

[Letter #—]
[Date:———]

Dear Carol,

1—*Rasool has been sent to London from MOIS as an agent to infiltrate the opposition groups.*

2—*His duties are to identify group leaders, sympathizers, and individuals connected to them who travel in and out of Iran. This information is used by MOIS to arrest members and*

*sympathizers upon their arrival in Iran and to assassinate
opposition leaders abroad.*

*3—Kazem told me that Rahim has also traveled to London to
meet with Guards' agents. Rahim is becoming increasingly
involved with the activities abroad.*

*4—Kazem told me that there is an unwritten pact with the
European governments, especially France, England, and
Germany, that allows Guards' agents to assassinate opposition
members without interference of those governments' security
services.*

*5—While in Kazem's office, two Guards from Central
Command showed up with news that Saddam is looking for
nuclear technology and desperately wants nuclear bombs.
This has been confirmed by Guards' agents in Iraq and
Guards' contacts with arms dealers in the black market.
Consequently, the Guards have also started their pursuit of
the nuclear bomb with the approval of Imam Khomeini.*

God Bless,
Wally

My preoccupation with the flurry of vital information I'd been
receiving distracted me from Kazem's upcoming wedding. As the
day approached, I realized that I'd have to prepare my grandfather
for the celebration, as he was quite old now and reluctant to go out.
He was slightly stooped and needed a cane to walk. His snow-white
hair and wrinkles testified to a lifetime of changes and experiences,
from the invasion of Iran by the Allies in World War II, to the shahs'
monarchies, to the mullahs he'd never respected now ruling his
country.

As I did regularly, I flashed back on the long-ago summertime
gatherings when Agha Joon and Davood would discuss their differences about the shah, democracy in Iran, and their favorite subject,
the influence of Arabs and Islam in our society. As a kid, I didn't
appreciate the extent of this influence and how it was changing the

vision of our nation. This great country—once ruled by Cyrus the Great and known for its rich culture and literature—was regressing now because of religion.

Although a Muslim, like many other Iranians, Agha Joon did not feel obligated to practice Islam the way my grandmother had. He didn't go to the mosque or pray five times daily, and he didn't think he was going to go to hell because of this. But he did live by the highest tenets of our religion: he always helped the poor, he never lied, he never stole anything—and, above all, he was not a betrayer. Agha Joon believed strongly in the separation of religion and politics. He would say, "Religion is in the heart. It cannot be forced upon the people. It is a private relationship between a man and his creator. You find the love within God, and with that love, you cherish life."

At first Agha Joon told me that he wasn't going to go to Kazem's wedding. He was uncomfortable being where henchmen of the Islamic government would be gathered. Unlike my mother, Agha Joon had never expressed his disappointment in my joining the Guards. He always gave me a warm smile, saying, "*Pesaram,* hopefully you'll find a better place to work." But he did not hesitate to show his resentment against the Islamic regime and the crimes it committed. When I told him that it would mean a lot to Kazem, and that Kazem's father had sent a special invitation for him, Agha Joon finally agreed to accompany me.

The ceremony was at the bride's house. When we arrived, a brand-new black Mercedes pulled up in front of us. At this point in the revolution, the regime had stopped the import of foreign cars for ordinary citizens. Only the authorities and high-ranking clergy were able to special-order the latest models and drive them. It did not surprise me when a chubby mullah exited the car. He was wearing a long black chenille robe and holding on to his white turban. He draped his prayer beads, shining on a gold string, in his hand. Two Guards escorted him out of the car, one opening the door and the other holding his hand to guide him out.

A small crowd, perhaps the bride's family, immediately surrounded the mullah. Agha Joon nudged me, winked, and with a wide grin said, "Look at this son of a dog. He steals people's money, drives a Mercedes, and I'll bet he has an honorary Ph.D. or a law degree, too."

"Agha Joon, please, hush." I was afraid someone who knew me would overhear him.

Kazem's father hustled toward the mullah. "*Bah bah,* Hojatoleslam Yazdi, you honor us today by your coming."

I looked at Agha Joon, who was now reaching into his pocket for his glasses. He mumbled *"Hojatoleslam!"* derisively spitting the honorific title representing authority in Islam. In those days, any mullah who had moved up in rank by any means received it.

Agha Joon finally found his glasses, stared out, and then turned to me in disbelief. "Reza *jon,* this is our own Mullah Aziz!"

Shocked, I looked closer and realized that he was right. It was Mullah Aziz—upgraded from a donkey to a Mercedes and with his title changed from Mullah to Hojatoleslam. I just shook my head.

Kazem came out to welcome the guests. He greeted us and took us over to Mullah Aziz.

"*Bah bah,* Agha Joon," the mullah said with great enthusiasm. "It is so nice to see you again."

"*Salam,* Mullah Aziz," Agha Joon said, not caring that calling this man "Mullah" rather than "Hojatoleslam" and using his first name was a sign of disrespect.

Mullah Aziz reddened at being addressed that way in front of his escorts. But I jumped in, trying to avoid any further embarrassment that would jeopardize my position. I paid my respects and introduced myself, certain the mullah would not recognize me.

"*Bah,* Reza *jon!*" Mullah Aziz said as he wrapped his arms around me. "Kazem has told me all about you, a true *pasdar,* a great Muslim."

I looked at Agha Joon to see his reaction. He was shaking his head, not happy with this reunion. I grabbed my grandfather's arm and we all headed inside the house, where the ceremony was to take place. But inside felt more like a funeral than a wedding. One room was full of men sitting on the ground with a couple of chairs in the corner, one especially cushioned for Mullah Aziz. The women and the bride were in a separate room, where they could not be seen or heard. Usually at a wedding, music played and people danced, but not here, not when religious radicals were the hosts. Only the smile on Kazem's face indicated that this was a happy event.

I could see that all of this displeased Agha Joon. All his life, he had been the center of attention, spoken his mind freely, and enjoyed the respect of everyone who knew him. Now he was being made to sit on the ground next to people who had stolen the dignity of his beloved country and he had to bow to a mullah who once performed a sermon at his house for a dollar or two.

"You know, Reza *jon*," Agha Joon said on the way home, "there are a lot of these *besharaf* mullahs out there. But do you know what this perverted bastard did while you were in the States going to college? He sent a messenger to your uncle's house to announce that he wanted to go *khastegari* for Haleh, your cousin. He had no shame. Haleh was half his age and this *binamoos* didn't know that my son would never have accepted him even as his daughter's butler." He shook his head. "I am glad it was before the revolution, otherwise God knows what he would have done to get them to accept. And thank God Haleh got married shortly after and left for Sweden with her husband."

He was right. During the wedding celebration, Kazem told me that Mullah Aziz's new position was as a judge in the Revolutionary Courts in charge of the trials of opposition groups. If he were interested in Haleh and my uncle refused, he could have accused my uncle of sedition, had him sent to prison, or even had him killed.

That night at home, I once again thought of Naser. I took his picture out, saw his bright smile shining back at me, and imagined that same smile on his wedding day, if he had lived. Earlier in the day, Kazem had described his wedding as the purest form of bliss.

The revolution had stolen that bliss from Naser and his siblings.

Early the next morning, I received a message from Carol:

Dear Wally,
  It's great to hear from you.
  We are so happy you are well and back on the job.
  We received all three letters.
  The information provided was extremely important and
valuable.
  Please keep us posted on any further information regarding
nukes.
  We have located both Rasool and Rahim.
Stay safe,
Carol

By the spring of 1985, the war was becoming more intense. Imam Khomeini and the ruling clerics were pushing for the removal of Saddam, conquering Iraq, and unifying Muslims in a bigger, holier war against Israel. Guards commanders said that Khomeini would go to his prayer room alone to talk to God for his approval before any offensive. Following one such talk with God in March of that year, he issued an order for a massive movement toward the city of Basra in Iraq dubbed Operation Badr, sending tens of thousands of soldiers to the front. The operation was successful, initially capturing part of the Basra-Baghdad highway, but it soon turned horrific when the Iraqi army again resorted to the use of chemical weapons. Saddam went even further by bombarding civilian targets in Iran.

Because of this, I told Somaya that even though most of the attacks came at night, she needed to take extra precautions when I was not there. She should keep the radio on at all times, and if the siren signaling an imminent aerial attack went off, she should take shelter in our cellar. She didn't like that idea, but for Omid's sake, she agreed it would be safer.

Taking such shelter became routine for us. First the siren, then antiaircraft guns, and then explosions, sometimes so close they would jolt our building. Omid, now three, would cry, Somaya would shake, and I would wrap my arms around them trying to protect them. Then there would be a quiet moment before another siren announced an all clear and we could leave the shelter. Calls to close family members and friends followed to make sure everyone was still alive. We somehow managed to continue to conduct our lives under these conditions, as did everyone who survived the raids.

That summer, a neighbor down the block invited Omid to a birthday party. I didn't want to let Omid out of our sight, especially because the party was in the evening. Even with the Iraqi air raids, Iranians maintained their custom of having parties, even birthday celebrations for the young ones at dinnertime. Although I knew Somaya would be by his side, still I was hesitant. That day, though, Omid woke up with a fever and Somaya decided not to take him. We had a quiet day, and Somaya got Omid ready for bed early, since he still wasn't feeling well. As she did, the siren went off. Before we had a chance to run to the cellar, a roaring explosion filled the air and the house shook violently. I grabbed Omid and pulled Somaya to a corner of the room away from the windows, covering them with my body. They were both screaming. For what seemed like an endless stretch, all I could feel under my body was the frantic beating of two innocent hearts desperate for survival. I prayed to God to let this pass with no harm. The growl of each antiaircraft missile shook Somaya's back and made Omid squeal. Windows and other glass shattered, and I kept praying.

I don't know how long we were in that position before the guns finally stopped firing. I left my family, still hysterical, in the corner. I stepped on picture frames that had fallen off the walls, broken vases, and other objects on my way to the far side of room, where I kept the emergency flashlights on the nightstand. I then led them to the cellar.

As we crumpled into one another's arms, the sky seemed quiet. But the sound of ambulances, police cars, and fire trucks filled our neighborhood. It was apparent that the explosion hit somewhere close to our house. When Somaya and Omid finally calmed down, I stepped outside to see what had happened.

Debris cluttered the neighborhood. Clouds of smoke and dust filled the air and I had to cover my mouth against this as I walked down the block. There, I saw that the top of a four-story building was missing, with bricks and concrete blocks in a pile on the ground.

Several neighbors were outside helping the police, the firemen, and the Guards pull bodies from the rubble. I saw several small bodies wrapped in cloth lying on the ground. The bodies seemed about Omid's size. Then it dawned on me: *Oh my God! This is where Omid would have been.* These were the kids at the birthday party.

I started digging furiously, helping pull out more bodies. Mostly small kids. Some still in their mothers' arms. Most dead. The kids and guests at that party on the fourth floor were all dead. Only a few from the lower stories of the building survived, suffering various injuries and burns.

A Guard was going around to the women's dead bodies and covering their hair as we pulled them to the side. They wouldn't allow even the injured and dead to be seen without cover.

The bombing and deaths of our neighbors terrified Somaya and me. After this event, Somaya would not leave Omid's side. She would hold him in her arms, and when he was asleep, she would sit next to his bed and cry. In the ensuing days, I pleaded for her to consider leaving, this time making sure not to offend her as I had when I'd proposed the same during her pregnancy.

"Just until this war is over," I pleaded. "And I promise to come and visit as much as I can. Do it for Omid. He is constantly crying and screaming through this madness."

Somaya wiped her tears, and bent and kissed Omid's hand as he slept in his crib. "I love him so much and I feel so responsible for him," she said, bursting into tears. "What if we were at that party and something had happened to him? What would I have done without him?"

I hugged her shivering shoulders, not mentioning that if they had

234 | REZA KAHLILI

been at the party I would have lost her as well. "I know. And we should thank God that Omid had a fever. That's why I am asking you to go to your parents. I know how much he means to you and you know how much you both mean to me. Your safety and happiness are all I am pleading for."

She pressed her body into mine. "Let's all go there and forget about this place. Reza, what are you doing here? What is so important about your job? I have wanted to go to London for a long time. The moment the war started, I did not feel safe. But I didn't want to leave you behind. I stayed for you. Now you should come with us—for me."

I kissed her head and wished that I could explain everything to her. "I will ask Kazem for permission to accompany you."

"But you will come back here after you take us." She let go of me and covered her face with her palms. "I have to do this for Omid now. But I don't know what to do with you, Reza. I am just so exhausted. If that's what you want, I cannot force you to love your family and to be with them." She walked to our bedroom and opened the closet. "I will start packing. You take care of the rest."

Kazem knew about the bombing in my neighborhood and about how close it had come to my home, so he understood when I told him that I wanted Somaya and Omid to go to England to live with her parents for a while. Fortunately, the restrictions limiting travel had been lifted and the airports were open to all who wished to travel outside. I told Kazem that I wanted to make sure my wife and son got there safely and asked if he could help arrange time off for me so I could escort them. Once again, he was instrumental in arranging this, but he told me that the following day Mohsen Rezaei, the chief commander of the Guards, would be making an important announcement. He asked me to accompany him.

We headed to the Guards' base southeast of Tehran, where Rezaei was holding the meeting. A flood of cars and bikes streamed down the street and poured into the base, filling the air with dust. Hundreds of Guards gathered in the compound, most being members of the Intelligence Unit. There was a host of regional commanders also in attendance.

The number of intelligence men in the crowd made me anxious. Some of them were longtime friends, but I couldn't look at them the same way I did before I became involved in the CIA. Every glance from one of them seemed to carry suspicion. I was churning on the inside, but I had no choice but to act normal.

I stayed close to Kazem while he shook hands with others. During this process, I met a Guard named Taghi. "You must be Baradar Reza," he said to me. "It's nice to see you here. Our great martyr Javad told me a lot of good things about you."

Mention of Javad's name caused my nerves to spike. This Guard had a higher ranking than Javad. If Javad spoke to Taghi about me, taking his concerns up the ladder, there was a good chance that the danger Javad caused me did not die with him.

"It's nice meeting you, Baradar Taghi," I said as I shook his hand. "We all miss Javad. He is indeed a great martyr. May God bless his soul."

Taghi said nothing else to me, leaving me to wonder what he knew and what he was thinking. I followed Kazem and the others into the meeting hall. Folding chairs were arranged in rows; pictures of Imam Khomeini decorated the walls. Kazem and I took our seats close to the front row.

Moments later, Mohsen Rezaei and his entourage entered the room and marched toward the podium. Everyone in the room arose and started shouting, *"Allaho Akbar, Khomeini Rahbar."* Rezaei eventually raised his hands and brought the gathering to order.

I focused on the speech, knowing that Carol and her team would want as much detail as possible and that I would have to rely on my memory to repeat it all. Rezaei began by commending the Guards for their bravery on the war fronts and reminding us of the importance of our duty to protect the Islamic Republic of Iran against our enemies. He emphasized that the U.S. and Israel were, at all times, planning to hurt Iran and suppress the Islamic movement.

Our vigilance was essential in this regard. The irony that I was sitting only a few feet from him, committing every one of his words to memory, was not lost on me.

Then Rezaei moved on to matters of business and made his most important announcement: with Imam Khomeini's personal authorization, the Revolutionary Guards' air, ground, and naval units were to be greatly expanded with sophisticated weapons. The plan was to turn the Guards' forces into a conventional army but with a martyrdom mentality. He talked about the formation of thousands of smaller units to provide air, ground, and naval support, and emphasized that while we might never match the air and naval power of countries such as America, these new ancillary units, with the proper weaponry, could overwhelm any enemy. He promised missiles, fighter jets, submarines, and the expansion of weapons production inside the country with the goal of reaching self-sufficiency. This was enormous news, something I could only begin to appreciate on that day. As it turned out, this moment was when the Guards truly began to seize control of Iran, exerting enormous power both inside and outside of the country.

"We will build a force that will demolish the enemies of Islam, continue the path of our great Prophet Mohammad, and raise the flag of Islam in all corners of the world," Rezaei said enthusiastically.

The chants of *"Allaho Akbar"* and *"Khomeini Rahbar"* filled the room again as the excited crowd roared its approval.

The plan to take Somaya and Omid to England now served another purpose. I needed to see Carol, to relay the important information that I had learned and discuss my fear that Taghi would be keeping an eye on my activities. I purchased our tickets to travel to London. Not wanting to take any unnecessary risks before taking my family out of the country, I did not write to Carol informing her about my travel plans.

But I knew that I would see her as soon as we got to England.

22

FAR FROM HOME

LONDON WAS FOGGY and hazy, displaying its typical sad mood. But there was no sadness about Somaya and Omid cuddling in the arms of Moheb Khan and Zari Khanoom on the way from Heathrow Airport to their house. I could see how relieved Somaya's parents were to have their daughter and grandson out of the country. They had called nearly every night during the war to make sure we were safe. As the taxi driver pulled up in front of their apartment, I felt a burden lift from my shoulders. Somaya and Omid would sleep safely and soundly here every night. I glanced up at the sky and smiled, knowing that there were no sounds of terror waiting to erupt behind those dark clouds.

At the dinner table that night, everybody enjoyed the peace and quiet. We shared love and laughter, which reminded me of something that was all too easy to forget in postrevolutionary Iran: that it was our right to lead a free and normal life. *This is an opportunity*, I thought. *I can stay here with my loved ones and move on, like the thousands before me who have left the country to seek peace and tranquility for their families. This is your chance, Reza!* But I was still not certain. I still felt I had a mission to accomplish.

"Reza *jon*," Somaya's mom said, interrupting my conflicted train of thought. "We are so happy that you finally decided to leave Iran."

"Yes," Moheb Khan added. "We prayed every night that all of you would leave. That country is no longer safe. I am so glad you are here in one piece. My house is small, but you should know that you are my children and we would love to have you stay with us."

"But, Dad . . ." Somaya interrupted.

"Somaya *jon,* we have enough room for all of you," her mother said, misinterpreting her daughter's interjection. "The house is not *that* small! And don't say no, Reza *jon.* At least stay with us for the first year and then find a place. I cannot get enough of you and especially my Omid *jon."* She squeezed another kiss onto Omid's cheek.

"But, Mom, Dad . . . Reza is not staying. He is going back."

"Chi?" Zari Khanoom looked at me in disbelief. "Why would you want to go back? It is not safe, Reza."

"Mom, we are still talking about this. He is going back in a couple of weeks, but he is considering coming back and leaving the Guards for good." She gave me an affirmative gesture that left me wordless.

Early the next morning, I put on my sneakers and told Somaya I was going for a walk. From the bed, she smiled and told me that we'd be so much happier if I'd stay with them and never go back to Iran. I winked at her and told her that I would be back from my walk soon. After jogging a few blocks, I looked around to make sure I did not see anything suspicious. Then I hopped into a phone kiosk and dialed the number for the station.

"Hello, this is Wally. I need to talk to Carol."

"Wally?" the man at the other end asked in shock.

"Yes, Wally. I am in London."

The man said something to someone, and I heard a few clicks before Carol's surprised voice came on.

"Wally? Is everything okay? Where are you?"

"I am here in London with my family and everything is fine. I just wanted to know if we could meet."

Carol was surprised that I had not informed her of my travel plans. I assured her that I wasn't here to escape and that I didn't think I was in trouble, but that I had brought my family to England to protect them from the war. She asked me to call her back the next day at the same time so she could arrange our meeting. I knew she had to check with the agency and discuss the situation with them as a precaution.

Somaya just nodded when I told her that I had to take care of some business for Kazem the day I was to meet with Carol at the Dorchester Hotel in Hyde Park. Once again, as I did most of my spy life, I carefully minimized my chances of being followed. I walked a few blocks, caught a cab for a couple of miles, hung around in a shopping mall, hopped on a bus, and then walked to the hotel.

It was nice to see Carol again. After all, she was the only person in the world I could talk to freely about my true feelings. She greeted me with a warm smile when I entered the room, but I could see the confusion in her eyes as she directed me to two big lounge chairs.

"I should have told you in my letter that I was coming to London. Since I was bringing my family here, though, I didn't want to do anything that would jeopardize their chances of leaving the country."

She was shocked when I told her about the bombing and how I helped to recover bodies from the fateful birthday party, explaining why I felt such urgency to get Somaya and Omid to London and out of the terror.

"Somaya has pleaded with me to stay here with them and not go back."

Carol, who had been reaching in her briefcase to get her notebook and a pen, stopped and looked up. She cleared her throat to say something, but instead she put her hand against her lips and paused for a moment. Then she went on.

"I understand, and I am sure that the agency thinks the same way as I do, Wally. As I said before, your safety and the safety of your loved ones is our priority. If you wish to stop now, we fully support you."

I don't know why it was that every time any of my contacts told me that he or she would support me should I decide to leave the agency, I felt how much they needed me. Were they playing a game with me because they knew I would react this way? Or was I simply realizing how much was still unfinished?

"You know, Carol, to be honest with you, I have thought about it many times. Given what happened at Evin and the possibility that I could have been killed at the front, I probably should consider leaving. And now that I am here in one piece with my family, knowing you would support me, it'd be the best time."

"But?" Carol asked. "There is a *but,* I presume."

I paused for a long moment before speaking again. "Carol, I love my family very much and I am glad they are safe here. But I cannot stop now. If you were in Iran, you would understand why people are sick and tired of being ruled by these Islamic radicals. Iranians need help. They need someone to speak for them, and I feel that I am that voice. Sometimes I think I am the only one they have."

Carol moved in her chair and uncrossed her legs as she listened to what I had to say.

"Do you mind if I smoke?" I asked.

"No, Wally, please go ahead."

I lit up a cigarette, took a long puff, and blew out the smoke. "So many injustices happen every day. Just last week, a teenager was talking on a public phone when the Komiteh forces approached her. At first they objected to her outfit. Then they realized she was talking to her boyfriend on the phone. They shot her right there.

"I was going to work one day during the month of Ramadan when I saw an old man being arrested for eating in public and not respecting the mandatory fasting. He must have been eighty years old, and Islamic thugs the age of his grandsons beat him mercilessly."

Carol listened quietly, her eyes downcast.

"A neighbor of my mother's, a Jewish man who converted to Islam out of fear, had his passport confiscated after returning home from a business trip. A few days later, they arrested him and took him to Evin Prison. He was beaten every night and taken in front of an execution squad, being told each time he was going to be shot. While blindfolded, he heard the sound of the gunshots and expected to die, but they didn't shoot him. That was how they tortured him. Then they would ask him to put others who had been shot in body bags. They wanted him to confess to spying for Israel. He never did, and he was released five months later after paying millions of rials in bail money."

"What do people do?" Carol asked, the incredulity and frustration evident in her voice. "How do they put up with all this?"

"People have not lost hope yet. In spite of all the arrests and executions, students, teachers, and workers still demonstrate for their rights. Women still do not adhere completely to the Islamic *hejab* even though they get arrested and whipped for that. But they need help." I sighed. "The West needs to do something."

I put out my cigarette in the ashtray. Carol sank farther into her seat. I could see that my stories touched her. She had tears in her eyes. Carol had lived in Iran and she loved the people and the country, so I knew she had more than professional interest in what I was saying.

"Wally, I hope the day will come when freedom returns to the Iranians. But it's most important to pressure the mullahs into accepting peace with Iraq and stopping this lunacy that is taking so many lives."

I knew that she didn't have the power to change anything herself, but what she said was enough to make me believe that America intended to make an effort. Now we had to get back to work. Carol asked me about the Evin incident and the death of Javad. She wanted to make sure that my safety was not at risk and that my position had not been compromised.

"I was convinced that Javad's death ended the suspicion about me. I even felt that Abbass, the guard at the prison, did not suspect anything. He just met with me because Javad asked him to do so. But there was this guy, Taghi, who also works out of MOIS and was present at Rezaei's meeting. Taghi implied that Javad had told him about me. That scared me, knowing that Javad might have left his unfinished business in the hands of somebody else."

Carol's brows knit. "What do you suspect he knows about you?"

"It's possible that Javad told him something that might

incriminate me. I don't know, I might be too sensitive about this issue at this point, seeing monsters around every corner. All I know is that I have to take extra precautions. I have no idea what was going on in Javad's mind, but I learned from other Guards that Javad was into everybody's business and that he did things on his own."

"Perhaps that's the case," Carol said evenly. "However, don't you think that if there were any suspicion about you Kazem would have known, and consequently not have divulged secretive information or taken you to important meetings?"

That was something I hadn't considered, and it made sense. "You know, Carol, sometimes I don't know what to think and how to feel. This double life is far more complicated than I ever imagined. But I am living it and praying to God that what I'm doing will help free my country."

I didn't want to continue down this path with her. We had too much business to do and this conversation wasn't helping with that. I made an abrupt switch in topic.

"The Guards have obtained authorization from Khomeini to formally turn their forces into a conventional army. They are now going to expand their ground forces and have a formal navy and air force. Rezaei promised surface-to-surface missiles with longer range and larger impact, fighter jets for the air force, submarines for the navy, and the expansion of weapons production in the country."

I also clarified that the Guards' power base and influence were going to expand greatly both inside and outside of Iran. The Guards' elite forces had infiltrated countries in the Persian Gulf, Asia, Africa, Europe, and even Latin America, setting up safe houses, recruiting volunteers, and training martyrs. I explained that the Guards had now mastered the production of chemical weapons, and were pursuing a nuclear bomb to counteract Saddam and to prepare for future aggression. I told her of Rezaei's plan to form thousands of small, lethal units to overwhelm the defense of any army, including America's.

"Carol, it's very important to understand this mentality of martyrdom and radical conviction. They truly believe that one day Islam will conquer the world. If we allow the Guards to go unchecked, the consequences could be devastating for the region—and the world."

Carol continued to write furiously. Then she stopped and looked up at me. "Wally, you should know that we consider you one of our best. The information you've provided has been very helpful in our understanding the situation in Iran and giving us insight as to the best way of dealing with it. I want you to be very careful, though. Don't put yourself in harm's way trying to learn about what the Guards are doing. Keep it limited to being eyes and ears. It's working great so far."

She reached for her purse, fished out an envelope, and handed it to me. "This is a bonus for your hard work."

I looked at her with a smile and said, "I should come to see you more often!"

We both shared a laugh. Since the bank they had originally set for my salary deposits was in London and I wanted to leave some of the money with Somaya, I accepted the cash with no hesitation. I peeked inside the envelope and guesstimated about five thousand dollars. I suppose I was learning that after all, I was an employee of the CIA no matter how I looked at it.

We spoke a while longer and then got up to leave. Carol hugged me warmly before we departed and reminded me again that I could stop doing this work anytime if I felt it was too dangerous for me to continue.

"Just promise me that you will take care of my family should anything happen to me," I said before leaving.

During the rest of my stay in London, I spent as much time as I could with Somaya and Omid. It was our best two weeks since Wally had come into our lives. Omid, who was now uttering full sentences, had learned how to take my breath away. The night before my flight, Somaya's parents left us alone at home. They said they had to be somewhere, but I suspected that they wanted to give us some space. The three of us sat on the floor in the living room, where Omid had his coloring books and crayons spread all over. While he drew, I held Somaya's hand.

"I will come back and visit," I promised her.

She shook her head in disappointment. Right up to that moment, I think she believed that I would decide to leave the Guards and stay with her.

Omid held a piece of paper aloft to show us the crooked red heart he'd drawn. *"Baba kheily asheghetam,"* he said. "I love you very much, Daddy." The innocence and purity of his words ripped at my soul. Then he dropped the paper and wrapped his little arms around my neck, kissing my cheeks.

I swallowed a lump in my throat and kissed him back. *"Manam kheili asheghetam."*

I looked at Somaya after I said this and said, "Oh, honey, I love *you,* too."

She got up and laughed. "You think everything is a joke."

I pulled her arm and had her sit next to us. "As soon as I have an opportunity, I will wrap things up. I'll come back here and we'll start a new life."

The next evening, I left. I had to say good-bye to my family on another foggy, hazy London night.

This time, the sad mood of England's never-starry sky was a perfect representation of my emotions.

2 3

GOD'S HOUSE

THE SCOWL ON the cabdriver's face disappeared when I passed a handful of 1,000-rial bills (about fifteen dollars total) to him after asking that he not pick up any other passengers. Usually, drivers in Tehran make several stops to get as many as five people in one cab. Arriving in the early morning following a six-hour red-eye from London, I was exhausted and I needed to catch a couple of hours of sleep before going to the office.

The driver counted the money carefully, turned toward me with a toothy smile, and said he knew a shortcut we could take to avoid traffic. I nodded agreement as I settled in my seat. Seeing Tehran's familiar landmarks out the cab's window reminded me that my wife and son were no longer with me. I felt both relieved and melancholy. I already missed them, but I was glad they were no longer in harm's way and that I would be free to pursue my commitment to being Wally without worrying about the consequences for them.

As though to reinforce that I'd made the right decision, we passed construction cranes with the corpses of three recently executed young men dangling like bait at the end of a fishing pole. A crowd stared blankly at the bodies silhouetted against the distant hills. People had become numb to the executions. At least most people had. Beneath one of the dead men, a black-veiled woman, likely the mother of one of them, wailed her heart out.

That afternoon, after my nap, I headed to work and went straight to Kazem's office with the souvenirs I bought in London for him and his new bride. Sitting behind Kazem's desk was a Guard I knew but whose name I could not remember.

"*Salam*, Baradar Reza, come in," he said when he saw me. "Are you here to see Kazem?"

"*Salam, Baradar,*" I replied, telegraphing some confusion. "Yes, I am looking for Kazem. Is he coming back?"

"Oh, no. Baradar Kazem has moved to the commander's office. He has replaced Baradar Rahim." He smirked. "I guess you were gone too long!"

I felt stupid not knowing what had happened in the two weeks I had been away. "Then where did Baradar Rahim go?"

"Baradar Rahim has moved to another base," he said as he pulled out a drawer and grabbed some papers, pretending to be busy.

I thanked him and rushed back to my building, where Kazem's new office was also located. I went to his office and Kazem jumped out of his chair as soon as I entered the room, happy to see me. He'd never greeted me at the office this way before. Maybe being in the commander's seat boosted his spirits.

"What did you do to Rahim?" I said brightly. "I'm only gone for a couple of weeks and you organized a coup and took over the base without me?"

Kazem burst into laughter and gave me a huge hug.

"After he came back from England, Rahim moved on to the MOIS. He is now involved with the organization and movements of our agents in Europe. Like it or not, I am your new commander."

"I guess I'll be okay with that," I said with a smile. "Oh, before I forget, these are for you and your wife—a small souvenir from Somaya and me."

I handed him a bag. Somaya had helped me pick up a sweater for Zohreh and a rain jacket for Kazem. Kazem thanked me for the presents and extended an invitation to stay at his house should I ever get especially lonely while my wife was away. It was a simple exchange between friends—the kind of thing that came naturally to people who'd known each other and had been as close to each other for as long as the two of us had been. I realized, though, that we would never be having this exchange if Kazem knew about Wally. This led me to wonder how, knowing me for as long as he did, he *didn't* know about Wally. How could he possibly have missed all my acts of deception?

The reality was that Kazem was not the shrewd, cunning person that so many Guards and clerics were. He was just a closed-minded one. My relationship with him was easily the most complicated in my life. I absolutely rejected everything he believed in, yet at the same time, I felt a deep attachment to him for everything we'd shared over the years. When I brought him presents, I was doing so from a source of genuine affection. At the same time, though, I never lost sight of how I could use my access to him to provide Carol with vital information, something that certainly fell outside of the scope of genuine friendship.

Shortly after my return to Tehran, I heard about William Buckley, the CIA operative Carol had asked me about who'd been taken hostage a year and a half ago in 1984. The evening news mentioned that the Islamic Jihad had announced the execution of Buckley in Beirut. Islamic Jihad was a front name for the Revolutionary Guards stationed in Lebanon, another example of their expanding power. They chose to create this front to generate confusion among American and Israeli intelligence. By doing so, they ensured that the enemy couldn't trace their terrorist acts back to Iran, instead believing that this was a homegrown movement in Lebanon. I knew the news of Buckley's execution had already reached Carol and that there was no point in reporting it to her.

By this time, Ali Khamenei had gained a second term as president in an election that saw stunningly few Iranians participate because they believed that the democratic process was a sham. They had every reason to feel this way, as the Guardian Council decided which candidates could run for office and the Council consisted of six members chosen directly by the Supreme Leader, Imam Khomeini, and six more approved by him after their nomination by the chief justice, who was also handpicked by the Supreme Leader, and their election by the parliament. This meant that no one could attain power if they posed even the slightest risk to the status quo.

The regime anticipated that voting would be light and worked hard to maintain the illusion for the West that the people still backed the mullahs. They ordered all Guards and Basijis to show up to vote dressed as ordinary citizens and they bused people who had been relocated from cities affected by the war to polling stations, offering them food and shelter—and threatening to withhold such necessities from anyone who didn't go along with their plan.

(Khamenei's prime minister at the time was Mir Hossein Mousavi, the man whose defeat in the 2009 presidential elections led to such violent outrage on the streets of Iran. The remaining moderates left in the parliament—a holdover from the pre-Khamenei days—still had enough votes to force Mousavi on Khamenei when he became president in 1981, foreshadowing the clashes between this group and the radical right that would explode on the world stage nearly three decades later. Mousavi lost his position in 1989, when constitutional changes eliminated the role of prime minister.)

Meanwhile, in Tehran and other major cities, the Iraqi jets continued dropping bombs on the rooftops of Iranian homes nightly. At the same time, Guards and young Basijis continued their battle against the Iraqis at the front. Saddam's weapons—including his vicious chemical ones—killed or severely injured many thousands of these brave men. The Mujahedin were also attacking our forces from their bases in Iraq after they moved their headquarters from France. This move brought more resentment and hatred toward the Mujahedin, not only from the Guards and Iran's military fighters but also from most Iranians who saw their alignment with Saddam as a despicable act. And as all of this went on, Islamic rules in Iran became even more stringent. I felt under siege at every turn, and I know that many of my fellow citizens felt the same way.

I had told Somaya that I would visit them for our New Year in the spring of 1986, but with the ever-tightening grip of the regime, I realized that it wasn't safe to do so and that I had to disappoint her. Taking another trip to England at this point would have drawn more attention to me than I was comfortable with. As much as I missed my wife and son, and as much as I wanted to be an active part of their lives, I had to stay away from them until I knew I could be with them permanently.

My house felt empty and I was terribly lonely, though I was trying my best to adjust. Somaya and I spoke a couple of times a week, but it was hardly a substitute for a life with my family. A few months after our New Year, Kazem invited me to his house for dinner and I was delighted to have the company. His wife had gone to Mecca in Saudi Arabia for the umrah, a lesser version of the hajj, where Muslims submit themselves to Allah.

Kazem and I rarely socialized away from work now that we were both married, and I had not been to the home he shared with his wife. He and Zohreh had decorated it simply, with a few old Persian rugs on the floor, just a few pieces of furniture, and a couple of pictures of Imam Khomeini on the walls in the living room. They had short-napped, coarse carpet cushions on the floor and a few low tables here and there. While Kazem had moved up in the world, unlike so many who ruled the country, he hadn't adopted the practice of decorating his home with goods stolen from those imprisoned or killed. This was yet another reminder that Kazem was a simple, righteous man. Sadly, he'd chosen the wrong ideology.

"When are you planning to go to Mecca and become a hajji?" I asked as we walked through the house.

"Maybe I will be lucky enough to have my name called soon," he answered. "I would be honored to do my hajj."

I was tempted to say something ironic—I tended to do this when faced with a concept I couldn't comprehend—but I knew this was neither the time nor the place to do so. *"Inshallah,* you'll be called soon" was all I said.

Kazem guided me to the kitchen, where the dinner he had prepared sat on a small table, waiting for us. He handed me a plate with rice and a ground beef kebab skewer. "It is nothing like your grandpa's kebab, but I tried. *Yadesh bekheir,*" he said with his eyes fixed on the distance. It surprised me to hear him refer to our childhood days as "good old times." *It was indeed,* I thought. I hadn't spoken with him much about the past, believing that it would hurt too much to talk to him of the spirited times he, Naser, and I had shared. Now that he'd mentioned it, though, I found that I welcomed even a brief reminiscence.

But before I could take this further, Kazem said, "Did you know your friends were here recently?"

Confused by what he meant, I swallowed a big chunk of kebab, which stuck in my throat.

"Do you want extra butter on your rice?"

I gulped some water. "No more butter, thanks." I cleared my throat. "What friends?"

He put two whole grilled tomatoes on my plate and said, "The Americans. They were here in Tehran."

I didn't really understand what he was saying, but still puzzled, I pretended not to be curious. "This stuff is good, Kazem. I haven't had a good hot meal since Somaya left."

"I'm glad you like it." He paused to take a bite and then said, "Reagan sent his men here to negotiate."

I crushed the tomatoes with my spoon over the rice. "He did? What were they negotiating? And why would we ever want to negotiate with them?"

"They met with Haj Agha Rafsanjani and his associates at Hotel Esteghlal. Listen to this: they brought a Bible, a cake, and a gun with them." He shook his head. "As a sign *of friendship.*" He put his spoon down, cut a piece of lavash, and pinched his kebab with it to eat it. "The dumb cowboys think we will help release their hostages in Lebanon and try to improve our relationship with them. They are giving us arms—lots of arms—and they think in return we will agree to be their puppets." He took another piece of bread and dipped it in the bowl of yogurt. "But Haj Agha Rafsanjani knows how to play with these bastards and how to milk them." He winked at me and put another piece of kebab on my plate. He laughed. "Dumb cowboys."

That night, back at my house, I wrote a letter to Carol about what Kazem said. At the time I didn't realize the importance of this new information and the potential impact it could have on my life. But when Carol didn't show any interest in these details and didn't ask any follow-up questions, I realized how foolish I had been. I had been risking my life to rid my country of the criminals running it and the Americans were negotiating with them. The CIA knew that the Guards were responsible for the barracks bombing in Lebanon that took the lives of 241 American servicemen. They knew that their own people, like William Buckley, were being kidnapped, tortured, and killed. Yet they were offering appeasement to these two-faced donkey-riding mullahs.

The notion of negotiations between America and the regime also chilled me for another reason. I began to consider the possibility that part of the deal-making process might involve exposing agents. Not long after my dinner with Kazem, three Iranians in the Foreign Ministry were arrested as spies working for America. Government papers disclosed the discovery of documents in these agents' homes very similar to the documents I had, including codebooks. I wondered if America would turn me in as part of a grand bargain.

In November of 1986, radicals leaked the news of the arms-for-hostages deals to Hezbollah in Lebanon, which in turn published this information in *Al-Shiraa,* a Lebanese magazine. This triggered the Iran–Contra scandal. I learned later that the U.S. meetings were not limited to those held with Hashemi Rafsanjani and his contacts in Tehran. They also met with the Guards in Geneva, Brussels, Frankfurt, and Mainz. The CIA assigned the Guards' negotiators the code names The Engine and The Relative, and they even facilitated a trip for The Relative to Washington, D.C., where he received a tour of the White House.

I was glad to see the embarrassment this revelation caused the Reagan administration. They'd sidestepped their principles to negotiate with people who committed heinous acts as a matter of policy. If these negotiations had gone further, any hopes I ever had for a free Iran would have evaporated.

With the news of the affair out and President Reagan putting an end to these Iran initiatives, I tried to stay focused. I continued my reports to Carol, hoping that the American government had seen the error of negotiating with Iran's rulers and would take a more aggressive stance in the future. They'd managed only to secure the release of a few hostages. In exchange, they'd provided the Guards with a stockpile of American weapons, some of which ended up in the hands of Hezbollah and the Islamic Jihad. Meanwhile, the Guards continued to take hostages and make greater demands.

Early in the summer of 1987, Kazem came to my office and informed me that his name for the hajj had been called. He was honored to visit Mecca, but he was intensely excited about this for another reason. Imam Khomeini had issued an order for an uprising to take place during that year's pilgrimage and Kazem believed he might play a role in this insurrection. I didn't doubt it. Kazem's being called to the hajj was no coincidence; I was sure Khomeini wanted him and other Guards from our unit there for precisely this purpose. The regime had tried in the past to cause turmoil in the Saudi kingdom. They'd been largely unsuccessful, but this wouldn't stop them from planning further criminal acts at the place many knew as "God's House."

"Everything is in place and the Saudi monarch is going down," Kazem said contemptuously. "These Arabs are the servants of America, and they will pay big this time." He then offered me specific details, which I memorized for my next report.

[Letter #—]
[Date:———]

Dear Carol,

    1—Kazem today revealed the Guards' plan for an uprising against the Saudi kingdom during the hajj.

    2—Thousands of Guards have been sent as pilgrims and flown by Iran Air.

    3—Knifes, machetes, and other arms have been transferred to Saudi Arabia by the Guards.

    4—Imam Khomeini gave the order for this uprising.

    5—The plan is to incite the Muslims for a demonstration condemning American and Israeli policies.

    6—They intend to escalate the demonstration to an uprising against the Saudi kingdom.

    7—The Iran Air flights are departing daily, carrying Guard members and transferring arms.

                                          Wally

About a week after my letter reached Carol, I heard that the Saudis were checking all the Iran Air flights and sending back many Iranian pilgrims who they found in possession of arms. I felt I'd played a direct role in this, believing that my information was put to use. Finally, I thought, some good was coming out of what I had been doing.

Still, in spite of my efforts and the Saudis' precautions, the Guards succeeded in causing a massive and violent demonstration. Thousands of pilgrims joined the fight with Saudi police, shouting "Death to America" and "Death to Israel," and demanding the overthrow of the Saudi kingdom. The riot led to a death toll of hundreds of Iranians, other pilgrims, and Saudi police. The Saudis ultimately quelled the revolt, but this led Khomeini to order a number of bombing attacks on Saudi agencies around the world and the assassination of several of their diplomats.

Tensions throughout the region were incredibly high. And in the midst of this, Carol sent me a chilling message:

Hello, Wally,

We have learned that Iraq has received shipments of long-range missiles from the Soviet Union. They will use them against civilians to force the regime to accept peace. We don't know what the timing is, but should you want to leave, we would understand.

Things are going to get ugly, but there will be peace in the end. Please take care,
Carol

24

BROTHER, MY BROTHER

"No, you cannot see her now. She is in the CCU. I am sorry." The nurse shook her head and left me alone in the hallway of Toos Hospital. I walked back to the administration area and found another nurse sitting behind the desk.

"I am here to see Fataneh Kahlili," I said desperately. "She is my mother and they just admitted her in here. She had a heart attack. Please tell me where she is and how she is doing."

The nurse looked up at me and narrowed her eyes. "We just told you. She is in the CCU. She is not doing well. How many times do you have to ask?"

Earlier that day, one of Mom's neighbors called to tell me that an ambulance had taken her to the hospital. The day before, I had pleaded with her to let me take her out of town, where she could be safe from the most vicious round of attacks civilians had experienced during the war. She refused. She even refused to stay with me. Of course she did. Why would she even consider that? Her only son was part of a ruinous regime and she couldn't forgive him for this. The birth of her grandson had brought us together physically, but this turned out to be a temporary rapprochement. After Somaya and Omid left, she returned to seeing me only as a member of the Guards. When I entreated her on the phone to allow me to help her get to a safer place, she told me that she would leave with her friends in a few days if things did not get better. But her voice was shaky, and I knew she was frightened.

This latest nightmare began when I was at home, having just hung up from a conversation with Somaya. A roaring blast jolted the building, the ground shook, and I thought the house would crumble. It was far worse than when Iraqi jets dropped bombs. I looked out the window to see which building had collapsed and found neighbors running and screaming outside. I couldn't see any sign of destruction within our neighborhood; just confused and rattled people. I turned on the radio, but before I could get any information, there was another jolt.

A few months earlier, Carol had warned me that there would be missile attacks. At the time, I could appreciate her message only in the abstract. The reality was so much more terrifying. BBC radio confirmed that Iraq was firing long-range missiles on Tehran and other Iranian cities. The BBC also said that there was a strong possibility that this was the first of many such attacks.

It was then that I called Mom, offering to take her away from this madness. Now, a day later, after more than a dozen missiles had hit Tehran, Mom lay in the cardiac care unit. I was devastated and I felt responsible for what had happened to her. I should have insisted on staying with her in such a situation, despite her protests and refusals, but I allowed the distance that had come between us to prevent me from doing the right thing.

While I was waiting to hear about her condition, an explosion jolted the hospital violently. Another missile had hit somewhere close by. Screams and howls filled the hallway. Nurses rushed from one room to another. People in waiting rooms hurried to leave. I just sat there on the floor and covered my face with my palms.

What has happened to us? Is this the kind of life we deserve? What is going to happen to Mom? I broke her heart and now she's suffered a heart attack. What if she does not make it? God, please save her and I'll do anything!

"Is somebody here for Fataneh Kahlili?"

I turned my head toward the deep, husky voice. I wiped my face with the end of my sleeve and raised my hand, still too choked up to talk. A man in light blue hospital garb approached. I felt his hand on my shoulder as I tried to get up.

"Please stay seated. Are you Mrs. Kahlili's son?"

I nodded.

"You know, *pesaram,* since last night we have had several patients with heart attacks. These missiles don't just destroy where they hit; you have to have a strong heart to survive the effect of their impact." He pushed his cap away from his forehead. "I am sorry to say that your mother did not make it."

Carol had also told me in her message that things would get ugly but that there would be peace in the end. Was this the kind of peace she was talking about? Would she consider my mother "at peace" now? I couldn't continue to live like this. By the time I buried Mom on a cold winter day in 1988, while Tehran was still under attack by Saddam Hussein, I had made the decision that would alter the course of my life.

The international phone lines had been jammed since the attacks started. Since we couldn't reach each other by phone, Somaya sent a telegram:

Reza, we are so worried. We are not able to call. Please let us know how you are. Please, Reza, call us ASAP.

I rushed to send a telegram back to her. I wished I could let her know about what I'd decided in the telegram, but I had to be sure I could follow through on this decision before I said anything. I did not even mention what happened to Mom and how devastated I was, how I was racked with guilt over her death and how much I regretted not telling Mom that I was not who she thought I was.

Somaya jon, I am safe and sound. Please do not worry so much. It is not as bad as it sounds in the news. I will be sending a telegram every other day until the phone lines become available again. I love you so much and I miss you. Please kiss my Omid for me and take care of yourself. Love, Reza.

"Are you sure you want to put in all these words?" the dispatcher at the phone company said. "You can delete 'I miss you' or 'I love you so much' to cut the cost."

"That's okay, I will pay for those."

"How about 'kiss my Omid'? Do you know how expensive every word is?"

"Don't worry about those. I will pay more to make sure they know I love them."

The dispatcher rolled his eyes and took the paper.

The always bustling Tehran had turned into a ghost town. Hundreds of thousands fled as soon as the first few missiles struck. Many took shelter in cities to the north by the Caspian Sea, as these places were too far away for the missiles to reach from Iraq. A three-hour drive had become an eighteen- to twenty-hour crawl because of the number of cars fleeing the capital. Others who could not afford to travel camped out in the outskirts of Tehran, feeling that this was somehow safer. Many people died in car accidents or from snakebite while camping in remote areas. Business in Tehran came to a halt.

I needed to talk to Kazem, but the timing wasn't right for a personal discussion. The base was chaotic. I had never seen Kazem so angry and rattled. Not long after the attacks started, I encountered him in the hallway and he asked me to follow him to his office. He slammed the door behind him and hurled himself into his chair. He mumbled some words and picked up the phone, but instead of dialing, he banged the handset back to its base.

"We'll teach this bastard Saddam a good lesson. These filthy Americans think they can force us to surrender by giving him missiles and a green light to attack us. The Iraqis claim the missiles are their own. They think we are donkeys."

"What is the plan, Kazem?" I asked. "We cannot just sit here and let this motherless plunderer destroy us like this."

"The U.S. has planned this. Imam just ordered us to expand the mining of the Persian Gulf to put pressure on American forces and oil shipments. And we are going to fire missiles at Iraq's major cities in return. They can take their dreams to their grave if they think they are going to demolish our Islamic movement."

It took several minutes for Kazem's fury to recede long enough for him to tell me how sorry he was to hear of my mother's death. This was an opening for me to discuss my decision, but remembering his tirade just moments before, I let it pass.

Later that night I wrote a letter to Carol:

[Letter #—]

[Date:————]

Dear Carol,

1—The Iraqi missile attacks have caused chaos. Innocent people are being slaughtered.

2—People are leaving the capital for safer ground.

3—Kazem told me that Imam has ordered a swift response to Iraq and to the American forces in the Persian Gulf.

4—The Guards will expand the mining of the Gulf in retaliation for Saddam's attacks.

5—The Guards don't know how Saddam has acquired these powerful missiles but they doubt they were built by the Iraqi army. They blame the U.S. for giving Saddam the green light for this action.

6—I will try to stay in touch, but the situation is very volatile.

Wish me luck,

Wally

Almost two months after the first strike by Iraqi missiles and while most of Tehran still looked desolate, the missile strikes stopped. But the war continued. After Imam Khomeini ordered the mining of the Gulf, a guided-missile frigate, the USS *Samuel B. Robertson,* struck an Iranian mine on April 14, 1988. The mine blew a fifteen-foot hole in the hull and flooded the engine room, injuring ten sailors. I knew that America would not take this lightly, and I prayed that the retaliation would not hurt innocent civilians. Four days later, the U.S. Navy attacked two Iranian oil platforms. The ensuing battle caused at least six Iranian speedboats and two navy ships to be destroyed or damaged.

The tension in the Gulf was later responsible for an ill-fated incident that ended the life of nearly three hundred innocent people. On July 3, 1988, while I was in the cafeteria at our base with Kazem and some other Guards, news came out that a U.S. Navy cruiser had shot down an Iran Air jetliner. Apparently, the USS *Vincennes* mistook the civilian jet for an attacking F-14 fighter. The news repeatedly showed footage of bodies of men, women, and children floating in the Persian Gulf.

The uproar among the Guards was immediate. "Death to America," the Guards chanted in the cafeteria. As always, this mob denied any culpability in the tragedy.

Later that month, Khomeini accepted peace with Iraq. But he did so with searing words that revealed the true hatred he had for his enemy.

"Making this decision was more deadly than taking poison. I submitted myself to God's will and drank from this cup of poison for his satisfaction. To me, it would have been more bearable to accept death and martyrdom, but I made this decision in the interest of the Islamic Republic."

After eight years of suffering, more than half a million people dead, injured, or wounded, and a great cost in economic damage, our Imam still held to the belief that he was sacrificing for the sake of the Islamic Republic. I could not feel more shame for what I once believed.

Now that the war was over and conditions on the base were less chaotic, I thought this would be a good time to talk to Kazem. I went to his office on a Wednesday afternoon. It was Somaya's birthday. I had called her earlier that day and she was in tears.

"Reza, it's been three years. Omid has started first grade. I cannot pretend everything is okay, because it's not. He needs you. I need you, too. I understand your love for your . . . whatever you love about that country, but I am sick and tired of this. You belong with your family."

She did not give me a chance to wish her happy birthday, but I told her that I would call her back later that night when she'd calmed down. I was hoping that I'd have things straightened out with Kazem by then and that I could offer her the birthday present she truly wanted.

I was surprised to find Rahim in Kazem's office because I hadn't seen him for some time. He hugged me when he saw me, saying, "*Salam aleikom,* Baradar Reza. It is so nice to see you again."

"*Salam,* Baradar Rahim. It's nice to see you, too."

I hoped Rahim would leave soon so I could talk to Kazem. Apparently, they were in the middle of a discussion about Khomeini's acceptance of peace. Kazem, who had earlier stated that the only acceptable end to this war was the destruction of Saddam and his allies, now acknowledged Khomeini's decision. But he was still furious with America.

"I wish that we had taught America a lesson and responded to its bullying," Kazem said.

"Rest assured, Baradar Kazem, that time will come," Rahim said. "But the Americans had sent a strong message that if we didn't accept peace with Iraq, they would use all their power, including nuclear bombs. Hajj Agha Rafsanjani has promised to retaliate for their downing of our civilian jetliner and much more. I know from many high commanders that if we had the atomic bomb, we would have used it against them. But there is a time to step back, get stronger, and then confront the evil powers of imperialism and Zionism. *Inshallah,* we will destroy them both."

Kazem looked at me and nodded. I could see he was satisfied with Rahim's response.

"I believe our Imam's decision was spiritually inspired," I said, playing the role I always played in the office. "As Imam said himself, we have to submit ourselves to God's will and Allah will empower us to defeat evil."

At some point, Rahim asked about my wife and son living outside the country away from me for such a long time. I remember telling him that they were with my in-laws in London.

"They are fine. My father-in-law, Moheb Khan, has a big apartment in the Mayfair district, and I am happy that my wife and son are safe and living with her family."

"Moheb Khan? I know this name. Is his last name Hadidi?" Rahim asked. I nodded, shocked that he knew my in-laws.

"Moheb Khan is a great Muslim and his contribution to the London mosque is well regarded. I was not aware you were related to him."

I did not know how to feel about having this connection. Would I earn more respect and credibility or be watched more closely? I knew Moheb Khan had a good reputation among Muslims in London, as he was a righteous man and a trustworthy businessman. But Moheb Khan was also openly against the crimes and unjust rule of the Iranian government. Would this put my family and me under more suspicion?

Rahim glanced at his watch and told Kazem that they should be going.

"If you are not busy, Baradar Reza, you should come with us, too," Rahim said. "You should witness justice in action."

Before I could ask where they wanted me to go, somebody knocked and opened the door to Kazem's office.

"Baradar Rahim, can I talk to you for a second?" the Guard asked.

Rahim got up and stood by the halfway-opened door, holding on to the handle with his arm twisted behind him. The two men whispered something. All I could hear was Rahim saying, "Sure, sure, I'll be there."

Rahim came back into the room and said that he had to go somewhere else immediately, as something had come up. He said that Kazem and I should go without him. I felt relieved, as going on a trip with Kazem alone would give me the opportunity to talk to him about my plan.

However, when Kazem told me where we were heading, I felt nauseous. He was taking me to a stoning.

"It is only a forty-minute drive from here." Kazem looked at his watch. "We can probably get there in time if we leave now."

I felt a surge of anger and directed all of it toward Kazem. How could he be so indifferent, so cold-blooded, to talk about this as though it were another appointment on his calendar? How could I possibly consider someone like this a friend? I was so livid that I couldn't speak to him about anything, let alone my plans, on the way there.

We arrived at the end of an unpaved, dusty road in a deserted spot in the shadow of the surrounding hills. A small crowd had gathered. Several Guards' and Komitehs' Land Cruisers were parked along the roadside. A short distance from the crowd, a couple of motorcyclists leaned against their bikes watching the event. Among the crowd were a few women in black chadors. In front of them were piles of fist-sized stones.

A young woman, wrapped in a white shroud and held on both sides by two policemen, stood in front of a hole dug especially for her. Behind them, five *pasdar* with machine guns watched the crowd.

A black-robed mullah announced the crime.

"Asieh Najmali, thirty-two-year-old mother of two, has been convicted of adultery."

The crowd sighed.

"Today we are here to bring justice. This is God's verdict. Asieh Najmali has committed a sin that can only be punished by the rule of Allah. She has brought shame and disgrace to Islam and her family. . . ."

"Let's go up farther so we can get a better view," Kazem whispered.

"You go ahead; I can already see."

Kazem frowned at me and forced himself into the crowd. I hid behind a row of men at the end of the circle they had made around Asieh. From what I could tell, her sin was trying to feed her two children by the only means available to a woman stricken with poverty because of the policies of the Islamic government: selling herself to a man for a few thousand rials. Now she was to face the punishment decreed by fanatical mullahs in Allah's name. I spied Kazem watching the proceedings avidly and wondered how my God could be so different from his.

"Kill this adulterer!" a man in the crowd shouted.

This set off a volley of epithets. From every corner you could hear people yelling, *"Binamoos . . . zenakar . . . kesafat,"* calling Asieh shameful, unchaste, and an adulterer. "Kill her, kill her!" they chanted.

I tried to think about what Somaya might be doing for her birthday in an effort to distract myself. I closed my eyes, but when I did, I saw Somaya in the hole. This set my nerves on fire. Driven by some force I barely understood, I pushed myself through the crowd. Suddenly, I felt that I needed to witness this moment with my eyes wide open. A young woman was being slaughtered, and I had to stop hiding behind my own shadow. I had to know her pain.

Asieh was now standing in the hole. They'd covered her body from the waist down with dirt. I saw no sign of surrender in her eyes. I could tell that she knew she was not guilty. She had submitted herself to the God she believed in, the God who would look after her two innocent kids, the God who had already forgiven her.

The Guards started shoveling more dirt in the hole until they buried Asieh up to her shoulders.

The crowd hushed.

A Guards commander reached into the pile of stones. He picked up a rock and aimed it at Asieh. I bit my lip and said to myself, *God, please, please put a stop to this. How can you let these savages contaminate the love you put into your creation. How can you watch and not be enraged.*

The rock hit Asieh's forehead and blood ran down her pale face.

She didn't plead and she didn't scream. Her God had given her strength and his love and protection.

The crowd attacked the pile of rocks. With all of the hatred they felt in them, they threw rocks at Asieh. Soon Asieh's face was veiled in blood and her head tilted to one side. She was gone. But the crowd continued to assault her.

"Die, you filthy, sinful woman. Die."

Eventually, the mullah stepped in. "Justice has been carried out. She is dead now, and God's will is satisfied."

The crowd started to scatter. Kazem was chatting with some Guards, but I could not take my eyes off Asieh. A pickup truck pulled close to the hole. A man stepped out and removed a shovel and a blanket from the bed of his truck. Then he opened the passenger door for an old woman, presumably Asieh's mother. The woman sat on the ground while the man dug out Asieh's body. She did not wail. She did not mourn. She just stared at the man digging out the bloodied body of her daughter. A mother watched her daughter stoned to death, a part of her being ripped apart, and could say nothing. She was not even able to shed a tear.

The man wrapped Asieh's body in the blanket, laid it in the bed of his truck, and drove away. Kazem and the Guards were still talking. I walked back to the car. I did not want to be a part of their conversation. I did not even care if my walking away from them insulted them. I was ready to spit on them and tell them how ashamed I was of them. Knowing that I was likely to say anything if provoked, I tapped the shirt pocket where I kept the rat poison capsules. I wanted to be sure they were with me.

The angry roar of the two cycles revving their engines in the distance caught my attention. Why in the world weren't they leaving? They'd seen what they wanted to see.

I turned around to find Kazem coming to the car. The other Guards were headed to their cars as well. Kazem put some papers in the trunk and waved good-bye as the last two Land Cruisers took off, leaving a cloud of dust behind them.

Kazem arranged some stuff in the backseat and hopped in behind the wheel. "What's the matter with you?" he asked as he turned the key in the ignition. I was convinced that he truly had no idea.

"I am leaving the Guards," I said in a voice filled with contempt.

Kazem scowled at me. "What?"

He had never looked at me with such derision. At another time in my life, I might have shrunk from this or tried to appease his anger, but it meant nothing to me now. I was ready to tell him how disgusted I was with him, his Islam, and his God. How for all those years I'd just pretended to be his friend. How I'd used him to get revenge for Naser and my lost country.

"Did the stoning bother you? You think a sinner like her didn't deserve that punishment? She was a disgrace to our society. Women like her are filthy. They should . . ."

"Kazem, stop it!" I shouted.

I thought in that moment that Somaya would never see me again. There was no way I could hold back the torrent of my feelings now. I had planned to discuss this with Kazem calmly, telling him that I wanted to leave the Guards for a while to stay with my family. I was confident he would accommodate that. But my outrage stripped me of any discretion.

"Kazem, it is not just the stoning." I shook my head. "No—not just that! It's all you do to these innocent people. All the injustices this Islamic Revolution heaps on this country. You are blind, Kazem. I've wanted to tell you this for a long time. This is not the real Islam. It is not God's will to kill and kill more."

Kazem floored the gas pedal. He maneuvered around cars and said nothing. He kept biting his lower lip and looking at the rearview mirror. I held on to my seat. People were honking at us, probably thinking that the driver had lost his mind.

I thought Kazem was doing this because he hated me for what I was saying to him. But then he adjusted his rearview mirror and said, "I think we have company."

"What?" I checked my side mirror and saw two motorcycles approaching us. "I saw these riders at the stoning."

"Are they friends of yours, Reza?" he remarked sarcastically. "You know what Javad once said to me? He told me you were not to be trusted, that you were either part of the Mujahedin or a spy for America." He shifted manically to another lane. "I slapped him in the face and told him, 'You get off Reza's back or I'll send you where you belong.'"

Another loud, long honk split the air as Kazem cut in front of an eighteen-wheeler.

"You know what else I told Javad? I told him that I'd give my eyes for you. 'If anybody, anybody among us is a pure believer and committed to this movement, it is Reza,' I said. And I would still like to believe that."

He turned his head to check the side mirror. The bikes were still behind us. He started to roll up his window and told me to do the same.

"Kazem, do you see what is happening here? Is this what you believe in? Is this the religion of love and forgiveness? Is this the same loving God you worshiped as the kid I knew? Or is this the one they want you to worship?"

A loud blast overwhelmed my words.

"Duck! Duck!" Kazem yelled as he pushed my head down and held it with his hand. We were under attack. The two bikers were shooting at the car. Kazem was zigzagging, trying to maneuver the car between lanes, and honking the horn. Then another blast shattered the back window, blowing shards of glass inside. I moved as far under the dashboard as I could and Kazem reached over to push me farther down. The car hit some bumps but we kept barreling forward.

Then came more gunshots and another window broke. We hit a heavy bump. I closed my eyes. The car lurched up and came down hard. When we landed, I realized that I could no longer feel

Kazem's hand on my head. The car was still moving uncontrollably. Suddenly, we came to a violent stop as we hit something. My head crashed into the glove compartment and pieces of glass showered over me.

After that, all was quiet, except for the howl of air rushing through the broken windows. I uncrossed my arms from around my head and carefully moved the glass away. I rose up and saw Kazem's head leaning to one side.

"Kazem?" I gave him a gentle push. "Kazem?"

I moved his head and saw the blood running down his neck where the assailants had shot him.

"Oh my God! Kazem!"

Smoke rose from under the smashed hood. I tried to open the door to get us out, but it was jammed. I removed my jacket and took off my shirt to wrap it around Kazem's neck.

Hesitantly, I reached for his pulse. There was none. I pressed on his wrist harder looking for a beat, moving my finger around. Nothing. I checked the pulse on his neck, but found nothing there, either.

I crumpled. *How many atrocities do I have to witness?* I screamed to the God in my head. *How many friends and family members do I have to bury? God, I am so tired of this! I am so tired.*

I submit myself to you, as I no longer have the strength.

I barely remember what happened in the ensuing days. Our base announced that Kazem fell victim to a Mujahedin attack. Rahim moved back to our base, telling me to take a few days off.

"Baradar Reza, you did what you could to save your brother. We all know you and Kazem were close. It must be very hard on you, as it is on all of us. We lost a great *pasdar*. He was a true Muslim and now he's a martyr."

But what Rahim did not know was that Kazem had saved my life and that I had not attempted to reciprocate. In the moments before the attack, I learned that he'd also protected me all those years. With the faith he had in me, he made it possible for a group of hard-core radicals to believe that Reza was like them, and perhaps even more dedicated than they were. He'd erased the damage Javad had caused. He'd secured for me the respect of Rahim, a shrewd commander of one of the most dangerous divisions of the Islamic Republic government. He'd saved my life more than once.

I stayed home for a few days, unsure what to feel. My relationship with Kazem had stopped being simple a long time ago. But as it turned out, he had never stopped acting as a friend. It would take me a very long time to process this and mourn it properly.

One thing was certain, though. With Kazem gone, I had no more security. If I were going to leave now, I would need Rahim's approval, and I assumed that this would be exponentially harder to attain than it would have been from Kazem. I decided that the only approach I could take was to have the evenhanded conversation I'd intended to have with Kazem before my fury overwhelmed me.

"Baradar Rahim, I know it's a very tense time with Kazem not being here, but I hope you understand that my family needs me in London, if I can have your permission. My wife is going back to school and my son has not seen me for a few years. They need me. . . ."

Rahim stopped me. "Baradar Reza, I know it has been hard for you to lose Kazem. I understand. You look so miserable. I think it is a good idea that you go there for a while. Be with your family."

I couldn't believe it had gone that easily.

"Leave your phone number and address with me and I'll be in touch," Rahim continued. "I know Moheb Khan and where he lives, but if I have your number, I can call should something come up. And perhaps while staying there, I'll connect you with some good brothers and you can remain active with the Guards."

Rahim's words sent me plummeting back to earth. How was I going to navigate my way through this? I decided that I couldn't worry about it at that moment. I had his permission to leave and I'd make the most of that. I made plans to leave the country in a few weeks, though I still didn't call Somaya to tell her so. I felt that I couldn't let her know what I was doing until after my plane landed in London because until that very moment things could go horribly wrong. I had Rahim's permission, my ticket, and the voucher of my freedom, but I had learned that none of this was a guarantee in Iran anymore. I just couldn't bear the devastation it would cause her if I got her hopes up and then someone with power over me squashed those hopes.

I was so anxiety-riddled in the time leading up to my departure that I could barely sleep. And when sleep did come, soul-ripping nightmares awoke me, leaving me stunned in bed. About a week before my flight, I woke up soaked to the bone in the middle of the night. I held my chest tightly because it felt as though my heart were about to burst out of it. I ran the sheet across my face to wipe off the sweat and sat up in bed, remembering the dream I had.

I am in a desert. There is nothing around me. I am stuck in a hole from the waist down. I feel something hit my head from the back and I feel intense pain. Then something hits me in the forehead. I see blood. Then something else hits me in the back of my head.

I turn and sigh. Kazem is standing behind me in his soccer jersey. He is ten or eleven years old. He has a soccer ball in one hand and is throwing rocks at me with his other. Another rock hits me in the forehead. This comes from Naser, who is standing in front of me. He looks skinny and old. He is behind bars and throwing rocks at me from a distance.

I scream, "I don't want to be the goalie anymore!"

Khanoom Bozorg approaches me. "Reza jon, *you should have done your namaz before getting in that hole."*

Agha Joon walks up and grabs Khanoom Bozorg's hand. "Khanoom, leave him alone. He is an adult and he knows what's right and what's wrong. He is in this hole just to be a goalkeeper."

Then Somaya comes toward me carrying a birthday cake. I try to blow out the candles from the hole, but no matter how strong I blow, I cannot do it. The fire is still there. The candles are burning and burning!

"I don't want to be the goalie anymore!" I scream again.

25

LEAVING HOME

MY LANDLORD WAS upset when I gave her short notice, but my offer to let her keep all of my furniture appeased her. Although I planned to be away for a long time, I packed light. I didn't want to take much. I even wished I could leave my memories behind, burying them with all of the people I loved whom I'd buried. All I wanted was a new future and for the past to hide in its own darkness.

Once on the plane, I closed my eyes and thought of Somaya and Omid's surprise at seeing me—how we would start the rest of our lives together and how different things were going to be. I was preoccupied with these pleasant thoughts when the plane hit air turbulence. The FASTEN SEAT BELT sign beeped and lit up. A commotion arose as the plane started to shake.

The woman next to me started to murmur prayers. *"Ey Khoda, Khodet hefzemoon kon,"* she said. *Oh God, please save us!* She held on to the arms of her seat and mine. The older man next to her on the aisle seat had his eyes closed as he rocked back and forth, a line of sweat traveling along the side of his pale face.

The plane dropped suddenly, causing several people to cry out in alarm. The sound of babies wailing and adults shouting for salvation was all too familiar to me. But a few seconds later, the shaking subsided. With another beep, the seat belt light went off.

"Thank God," the woman next to me said as she took a deep breath. She turned her head toward my seat to look out the window and I saw tears in her eyes. "Even to leave this ruined place does not come easy."

All I could do was nod and force a smile.

She shook her head. "Thank God, I am not going back. Never!"

Before I left, I went to see Agha Joon to say good-bye. By this point he was battling Alzheimer's, but he remembered me. He asked when I was planning to return, and I just told him I'd be doing so soon. I wished I could tell him that I might not be back for a long time and that when I did return, he might not even be around, but I couldn't be that candid.

Thinking about my grandfather, thinking about how he'd helped form me and how much he meant to me, I realized that I didn't truly want to bury my past. I needed to look forward, but I should never look away from what made me who I was.

The Iran Air Boeing 747 landed smoothly at Heathrow. After the sometimes rocky ride, the passengers applauded the pilot's gentle touchdown. I saw this as a metaphor for my future and the freedom I was about to enjoy.

I called Somaya once I got off the plane. All flight, I'd been thinking about how to explain my arrival. Ultimately, I just decided to make it as clear as possible. "Somaya *jon, salam*. Please forgive me. I know I should have called before, but I am in London."

I paused for her reaction. All she said was "What?"

My voice was shaky. "I am catching a cab and will be there in less than an hour."

Somaya and Omid greeted me at the door. I held Omid in my arms, and all I could do was cry. Somaya looked at me in disbelief. Her expression said, "Only you would show up this way." Somaya's parents were happy to see me and we all celebrated my appearance. I knew things would be different later, when I was alone with my wife. She had every right to be angry with me for being away from her for so long and then for not telling her that I was coming to England.

In some ways, I dreaded that conversation. But Somaya never

failed to come through for me. When I told her about my mom's and Kazem's deaths, she held me in her arms and let me weep till the last drop of my tears dried on her shoulder. Though I knew she could have criticized me for the way I'd handled things since she moved to England, she didn't do anything of the sort.

When I was cried out, I said to her with shaking voice, "I promise, I will never, ever leave your side again and . . ."

She put a finger on my lips. "Don't, Reza. Please, I don't want you to promise anything anymore. You are here, and that means the world to Omid. For a long time, I've wanted the three of us to have a happy life. I am sure that's what you want, too. I waited for you all these years. Let's not let your promises ruin it, at least for Omid's sake."

"Do you still love me?" I said apprehensively.

She looked in my eyes and tried not to smile. "You know, Reza, I sometimes ask myself the same question." Then her eyes brightened and she said, "Yes, I still love you." Hearing this from her made me feel incredibly strong—and incredibly lucky that I'd managed to find a woman who would support me the way she did.

For the next several days, while I enjoyed the life I had missed for years, Somaya and I talked about our future. She agreed right away when I proposed that we move to America.

"Oh, California! I'd love to go to Los Angeles. The weather . . . Malibu Beach . . . Hollywood. And, oh my God, we can take Omid to Disneyland every day!" She closed her eyes and smiled like a child.

I laughed. "You've been watching a lot of American movies, haven't you?"

She patted my arm and said playfully, "You are so mean." Then she added, "It is not all about that. I could finish school there." Somaya had started going to college in London part-time. She was not sure of what she wanted to study, as she had several majors in mind. "I can decide what I want to do in America."

"You'll be good at anything you put your mind to."

Next, I had to call Carol to advise her of my decision to leave the agency, and to ask her help in arranging our trip to America. She had told me several times previously that when I was ready to go to the U.S. she would have our paperwork processed to attain our residency status.

Carol was shocked when I called and told her I was in London. She said she hoped I had a better excuse this time for not telling her about my trip. She asked me to meet her at the same hotel where we had met the last time. This seemed unusual, but it didn't matter to me anymore.

Seeing Carol, of course, meant that I had to lie to Somaya again about what I was doing, something I could barely reconcile any longer. I made up a story about contacting an immigration lawyer and planning a meeting to see what our options were.

"I'd like it if we could do these things together from now on," Somaya stated flatly.

"We will. This time is just a consultation. If the lawyer is any good, we'll go together next time." As the words left my mouth, I pleaded with God to make it possible for me to end my double life as soon as possible.

Carol gave me a warm hug as I entered the hotel room. "What brings you here this time? Visiting your family?" She didn't seem at all worried about why I'd asked to see her, perhaps because I was projecting the strength and serenity that several days with Somaya and Omid had provided.

"Yes, I am visiting. But there is more." I hesitated for a moment. "I need you to help me and my family move to the States."

Now concern crossed her face. "Is everything all right?"

"I lost my mother during the missile attacks. And a few weeks ago, before I came here, Kazem was killed. . . ."

"Oh my God! I am so sorry, Wally."

I didn't want to hear the name Wally now. For the past few days, I hadn't been thinking like Wally at all.

"What happened to Kazem?" she asked in disbelief.

I related all of it to her, explaining that the stoning and Kazem's assassination were the final straws for me. I told her that I was convinced that it was impossible for me—emotionally and physically—to remain in Iran.

"I am sorry," she said, rubbing her eyes and shaking her head.

"I talked to Somaya and we think it is better for us and for our son to live in the States instead of England."

Carol nodded thoughtfully. "Is this your final decision, Wally?"

I didn't hesitate in my response. "I am afraid it is," I said, surprised at how good it felt to get out those words.

"Then I will do my best to get everything ready," Carol said with a warm smile. "Give me a week and I'll have your papers prepared. But call me in a few days so we can set up another meeting."

When I heard her say this, I realized that I was truly committing to ending my double life. I'd wanted to do this for a long time, but I wasn't prepared for the ambivalence that struck me now. What about the madness still going on in my country? Was I truly prepared to leave so many good Iranians behind?

At the same time, though, I had to wonder if my efforts as Wally had really helped anyone. Did my reports accomplish what I hoped they would? I'd told the CIA about Iraq's use of chemical weapons, but this led to nothing more than the U.S. government's condemnation of the practice while they continued to provide Saddam with military intelligence and training, along with billions of dollars in economic aid. I reported China's secret military cooperation with the Guards, and again, this led only to a condemnation. I reported the ruthless torture and killing of men and women opposing the mullahs and how some European countries even allowed such practices within their own borders, and yet the West continued to sidestep its principles of supporting democracy and defending human rights because of the lure of Iranian oil.

You did all you could do, I told myself. *You did as much as one man* can *do*. For many years I had been certain that I was working for the freedom of my country. But now I realized that I was just another employee of the CIA.

Carol held up an envelope. "This is for you."

I stared at the envelope, wondering why she was giving me money after what I'd told her.

"It's for your hard work," she said, as though reading my mind.

I slipped the envelope inside my breast pocket. "Thanks."

"Wally, I'm not trying to change your mind, but if you decide to go back to Iran, even for a short while, and continue the work, the agency will provide you with a new car, a house, and a guaranteed job with a good salary at the headquarters when you return to the States."

I felt somewhat insulted that she would suggest this after what I told her I'd been through, but I decided to let it lie. "That is a very generous offer, Carol, but I have to pass at this moment." My voice was a little husky. "For the sake of my family."

The next time I saw Carol to go over our papers, I had Omid with me. Somaya was at school and I had told my in-laws I was going for a walk with my son. Carol was surprised when she saw the boy. It didn't dawn on me until that moment how stupid it was to bring Omid along. He was six years old and he was likely to tell Somaya how we had spent our day.

"This is my son, Omid, Ms. Lawyer," I said, trying to spin this on the spot. "Omid *jon,* please shake hands with our lawyer. She is working on our case so we can go to America."

Omid shook Carol's hand. My *six-year-old son* was shaking hands with a CIA agent in a covert meeting. The moment bordered on surreal.

The hotel room arrangement was a little different this time, thankfully. We were in a suite, the bedroom closed off by a double door. In the living area with us was a couch, a coffee table, and a huge working desk piled with Carol's paperwork, her briefcase, and a portable computer, perhaps one of the very first laptops ever available to the CIA's agents. It did not look like a lawyer's office, but I hoped it was convincing enough for a six-year-old to think it was.

"Hi, Omid. Nice to meet you," Carol said as she gave him a delightful smile. She looked up at me. "Your son is very handsome."

Though having Omid there was a little awkward, we were able to get through some of the paperwork. Carol said she would start the procedure with this and that she would let me know what else we needed to do.

"I think it is important to bring my wife along so she can be part of this process without . . ."—I looked at Omid, who was on the couch looking at a magazine. I lowered my voice—". . . without being suspicious."

"I'll plan something to make it look real and official," she whispered. "Call me tomorrow and we'll talk."

I felt embarrassed having to put Carol in that position. She obviously had more important things to do than prepare an elaborate ruse for my benefit—especially now that I was walking away from my role. Still, I needed the kind of help that only she could provide if I were going to maintain the secret that the CIA needed me to maintain.

After the meeting, I took Omid to Hamleys, a toy store, buying him a remote-control police car and a two-hundred-piece Lego fire station to keep him busy for the night so I could explain that day's meeting to Somaya without his comments.

As promised, Carol set up a meeting to which I could bring Somaya. The two of us entered a three-story building on Regent Street where the "law office of Harriet Johnson" was located on the second floor. There were two offices across from each other in a narrow hallway and I wasn't sure which was Carol's.

"Weren't you here before?" Somaya asked.

"Not here, no," I said, coming up quickly with yet another fabrication. "I thought I mentioned that Harriet just split from her old law partner. She moved here only a few days ago. Oh, there it is."

I knocked and entered the room. Carol was sitting behind a desk piled with files, books, and papers, taking notes on a pad. Behind her desk, there was a bookshelf across the back wall filled with hard-cover books. She was in a blue suit, her hair up, and her bifocals down on the tip of her nose. It was the first time I'd seen her with glasses and it surprised me that these made her look much older.

"Please have a seat," she said without looking up at us. "I'll be with you in a minute."

I was nervous and shifted in my chair, not ready for this, not sure if I could act my part. I'd been "performing" through most of my life as a CIA agent, but this scenario was different. I'd never been asked to deceive my wife in front of my employer. Somaya looked at me with a frown on her face. She noticed my discomfort. I bent my head toward her ear and whispered in Farsi, *"Ageh nashe chi?* What if she says we can't go?"

"Sorry for the delay, Mr. Kahlili," Carol said a few minutes later. She reached a hand out to Somaya. "This must be your wife. My name is Harriet Johnson, and it is a pleasure meeting you, Mrs. Kahlili."

"Please call me Somaya. Nice meeting you, too."

Carol and Somaya proceeded to discuss the process with each other without involving me at all. As odd as that seemed to me under the circumstances, I was fine with it because I didn't want to be any more of a part of this game of pretend with my wife than I needed to be.

"Then you think that political asylum is our only option to obtain our residency in the U.S.?" Somaya asked.

"It is indeed. Since Mr. Kahlili worked for the Iranian government, this way you can have amnesty. As I've already told your husband, the other options are an H-1 visa, a business visa, or a work permit. None of those fit your situation."

"But this way we cannot go back to Iran? Ever?"

"That's right. At least not under the current government."

Somaya looked at me sadly. "Are you okay with that, Reza? I

know I have no interest in going back as long as the mullahs are in power, but how about you?"

Carol left the room to give us some time to discuss this, though we had only one option. I already knew this because I'd already discussed it with Carol. I let Somaya make the final decision. With little hesitation, she gave permission to "Ms. Johnson" to start our petition for political asylum.

"It might take six months to a year," Carol said. "I will be in touch."

While the wait sounded long, Somaya seemed perfectly relaxed about it. She would happily be patient about getting to America as long as we were a family again and we could live together away from all that had separated us these past years. I knew she was especially happy that I'd agreed to an arrangement that would keep me out of Iran permanently, or at least until the current regime was gone.

On the way back home, we held hands and talked more about the future. We decided to rent our own place in London while we waited for the final paperwork. We also thought it would be a good idea to not tell anybody, even Somaya's parents, about how we were getting to America. We would simply let them know that we were planning to move there soon.

At the dinner table that night, while Somaya was happily announcing our plans, the phone rang. Zari Khanoom answered in the kitchen and let me know that the call was for me.

I picked up the phone and my blood chilled. After I finished the conversation, I stared at the wall.

I should have known. He did tell me he would be in touch. He did say he would not just leave me alone. How in the world did I think I could get away from him and my contorted past?

Rahim was in London. And he wanted to see me.

26

BACK INTO THE COLD

THE FACT THAT Rahim wanted to see me at the Iranian embassy alarmed me. The Guards used this tactic regularly to bring in people of interest, kidnap them, and transfer them to Iran and then on to Evin Prison. Was I walking directly toward my doom? Did I have any choice? I couldn't avoid this meeting, regardless of my sense of trepidation.

I needed to call Carol and inform her that I was to meet Rahim the next morning. This required some finesse, as I had to do this without drawing the attention of Somaya or my in-laws. After I helped clean up the dinner table, I told Somaya that I was going out to get a pack of cigarettes.

"I thought you just bought a pack this afternoon," she said with a puzzled expression. "You need to quit this soon."

I kissed her forehead and told her that I would.

When I called Carol, she assured me that even on such short notice, she would provide me with as much protection as she could. "If you don't come out by the time they shut down the place, we will take action. Our people will be there."

The taxi driver dropped me off at the corner of Ennismore Mews and Princes Gardens. I walked west, checking for lookouts. On the left side of Exhibition Road, a man in a black corduroy jacket was reading a magazine. I presumed he was one of the lookouts. On the other side, at the corner of Prince Consort Road, a man in a beige trench coat was carrying a map. Carol had said that I should look for the men with big overcoats holding newspapers or magazines. Because she was putting this together so quickly, she couldn't give me any more detail than this.

Before I got to Princes Gate, at the first entrance to Montrose Court, I saw a familiar-looking woman in a red suit waiting for a cab. I held my head down and tried to compose myself. I never imagined Carol herself would be there. I felt more secure knowing that the CIA was watching out for me, but I also knew I could never be fully secure as long as I was in the orbit of the Revolutionary Guards.

Around the corner, Rahim caught my eyes. He was standing next to the iron fence that surrounded the embassy, smoking a cigarette. He was wearing a buttoned-up white dress shirt under his army jacket and his black pants were creased in several spots. I turned my head to see if I could still locate any of my lookouts, regretting this instantly, as I realized that I was acting suspiciously and that Rahim might notice.

Rahim greeted me with a hug and a pat on the back. "*Salam,* Baradar Reza. It is so nice to see you." He kissed either side of my face. "Let's go in. Baradar Amiri is waiting for us." He crushed his cigarette butt under his shoes.

We went to the second floor, where we were to meet Amiri in his office. Amiri, a short, skinny man with a unibrow and a full black beard, got up and hugged Rahim when we arrived. He looked to be in his early forties. Amiri seemed to know a great deal about me, mentioning my service in the Guards, my relationship to Moheb Khan, and the Mujahedin attack that killed Kazem.

We sat down and Rahim immediately went off on an extended monologue about how every devoted Muslim needed to pay his dues to our revolution and about how we had enemies in every corner of the world. "It's our duty to look out for our country no matter where we are. And, Baradar Reza, you are a devotee and you owe it to your country to start being active soon. You are still a member of the Guards, and you have had enough time to recover from the terrible experience you had in Tehran. I think you should start work-ing *forran* right away. Your stay here will be questioned by the *Sepah* back home. As your commander, I have to make sure you continue to serve your country."

As shocked and terrified as I was by the gravity of Rahim's tone, I gave him an affirmative smile. "Of course, Baradar Rahim." I cleared my throat. "I am and will be at your service, and will do anything you ask me to do."

Rahim turned to Amiri. "Baradar Reza will be in your hands now. The work we need from him will be quite different from what he did at home, but he is a smart guy and a fast learner." He laughed.

He then looked back in my direction and regarded me ominously. "By the way, how long did you plan to stay here?"

"My wife is still in school for a while," I said nervously, "but it shouldn't be too much longer."

"I am sure you will do as great a job here as you did back home. We will then see what's best for you and what you need to do."

Rahim then told me about the vicious bloodbaths that had taken place in the couple of months that I'd been away from home. "Bara-dar Reza, God took revenge for the unjust killing of *Shahid* Kazem and all the other crimes. Imam Khomeini issued a fatwa."

When Khomeini had announced the campaign, he said, "If the person at any stage or at any time maintains his [or her] support for the Munafeqin [Mujahedin], the sentence is execution. Annihilate the enemies of Islam immediately." He also ordered the deaths of leftists because they were apostate. The fatwa led to the execution of thousands of innocent men and women of all ages in a very short period. Among them were girls as young as Parvaneh and Roya, raped before their bodies swayed on the hook of the cranes. Inno-cent young men like Naser and his brother, Soheil, were lined up for several hours before they were hanged. This massacre was one of the most heinous acts of Khomeini's rule, yet the rest of the world paid little attention to it. This was the first I'd heard of this barbarism, and I learned that the British media had barely reported it.

To legitimize this act, a Death Commission carried out mock trials behind closed doors. They interrogated prisoners about their associations, affiliations, and allegiances with a series of questions designed to elicit an answer that assured the death sentence: Are you willing to denounce the Munafeqin on television? Are you willing to name and identify other active members? Are you willing to help us arrest these people? Are you willing to die for Islam? A negative answer led to immediate condemnation. But answering positively eventually led to the same, as the questions had been designed to generate only one result. The prisoners had no idea why they were being questioned, and many of them had been arrested for minor infractions and were coming to the ends of their original sentences.

Amiri shook his head as Rahim described this, adding, "Yes, God took revenge. And hopefully we will soon arrest and execute the rest of them."

"*Inshallah!*" Rahim said.

"*Inshallah,*" I replied, feeling shame, remorse, and repulsion.

Amiri and Rahim continued to talk about how important it was to identify those who opposed us outside the country and punish them in the same way. I felt an ache in my heart. These criminals were running rampant while the superpowers turned a blind eye. How could there ever be peace in this world as long as this was the case?

When this insane discourse was over, Rahim rose and shook Amiri's hand. "Okay, then. You let Baradar Reza know what you need, and he will be at your service. I'll leave you two to work out the details." He turned back toward me. "Reza, I have your phone number and will be in touch before I leave."

I watched Rahim exit, feeling disoriented by my sudden and quite involuntary conscription back into service. Amiri got down to business immediately, suggesting that if I did not have a car, I should rent one.

"Two of our brothers are here in London to purchase some material, and I'd like you to take them where they need to go. They are staying with Baradar Sadri." He handed me a piece of paper. "Here is his address and phone number. Tell him Amiri asked you to call him. We will reimburse you for any costs you incur."

I nodded as Amiri directed me, but as he spoke, I kept wondering why they were giving me such an assignment. What I did for them in Iran had nothing to do with driving dirty bearded criminals around town. Why did they think I was the right person for this? I had to assume it was because Rahim trusted me. And this was because of Kazem. *I wish Kazem were here,* I thought as Amiri continued with his instructions. He'd always been my safe harbor with the Guards. Now I needed to navigate these waters by myself and I wasn't at all sure I could handle it.

Later that day, I called Carol to arrange another meeting right away. I felt as though she was my only source of support at this point. I needed some additional reassurance that the CIA had my back. I also felt an obligation to inform her about the underground activity going on in England. Carol set our rendezvous at a safe house. When I got there, another agent was waiting with her. Eric seemed affable and easygoing, and I quickly learned that he would be my new contact. While I'd had a number of contacts in my tenure in the CIA, I'd been with Carol for all of my active spying days. Given how uneasy I was feeling at this point, I didn't need this kind of switch now. I had felt very close to Carol and I worried that a new handler wouldn't have the same commitment to me. But like the rest of the events happening in my life at that time, I knew I needed to put myself in the hands of destiny.

I told Carol and Eric about the meeting at the embassy and about how Rahim had put conditions on my stay in London by insisting on my cooperation with the Guards.

"Wally, I think it just makes sense that you do what they want," Carol said. "It's going to take some time to prepare the papers for your move to America, so meanwhile you could continue your work here with us."

"I don't know, Carol. I promised Somaya that we were starting a new life. To endanger my family again by getting involved with the Guards here . . . I am just not sure."

Carol gave me a warm smile. "It's your decision, Wally. But remember that you are out of Iran now and that we will protect you and your family. I don't think you want the Guards to become too suspicious about your stay in London."

"Wally, you have nothing to fear," Eric added. "We will take care of you. You have done a great job so far and your commitment to your country and your cooperation with us is much appreciated."

In spite of their assurances, I felt like a vulnerable child seeking shelter and security. I'd hoped Carol would have better ideas about what to do in my situation, but her only solution was for me to dive back into the world I longed to leave. Again, I felt I had no choice but to comply. I was leading two lives, but neither of them was my own.

Before I left, Carol stood and gave me a hug.

"I wish you luck and hope to see you back in the States," she said warmly. That would be the last time I ever saw her.

Explaining my decision to Somaya that night was another task. On my way home, I tried out various stories, but all of them seemed artificial and transparent. I so hated lying to my wife, especially because my lies once again had the potential for dire consequences for both her and Omid.

I finally decided to avoid preparing anything in advance. Instead, I would come up with something on the spot. When I saw Somaya, I told her that Rahim was in town and needed my help. At first she said nothing in response. Then her expression darkened.

"Why didn't you tell him no?" she said with barely controlled anger.

I tried to hold her hands, but she pulled away.

"You know that I did not quit the Guards when I came here," I said. "I just asked for a few months off because that was safer."

"So what? You are here and don't want to go back. In fact, you *cannot* go back now. You said you were through with them! They are not even paying you anymore."

I reached for her hands again, beseeching her to sit next to me on the bed.

"It's not that easy with the Guards. Rahim said . . . You know I am still officially part of the organization."

She turned her head away from me. "I can't believe you, Reza. I don't know what is in your empty head. I wish you did not even come here."

"I'm just going to do this until our paperwork is ready. I told Rahim that as soon as my wife is finished with school I am done with the Guards, and he agreed." The pain of that lie gnawed at me.

Somaya glanced in my direction, narrowed her green eyes, and shook her head. Without another word, she got into the bed, covered her head with the blanket, and turned her back to me. Once again, guilt overwhelmed me.

That sleepless night, I thought once more about the complicated journey I'd chosen to take. There was no way I could say no to Rahim without raising dangerous suspicions. There was also no way I could witness the Guards' activities in England and not let the CIA know about it. If only I could explain it all to Somaya, I knew she would understand. But this wasn't an available option, and none of the explanations I created instead of the truth satisfied her in any way. She was sticking with me because she loved me, but I was giving her every reason to question her continued loyalty.

The next morning, I stood in front of Sadri's small apartment building off Queen's Road by Richmond Park. A tall, skinny man in striped blue pajamas opened the door. I had called Sadri the night before and he was expecting me. He threw down his cigarette butt, gave me a quick hug, and guided me inside. "Come in, Reza *jon*," he said, the first time any Guards member had ever addressed me with this term of endearment rather than the usual "Baradar." Something about Sadri made me even more uncomfortable than I already was. My instincts told me that I shouldn't trust him, and I'd learned to pay close attention to my instincts.

The two Guards I'd been assigned to drive around were inside, sitting at a small square dining table having tea and English muffins. Even though Sadri knew Amiri had sent me, he started questioning why I was in England and where I was staying, and asking details about my family. I answered calmly, offering enough information to placate him and nothing more. I suppose I passed some sort of test, because after this he gave me the directions to a chemical factory in Billingham, a city about two hundred miles northeast of London.

"The meeting has been arranged with a sales manager named Charles Winston," Sadri said. "If you just take them there, they will deal with the salesperson themselves."

Sadri told me that the two men were in agriculture and that they had come to England to purchase a chemical to protect and preserve the soil of their farmlands. I pretended to believe this story and went about my job. I drove them to Billingham and waited several hours outside the factory for them to return.

On the way back, I sharpened my ears to listen to their whispered conversation, trying to read their lips via the rearview mirror as well.

"Sadri was right," the man sitting directly behind me said. "This Winston guy seemed easier to deal with than the one in Manchester."

"They are all stupid," the other man said with a smirk. "This white powder will turn all of them into *fertilizer.*"

I peeked at the man behind me again, and this time our eyes met. This startled me, so I quickly shot my eyes to the rearview mirror, elaborately surveying the road behind us. "That stupid car!" I said agitatedly. "Did you see that?" They both turned their heads to check the road. "The British think they are the best drivers in the world, but he was about to hit the car next to him." I shook my head and hoped this ruse stifled any suspicion.

Later, when I met Eric at a safe house outside London, I told him what I overheard on the trip back from Billingham about the chemical they sought to purchase. Eric recognized the compound right away, as well as its more nefarious function.

"The white powder—ammonium nitrate—is a dual compound

chemical. It's mainly used in agriculture as a fertilizer, but it is also used as an explosive agent. Having an agricultural use gives it certain legitimacy and makes it easier to acquire. Smart people!"

In our next meeting, Eric told me that Sadri was a fake name and that the apartment at Queen's Road was a safe house. I never saw Sadri again and I never learned his real name.

Rahim left London a few days after I drove the two agents to Billingham without my seeing him. He just called to say good-bye, telling me that I should take care of Amiri.

Amiri was in touch with me constantly, and I met with him nearly every week. I joined him in meetings held in the back rooms of mosques, in safe houses, and at the embassy. The Guards were infiltrating the opposition groups, especially the Mujahedin. They tracked the supporters of the Iranian monarchy who had made London a hub for their operations. They were also recruiting radical Muslims from the Pakistani and Afghan communities in England for their aid in transferring arms and explosives, assassinating Iranian opposition members, and plotting terrorist acts.

I'd come to London to initiate my escape from the Guards. Instead, I was becoming enmeshed in their dealings at a higher level. Meanwhile, I was reporting their activities to the CIA with increased fervor. I was once again fully ensconced in my double life.

27

EYE FOR AN EYE

IN DECEMBER 1988, Somaya found a small, furnished flat close to her parents in the Mayfair district. The one-bedroom apartment had a tiny den that barely accommodated Omid's bed. The kitchenette and the living/dining area were all in one room. Still, it was good to have our own place again—even though it gave Somaya the chance to complain freely about my continued work with the Guards.

"I hate this, Reza! You don't need to work with them anymore. Look at you—you still look like a *pasdar* with your unshaven face. *Ugh!* You promised that they would be out of our lives."

I explained to her that they had started paying me a good salary again for the little work I did in England, and that this money would help toward our start in America. I'd been making up many stories about money to explain why we had much more than we should. The income and bonuses I had been receiving from the CIA were in the bank almost untouched for several years, and the agency was now paying my expenses in London. I told Somaya that my mother left me an inheritance when she passed away. I told this same lie to Amiri. Then, when he offered me a few hundred British pounds in addition to the reimbursement costs for the rental car, I refused to take it, believing that this showed modesty and commitment to the revolution.

Around this time, Moheb Khan introduced me to a man named Fallah, and we established a good relationship right away. Fallah was a close friend of Somaya's family and he loved my son, which predisposed me to him quickly. He was an influential businessman in London, a broker for industrial supplies manufactured throughout England and most of Europe.

Amiri, who knew of this acquaintance, urged me to arrange a meeting with Fallah and a few newly arrived agents in town looking for industrial parts. The three newcomers were different from the other agents I'd met in London. They dressed in finely cut expensive suits, acted in a businesslike manner, and even drank alcohol at restaurants and ordered pork.

I rented a car and took them to Fallah's warehouse in the Stratford area of east London. Fallah greeted us and took us to his office, which was located at the end of a dark cold storage area lined with stacked boxes and large cartons on both sides. Some boxes were labeled with handwritten markings and some had diagrams of industrial materials and products. For the size of the warehouse, it was sparsely populated.

"Please have a seat," Fallah said as he pulled an extra chair from the corner of the room. "Sorry for the mess. I am getting orders on a daily basis and I am here by myself." He laughed. "My two colleagues are both making deliveries."

Hushang, one of the agents, handed Fallah a list of the tools they needed for high-precision machinery. He did not mention the use he planned for this machinery, but stressed that it was essential for the new company he and the others were running in Esfahan, a city in the heart of Iran. Fallah noted the considerable size of the order and promised to make the necessary calls to fill it.

"Fallah Khan, don't forget to give us your special discount," Hushang said as we were leaving the warehouse. "Reza is a good friend of ours."

Hushang invited me to have lunch at their hotel when I dropped them off. The other two men excused themselves and went to their rooms. I agreed, though I found Hushang a little intimidating. He was well mannered and polished, but his eyes carried an intensity that made me uncomfortable. At the same time, if Amiri had not introduced me to him, I never would have suspected that he worked for the Islamic government. Amiri had told me that Hushang had strong ties with Imam Khomeini's office. Since the English Secret Service kept an eye on people coming in, especially from Iran, it was imperative that he blend in.

In broken English, Hushang greeted the doorman, clerks, and bellhops as we entered the hotel. He grabbed a newspaper and led me to the restaurant off the lobby.

"They have good burgers here and the potatoes are delicious," Hushang said as he unfolded the *Guardian*. I reviewed the menu and decided to have the burger on his recommendation, realizing that the potatoes he referred to were fries, or what the British called chips. After the waitress took our order, he passed me the first few pages of the paper. I scanned the headlines.

"Were you here when this happened?" He folded the bottom half of the page, put it on the table over my setting, and pointed to an article. It was about the bombing of Pan Am Flight 103—the Lockerbie air disaster. I had learned about it at Moheb Khan's house when we were packing our belongings to move into our new home. A Boeing 747 jet had exploded over Scotland, killing everyone on board and several others on the ground.

"Do you know what they say in their Bible?" Hushang said, narrowing his eyes. " 'And if any mischief follow, then thou shalt give life for life, eye for eye, tooth for tooth, hand for hand, foot for foot, burning for burning, wound for wound, stripe for stripe.' "

A shiver ran along my spine as he uttered this passage in perfect English, though his diction had been tortured earlier. *Who is he?* I wondered, taking a gulp of my drink.

"What do you mean?" I said, knowing it was a stupid question.

The waitress came with our food. I was thankful for this, as I needed the distraction to gather myself.

Hushang picked up his burger and took a big bite. "Rahim told me you were a smart guy, Reza." He wiped the ketchup on his chin with his finger and then leaned toward me. "Do you think we would let these bastards get away with their deadly attack on our civilian airliner? Do you think *that* was an accident?"

I remembered watching the news with Kazem less than a year ago in the cafeteria at our base about the Iran Air jetliner shot down by the U.S. Navy, killing three hundred civilians. Rahim had told Kazem and me that Rafsanjani promised retaliation.

"Kazem also said that it wasn't an accident. He thought the Americans did this in an effort to destroy our movement." I sipped my drink. "God bless his soul."

"Yes, Kazem was a great *pasdar*," Hushang said with sadness in his voice. Then his tone grew stronger. "Well, they got their punishment, Reza. Eye for an eye."

"They deserved that," I said, feeling the now familiar self-reproach associated with playing along.

Hushang looked around. Since we were there later than lunch hour, we were the only diners in the restaurant. "We have Hajj Agha Rafsanjani to thank. He delivered on his promise for retaliation. We also must thank our Palestinian brothers who helped us with this. The German police are even investigating the contacts of one of the Palestinians over the radio transmitter that carried the bomb."

I couldn't believe he was telling me this much. "Hajj Agha Rafsanjani is an asset to our Islamic Revolution. He is a smart man," I said. I took a bite of my meal and swallowed hard. "You were right, the burgers are good here."

"I'm surprised that you eat *haraam*."

This stopped me cold. I couldn't believe I'd made this mistake in front of him. Muslims were not supposed to eat unlawful meat—only the meat from animals killed by Muslims according to Islamic laws.

"It's hard to live outside and do all your duties, isn't it?" Hushang said as he folded his napkin and put it on his plate.

"I usually eat *halal* meat," I said quickly. "But today, just because you suggested the food . . ." I let my voice trail off. I knew that I had made a rookie mistake and I beat myself up for it. My job was to act and behave like a devout Muslim so that everyone associated with the Guards would trust me. In my mind, I heard Steve, my first CIA contact, saying, "Never let your guard down. You'll stay alive longer."

"Hushang! Hushang!"

We turned our heads to the voice. It was one of the other brothers.

"Come on upstairs," the man said. "You missed some phone calls and they will be calling back shortly."

Hushang looked at me, and I told him that I would take care of the bill.

"Next time on me, then," he said, pressing my shoulder with his hand before he left with the other man.

I sat in the restaurant for a short while after they left, trying to clear my thoughts. I was frightened. Frightened of Hushang and what he said about the Pan Am flight—the "eye for an eye" comment; how he emphasized "burning for burning" with such menace in his voice. Frightened of how he stared into my eyes and the surprise he expressed at my eating *haraam* meat. Once again, I felt that no matter how much the CIA covered me while I was in London, I had to be even more cautious. I was not just among fanatic Islamists; I was among ruthless criminals.

I left a generous tip for the waitress and decided to call Eric to let the CIA know what I had learned about the Pan Am incident. As I was about to open the double glass door of the hotel to go out, I saw the shadow of a heavily built man behind the door. I moved to the side to let him in before I exited.

"Reza?"

I raised my head and saw Rasool.

"Rasool? *Salam*, big guy! What are you doing here?"

Rasool hugged me and lifted me off the ground. "It is nice to see you, Reza."

I had not heard from him since the last time I saw him at our base when he was ready to go to England to "pursue his education." He was still well groomed in a nice gray suit with a long black wool coat over it.

We stepped outside the hotel and chatted a little bit. Rasool knew about Kazem's death and spoke mournfully about it. He told me that he was going to meet with Hushang and the other men. He said he would be in touch and suggested that we get together.

"I have to go now, but don't hide yourself," he said, handing me a business card. "Call me."

The card read RUSSELL CONSULTING SERVICES. It had no address. Only a phone number and the name Russell rather than Rasool.

I arranged a meeting with Eric for the next day. Feeling especially apprehensive about getting to the safe house, I transferred several times in the Tube, walked a number of blocks, caught a cab, and went to a bookstore, where I bought a few books.

When I got to the safe house, Eric was not alone. After many years with little change in my interactions with the CIA and building a bond with Carol, the agency had started rotating my contacts. I'd quickly built a good working relationship with Eric, but now he introduced me to my new contact, Andrew. Unlike Carol and Eric, to whom I'd taken an immediate liking, Andrew seemed chilly and opinionated. I wasn't happy with this sudden shift, especially now. Regardless, though, I had a job to do. I passed along the information about the Pan Am flight, as well as the names and descriptions of Hushang and the other agents, and both Eric and Andrew expressed shock at the possibility of Iran's involvement in the bombing. As I did this, though, I grew increasingly uneasy with how things were unfolding for me in England. Things were becoming too tense with the Guards, and now I had a CIA contact who made me uncomfortable.

I wanted out of all this.

28

DOUBLE AGENT

THE DEATH OF Khomeini in June 1989 brought all of the Guards and Khomeini's adherents in London together in the Iranian embassy. Disbelief, feelings of emptiness, and the grief at the loss of an icon caused weeping to run infectiously through the crowd. A mourning ceremony was held for him at the central mosque in London and many Muslims from different nationalities gathered to share their sadness. I attended the event because I had to, but I sat in a corner by myself, closed my eyes, and thought about all of the damage he had done to Iran—how he'd ruined a nation and killed so many innocent people. I wished his legacy would be buried with him. I wished the West would help us restore the Iran I loved. If ever there was a time to do so, this was it.

"Consider Rafsanjani the new king of Iran," Andrew said casually in a meeting we had a couple of months after Khomeini's death. As was the case with so much of what he said to me, this rubbed me the wrong way. I had just finished telling him that America needed to do more to free the people of Iran from the tyrannical rule of the mullahs, but Andrew believed that George H.W. Bush's plan to encourage better communications with Rafsanjani was the best approach toward improving relations between the two countries.

Rafsanjani became the president of Iran after Khomeini died, and Ali Khamenei, who had been president, became Khomeini's successor as Supreme Leader. Khamenei was not even an ayatollah. Yet he was enough of a radical to ensure that the regime retained the power for which it lusted. Before the revolution, Ali Khamenei was a mullah performing Rowzeh Khooni in the city of Mashhad. Just like Mullah Aziz, he had charged a few dollars for the sermons he performed and owned a donkey. Now he was the spiritual leader of a once great country.

Andrew further incensed me by suggesting that Rafsanjani was a reformer who could make life better for Iranians. "Negotiation is our best policy," he said.

"Rafsanjani is no different from the rest of them," I responded angrily. "You can't trust him. Have you forgotten his involvement in the Marine barracks attack in Lebanon along with the radicals ruling Iran? Or his involvement in the Lockerbie bombing? He encourages terrorism."

Andrew did not respond, other than looking at me disdainfully. Without saying so explicitly, he was making it clear that my opinion wasn't welcome.

President Bush, who was the vice president during the Iran–Contra affair, was aware of the negotiations back then. Now, as the leader of the free world, he was hoping that Rafsanjani would deliver on the promise he had once made to Robert McFarlane, President Reagan's national security adviser, to normalize relations between the two countries once Khomeini was dead. This amazed me. Hadn't the Americans learned their lesson from the deceitful promise Rafsanjani made them to aid in the release of American hostages held in Lebanon? After the Iranians received the many shipments of weaponry offered as an overture, they not only didn't develop a healthier relationship with America but, in fact, assisted Hezbollah in taking more hostages. Believing that Rafsanjani would bring positive change to Iran was dangerous not only for my country, but for America as well. One hundred and eighty Americans had died on Pan Am flight 103. This seemed like an especially foolhardy form of political maneuvering. After all, the CIA was aware that the information Hushang provided me during lunch was neither publicly available nor confirmed by the investigators of the Pan Am crash at the time. (Interestingly, this maneuvering continues to this day. In August 2009, Scottish authorities freed Abdelbaset al-Megrahi, the Libyan convicted for downing the plane, just when his legal team was ready to present U.S. Defense Intelligence Agency documents implicating Iran.)

My relationship with Andrew continued to get frostier. Then, one day, on my way to the embassy to meet up with Amiri, I called Andrew to set up another meeting.

"It's good that you called, Wally," Andrew said. "We have to meet as soon as possible. It has to be by tonight."

His tone concerned me, and I wanted to meet him in the safe house immediately to find out what was so urgent. But I could not be late for my meeting with Amiri. Apprehensively, I made my way to the embassy. Amiri had someone else in his office when I got there and I needed to wait about fifteen minutes before he summoned me.

"Reza, I have a very important assignment for you," he said when he called me in. He handed me a piece of paper. "There's a certain individual who we suspect is involved in antirevolutionary activities. You'll find the details on that paper. We need to know who else he's involved with and what they're up to. Rasool is to be your partner, so call him and get started on this right away."

This alarmed me. Why would Amiri pair me up with Rasool?

As I left the embassy, chimes from the nearby Patriarchal Cathedral announced that it was four o'clock in the afternoon. My meeting with Andrew was not until seven. That left plenty of time to hang around town and make sure I was not being watched or followed. But instead of going through my usual routine, I simply decided to walk along the Thames to gather my thoughts about the latest complications in my twin life.

"Come on in, Wally," Andrew said officiously as I entered the safe house. My dislike for him had grown to the point where even hearing his voice set me on edge.

Andrew was not alone. A well-built man in his midthirties with a buzz haircut was sitting in the living room and looked up at me with anticipation. He rose and introduced himself as Gary. I learned quickly that he would be my new contact. Andrew was leaving because his father had passed away in the States.

"I'm sorry for your loss," I said to Andrew, hiding the fact that while I was indeed sorry his father had died, I was glad our association was ending. While I'd never gotten along with Andrew, I got the immediate sense that I would have a good relationship with Gary. His firm handshake and his clear enthusiasm for what I was doing encouraged me.

I told Gary about Amiri's assignment and about my growing, though somewhat confusing relationship with Rasool. As I got to know Rasool more, I realized he was not like the other Guards. He cared about Iran and expressed outrage at the assassinations of the opposition inside and outside the country. And while he was a devout Muslim, he did not seem happy with the Guards' activities in England. I related conversations to Gary where Rasool revealed this, and I told him that I thought Rasool seemed sincere. But as was always the case with anyone associated with the Guards, he could have been trying to trap me.

Gary made a note and promised to find out about Rasool and what he was up to. I did not know how Gary was going to find out if the big guy was a committed Muslim or whether he cared about Iran, but I trusted that he knew what he was doing. I got up to leave and he patted me on the back, calling me a great man.

"There are only a few men who can make a difference, Wally. And you are one of them."

After my difficult association with Andrew, I found these words welcome and inspiring.

Amiri had instructed me to shave my beard for the mission and dress in a nice suit. The experience had a surreal quality to it. I was shaving now to participate in an undercover activity for the Guards. For so long, the very beard I was shaving had protected me as an undercover agent for the CIA. Once again, I felt my identity shifting in ways that left me feeling unsteady.

Rasool picked me up a few blocks from my house. Our instructions were to set up surveillance in a Muslim neighborhood in the Tower Hamlets area in the shadow of the Tower of London. A prominent Iranian professor who had been teaching for some time in London was the target. Rasool knew where to go and what to do. We drove for a few miles and parked in an alley off Artillery Lane; we would walk the rest of the way. The entire exercise made me intensely nervous, but Rasool seemed extremely calm, talking casually about aristocrats who had been beheaded at the Tower prison and pointing out different buildings and restaurants.

We walked for several blocks. The entire time, I tried to keep up with Rasool's big strides. As we got closer to the Tower Hamlets district, we made the transition from a thriving business area to a working-class neighborhood.

"This way!" Rasool said, pointing to a three-story commercial building with a Bangladeshi restaurant on the first floor. I followed him into the restaurant, not knowing what we were to do in there. He walked into the kitchen as if he had been there before, waving at the men by the stove, and then to a door at the end of the kitchen. Despite an EMPLOYEES ONLY sign, Rasool opened it. The door led to a stairway and we went up two flights, then down a narrow hall to an empty warehouse.

It dawned on me that all of this could have been a setup to eliminate me. If the Guards had somehow found out about Wally and wanted to assassinate me, this would have been a perfect location. For all I knew, Russell Consulting Services regularly provided this kind of "consulting" for the regime.

"Walk toward that window," Rasool said as we stood in the bare room. He pointed to the left corner as he bent toward his shoes. *He is getting his gun out,* I thought. But he'd only been bending to tie his shoelaces. I allowed myself one deep breath.

"Take a look out the window," he said.

I moved to do so when I saw Rasool take a small black item from inside his jacket. How stupid for me to think he'd hid a gun in his socks when he could carry it in his pocket. That's when I knew he was going to shoot me in the back while I looked out the window. My chest tightened.

Palming the black item, he stuck out his arm.

I backed up and tripped, landing hard on the floor.

"*Cheteh,* Reza? What the hell is wrong with you?"

He was pointing a pair of black binoculars at me.

I said nothing for a few moments, and then blurted, "I thought you had a gun."

He frowned and shook his head. "What? I wanted you to take a look at the apartment building across the street."

I tried to think quickly. "Oh. I thought you wanted me to shoot somebody."

He sat down next to me, dropping the binoculars on the floor and wiping his face with his palm.

"If the time comes, I definitely would not recommend you." He offered a bittersweet smile. "But pray to God that time never comes."

He slid backward on the floor and found the wall to lean on. I followed his move.

"Reza, I don't understand why you want to be part of all this. You seem like a nice guy. You don't even look like any of them. You should pack your bags and leave. Go back to America. I know you were there once. I wish I could get on with my life, too, but I am too deeply involved."

This confession struck me mute. Was he trying to get me to say something incriminating?

He closed his eyes and blew a deep breath. "I wish I could go away, far away, perhaps to America. Reza, you don't want to be part of this. Assassinating innocent people . . ." He loosened his necktie. "They killed a father and his son in their apartment here in London. They were monarchists, supporters of the shah. Did you know that our government had our agents contact Ghassemlou, the Kurdistan Democratic Party leader, in Vienna for a meeting to offer peace?

Then our agents killed him and his aides. Did you know that Ahmad Talebi, a fighter pilot who had sought refuge in Switzerland, was shot dead in the streets of Geneva? He was married. He had children."

A few weeks earlier, Rasool had talked about how he resented the killings and how unjust the ruling Islamic government was. I felt at the time that he was just testing me. But now, sitting there next to me with his hands wrapped around his head, I knew he trusted me. Did I dare trust him back?

Rasool bent to grab the binoculars and slowly got up to look through the window. "Here is the professor in his library," he said, adjusting the lens. "Do you see it in yourself to kill this man? And after him another one and then another?"

"I would never kill anybody," I said under my breath, mostly to myself.

He sat back on the floor. "They'll make you, Reza."

I shivered. I forced my shoulders against the wall and sat up straight. Had he already killed someone? Many people? He grabbed a pack of cigarettes from his jacket and offered me one. I still had not said anything, still wondering if I could safely express my feelings to Rasool. I decided that I couldn't risk it.

"We will tell Amiri that this guy is not involved in anything," Rasool said to break the silence. "We'll wait a week before telling him, though."

"We'll do whatever you suggest. Amiri said I should take your lead."

When Rasool looked at me, I saw confusion on his face. Was he expecting me to engage him?

I couldn't take the chance of finding out. We left the warehouse and he suggested that we go in different directions. He headed to his car and I took the Tube back home. I stopped at a phone kiosk on my way to the Tube and called Gary, telling him what happened at the warehouse. I must have sounded upset, because he made an effort to comfort me and said that he had some news on Rasool. We set up a meeting for the next day.

When I got home, I found Somaya sitting on the couch crying. She lifted her head as I entered, wiped the tears away, and looked at me in shock.

"You shaved," she said, choking back tears.

I touched my face. "Yes, I did." I sat down next to her. "Is everything okay? Is Omid all right?"

"Oh, yes. But . . . but I just had a call from your uncle." Her shoulders shook. "It's Agha Joon . . . he has passed away." She sobbed. "I am sorry, Reza." She held on to my hand as I got up to leave the room. While I knew Somaya wanted to offer me comfort, I needed to be alone. I couldn't talk about my grandfather with anyone right then. Instead, I allowed guilt to overwhelm me. It seemed so foolish now that I hadn't tried harder to stay in touch with him since I left Iran. Ridiculously, I'd left that to Somaya. I was too busy. Too busy with things I should have never allowed get between me and a man who was like a father to me—or even more. How could I have had no time to maintain my bond with the man who shaped me, the man who I spent most of my childhood with, the man who taught me to love life?

I went back outside, sat on the steps in front of our building, and looked at the sky peeking through the clouds. Like my own life, the sky of London was in conflict. There were no stars shining, no rain clearing the air, and for a long time, no sun to brighten up life—just an ominous wind blowing in uncertain directions.

My grandfather was gone. He was all I had left of my past. Every time I thought of Naser, Agha Joon was there. Every time I thought of Kazem, Agha Joon was there. Every time I thought of the mess I was in, I thought of Agha Joon and his faith in me. While I feared that I might never see him again when I left Iran, the reality hit me so much harder than I expected. I wanted so badly to go back to Iran. Being present at his funeral was the least I could do. But that wasn't even remotely possible. I held my head in my hands and choked the scream inside me as I begged God to free me from the constraints that kept me from grieving as any normal person might. I allowed the rage and frustration to build within me.

And then I had no choice but to let it go. Agha Joon was gone, Reza had to share his life with Wally—and Wally had a job to do. I had to persevere through the pain. I had to conduct the role fate had presented me.

My next meeting with Gary was at a small hotel downtown instead of the safe house. It was a few miles away from my flat. I was tired, as I had spent the entire sleepless night mourning for Agha Joon, but I decided to walk anyway. I checked the map, memorized the route, and continued to think of Agha Joon and the past. *Naser and me splashing in the creek behind my grandfather's house that led all the way to Kazem's neighborhood . . .*

I saw my turn, left on Victoria Street.

. . . Naser whistling and playing with the toad in his pocket.

"Let the poor thing go, Naser. . . ."

The sound of a car horn—unusual in England—shook me from my reverie. I realized I was crossing the street against the red light. Embarrassed, I quickened my step, noticing a man in an oversized green jacket walking on the other side of the road and going in the opposite direction.

. . . Kazem joined us, and the three of us walked back to Agha Joon's. We talked about our soccer matches. We'd won for a third week in a row. . . .

I thought I saw the man in the green jacket again at the corner of Marshman Street. How could that be possible? He had been going the opposite way.

. . . "What are you going to be, Reza, when you grow up?" Kazem asked.

"Not a mullah, for sure!" Naser said, laughing loudly. I laughed with him. Kazem frowned at us. . . .

I was sure I saw the man again before I turned to Kensington. Yes! I remembered his jacket. But now he was waiting at a bus station there. I hadn't planned for a detour because I was following the route I memorized from the map. I chastised myself for my laxity. But when I looked at the bus station again, the man was no longer there.

To my right was a small alley leading to another street. I walked through the alley with plans to go to the next main street, walk a few blocks, and then come back to where I was. I took one more careful look around, not seeing anything suspicious. Perhaps I was worried for no reason.

. . . The double door to Grandpa's house was halfway open and Khanoom Bozorg was there talking to her guests. Naser told us to untie the reins of the donkey. . . .

Having walked several blocks, I backtracked before I got lost. I eventually found the same alley and went back through. I checked around me again before continuing.

. . . The trembling voice of Khanoom Bozorg calling my name . . . "Reza . . . Reza . . ."

She was biting her lips. I looked for Agha Joon. I needed him to protect me. I needed to hide behind his robe. . . .

With a thump, I ran directly into a pedestrian. I looked up. I was face-to-face with the man in the green jacket. My heart stopped beating and I started to sweat.

A strong English accent rang in my ears. "Oh, dear, I am so sorry. I did not see you."

He seemed as shocked as I was. I knew he was up to something, but he continued to walk in the other direction. My heart started pounding now. How had I let my guard down? Who was he?

For the next half hour, I walked back and forth on the same street, pretending to window-shop but using reflections to check around me. I sat at an outdoor café, acting as though I was casually people watching when I was specifically looking for one person. I didn't see the man in the green jacket again.

"British Intelligence—MI6," Gary said when I met up with him. "They must be on to you."

What in the world is he talking about?

"Maybe it's time to let them know," he said.

As unnerved as I was, Gary calmed me down, explaining that British intelligence might know about my activities with the Guards. He told me that he would let them know that I was with the CIA, and that he would arrange for us to meet with them. He assured me that MI6 would not create problems for me from that point on.

I wasn't sure that I could handle a meeting with yet another intelligence agency. But what was causing me the most stress at that point was Rasool's suggestion that the Guards might want me to kill somebody. Gary told me that he learned that Rasool had been under agency surveillance—based on my report to Carol—since he moved to England in 1984. Gary said there was a strong possibility that Rasool was not entirely devoted to the Islamic government. He had secretly dated an English woman for a few years, and they even spotted him with her on a beach in Istanbul.

"Rasool told me he was too involved to get away," I said. "What if they make me get more involved? I might never be able to leave."

"You have *us*, Wally!" He smiled. "As soon as your papers are ready, you are on your way to freedom."

I told Gary that Rasool told me he wished he could go to America. This caught Gary's attention, and he didn't say anything for a few moments. He crossed and uncrossed his legs and finally said, "How about you introduce him to us, Wally?"

I could feel my eyes popping out of my head as I tried to understand what he was implying.

"Not like that, Wally! You can bring up the idea of going to America and tell him that you know an immigration lawyer or something. Once you introduce us, I'll take it from there."

I knew what he was thinking. He wasn't suggesting that he could help Rasool get a visa. He wanted to recruit him as an agent. I told Gary that I needed some time to think about it.

There was a British intelligence officer present at our next meeting, a stiff, very proper man named Ted Smith. Smith was eager to get as much information as he could from me. He had a list of names and photos of suspected Iranian agents. Among them I was shocked to see pictures of Moheb Khan, Somaya's father, and his friend Fallah, the owner of the industrial machinery warehouse where I took Hushang and the two other agents. I identified as many faces and names as possible, specifying those I knew to be working for the Guards and feeling an even stronger commitment to weed out the innocents, like Moheb Khan. Apparently, Fallah was involved more than I knew. Smith told me that his company was a front.

Connecting Rasool with the CIA was a huge risk. It could jeopardize my chance of getting my family to America and even put my life at risk. But taking risks had become a matter of course with me. One day, when Somaya and Omid were out, I invited Rasool to my apartment. To my surprise, the subject came up naturally. Rasool commented on a picture of Somaya holding Omid and I told him that my wife had a dream of finishing her education in America.

"She wants to be a pediatrician and she's thinking about Harvard or Stanford," I said, inventing this on the spot. In reality Somaya was still unsure what she wanted her major to be. "But if she gets accepted to UCLA, that would be ideal. I used to live in LA and UCLA has one of the better programs for medicine in the country."

Rasool stared at the distance. "I'd like to go to America." Then he made eye contact with me. "I told you that before. It is my dream, Reza."

"Why don't you go, then?"

"You are joking, Reza! I need a visa."

I shrugged. "Why don't you just apply for one?"

"If it was that easy to get a visa, Reza, half of the population in the world would have gone there by now."

"If you are serious about it, I am sure there is a way. People travel to the U.S. every day. You should be able to get some kind of visa . . . wait!" I walked toward the dining table, which was piled with newspapers and magazines, leafing through them. "Somaya showed me something the other day. Let me see if I can find that ad. It was in one of these papers." My hands started shaking as I continued my "search." I knew exactly where the ad was.

"Here it is," I said at last, holding up an Iranian newspaper. Gary had perfectly doctored one page to include an ad for me to show to Rasool. "'Immigration Lawyer for Iranians,'" I read. "'If you need a visa to travel to America, we can help. Contact Gary Sullivan . . .'"

Rasool came over to look at the ad. "Between you and me, I wouldn't mind trying him."

"Maybe he could get your visa," I said nonchalantly.

"How about you? Do you think you'll go to this guy for one as well?"

I'd prepared for such a question. "We will if Somaya gets accepted to a university in the U.S. She definitely wants to continue her education. But I need to ask Rahim. He is still my commander. He is expecting me to go back home after I am done here. If he wants me back, I will arrange for Somaya to go to America by herself."

Rasool nodded. "You won't be asking Rahim."

"What do you mean?"

"Rahim is no longer at our base. He had a heart attack. He resigned and moved to Kerman with his family."

I sighed. Rahim was not very old, but he was overweight and smoked heavily. Rasool told me that Rahim had had heart problems for a long time.

"You should come to this lawyer with me," Rasool said. "Call him and arrange a meeting. We'll go together."

I hadn't prepared for that. And even as I agreed to do as Rasool suggested, I wondered if he was playing me after all. Though my conversation with Rasool had gone extraordinarily well, connecting him with Gary could still turn out to be a grievous error.

29

FREE AT LAST?

WE SET THE appointment with "Gary Sullivan" for the following week. Gary mapped out the route and went over the details
involving the lookouts and the signals. If there was any evidence we
were being followed, the deal was off and Gary would not show up.
Making the excuse that the law office building was being remod-
eled, I told Rasool that Mr. Sullivan arranged for us to meet at the
Red Lion Inn, an intimate and dimly lit restaurant near St. James's
Palace.

My anxiety increased as we got closer to the meeting day. I
called Gary to see if we could meet one more time before we got
together with Rasool. It was not that I needed to rehearse things
or go over the plan; that part was quite clear. I needed to clarify
my situation with the agency. The fact that this latest undertaking
could possibly be the riskiest made me uneasy regardless of how
many times I played it out in my head. I could have told Gary
that I didn't want to help him recruit Rasool—there was already
enough tension in my life. But the same thing that made me take
this dangerous journey in the first place was forcing me to put
everything in jeopardy again. I believed that Rasool would serve as
my replacement. He'd watch over the Guards' activities from that
point on, delivering information to the CIA that would eventually
lead to Iran's freedom. And his reward down the road would be a
visa to his dreamland.

Gary understood my concerns and agreed to see me that afternoon at the safe house.

"I know that our papers might not be ready yet," I said when we sat down, "but it is very important for us to agree that should you and Rasool reach an understanding, I cannot be involved with the agency anymore. Two reasons . . ." I paused. "First, it's possible Rasool could turn on you and tell Amiri or the Guards that the connection with you was through me. Second, I would not—could not under any circumstance—continue my acquaintance or contact with him if he joins the agency. That would be too stressful and alarming for both of us, being in the Guards. Is there any way you could put our papers on the fast track?"

"Actually," Gary said, "before I left my office today, I got a call from the American consulate. Your papers are ready, Wally. You are good to go. Isn't that exciting?"

It could indeed have been. But I couldn't help feeling that this "coincidence" was a form of betrayal on the part of the CIA. Could it be that my papers had been ready long before this and that they did not tell me because they wanted me to reel in Rasool?

"You don't seem happy about it, Wally. Is everything okay?"

"Oh, sure. I'm just worried about tomorrow."

Gary patted my shoulder. "We have taken care of all of the details. Just do what you have been doing all these years. You've done a great job, Wally, and if things go wrong, we have you covered."

After I left the safe house, before getting to the Tube, I walked along the Thames. The colorful lights from the barges, ships, and ferries populated the river and cast a dancing sparkle on the water, reflecting a memorable picture of a lively night in London. I leaned against a wall, lit a cigarette, and looked out at the river. I thought about how close I was to freedom. So close that I could feel it, just like the breeze from the Thames moistening my face. *Somaya is going to be so happy when I tell her that it is all over,* I thought. This made me feel better than I'd felt in a very long time.

"And it is over," I said to the water. "It is all over."

The next morning, I got up early. Before Somaya and Omid left for school, I told my wife that I would check with Harriet Johnson, our immigration lawyer, to see if she had any news for us.

"I might even go to her office today," I said.

"You should. Why is it taking so long? She said six months to a year. It is way more than a year now. Tell her we need an answer soon."

"I told her that the last time I called her. She said it was just a matter of time now. Hopefully, she has something for us today."

When Somaya left with our son, I got ready for what could be the most momentous day of my life—if I made it through. Even though the CIA had me covered, considerable danger existed. Maybe this was a trap and Rasool was planning to assassinate Gary and me at the restaurant. Anything was possible.

When I put my suit on, I felt a twinge in my back. I was only thirty-four, but the burdens of my life bowed me like an old man. "What have you done, Reza?" I asked my reflection in the mirror, thinking about how freedom and life itself could still be snatched from me in the final hour. I felt a ball wadded in my throat and tears coming to my eyes. Why couldn't this have been simpler? Why did I need to suffer through every step of this experience?

Seeking reinforcement, I turned to the closet where I kept some of my old books and papers and scrambled through the pages of a book to find Naser's picture hidden inside Roya's letter. The picture was fading. Roya's letter was torn at the creases, not readable anymore. But I knew every word of it. I could see Naser under the peeling layers of the picture still looking at me.

For many years, those two pieces of paper had motivated me to go on. I was not sure that strength was still there. Like Roya's torn letter and Naser's faded picture, my conviction was vanishing.

Still, I grabbed my coat and left the house.

The signals were all cleared, the lookouts at their posts. Apparently, no one had followed Rasool and me. We entered the restaurant, and I spotted Gary already seated at a table.

"Shoot! I should have asked him what he looked like, or what he would be wearing." I shook my head, realizing that Gary and I had forgotten to discuss how we should show acquaintance at the restaurant—not so smart for a CIA operative and a spy.

Gary glanced at us and looked down at a piece of paper on the table. I turned my head away.

"Could that be him?" Rasool said, pointing at Gary. "He has a bunch of stuff with him."

"Where?" I asked. Rasool pointed again. It was a small restaurant, but busy enough for me to be able to pretend. "Oh, that man? Maybe. Should we go and ask him?"

Rasool stopped a passing waitress. "Excuse me, but we are here to meet somebody. I think that's him. Could you ask that man over there if he is expecting anyone?"

The waitress went to do as Rasool asked. Meanwhile, Rasool continued to study Gary. "That man looks more like a military man than a lawyer, if that's him," he said.

Indeed, Gary was ex-military, and his broad shoulders, physique, and, of course, the buzz haircut testified to that.

"But, big guy, you can take him down in a second if he tries to mess with us," I joked.

At that moment, Gary got up and came toward us. "Thank you so much for agreeing to meet with me here." He offered his hand. "I am Gary Sullivan, and you are . . . ?"

I reached his hand first. "I am Reza Kahlili."

"Glad to meet you, Reza. And you must be . . . ? Sorry, I did not get your name."

"I am Rasool. You can call me Russell."

After we settled at our table, Gary sensed my nervousness and knocked over a glass of water as he bent to grab his briefcase. The time required to clean up the spill allowed me to compose myself.

Then Gary moved on to the reason for the meeting. "A tourist visa is possible if you have somebody in the States offering an invitation and an affidavit of support. We can try that if you just want to go for a short time. If a company in the States sponsors you, perhaps an H1 visa would be another option. A student visa, if you apply at a university, is one way . . . or a business visa . . ." Gary continued with the other possibilities. I was afraid he'd mention political asylum. That would be a red flag for all of us. But he was smarter than that.

"Why would I need a lawyer if I had a family member who could send me an invitation?" Rasool said casually. "If I got accepted in a school, or sponsored by a company, I could apply on my own."

"You are right, but if it were that easy, there would not be a line at the consulate door and a disappointed rejected crowd leaving it. Even for those who have the invitation or sponsorship, it is unlikely to get permission to enter the States. And not everybody is lucky enough to have a relative there to prepare the ground for them. That's where I come in."

"But how likely is a visa for somebody like me who has nobody in the States?" Rasool asked.

"I have done this a lot, Russell. Ten out of ten get their visas." Gary paused. "Of course, there is money involved."

"How much are we talking about?"

"What I would like to do is . . ." Gary looked at his watch. "I have another appointment soon on the other side of London, but what I'd like to do is to set up another meeting with you to go over everything. I need to get some information from you and examine your options." Then he looked at me. "Reza, are you also interested in moving to America?"

"My wife is. She is in school now, but she thinks finishing her education in America would be ideal. Unfortunately, all of her family members live in Europe. It will be hard for her to be away from them. We have discussed this briefly, but I will talk to her again and see if she really wants to live in America. I'll get back to you."

Gary then excused himself to make a call, informing his "next client" that he might be a little late. That was part of our plan. He wanted me to see what Rasool's reaction was. If Rasool was not sure,

I had to convince him that he should make another appointment with Gary. And if he was already set to do so, my job was easier. But either way, Gary needed my signal to do his part.

"I think I like this man. I trust him. I should keep going with this," Rasool said.

"Whatever you do, big guy, don't pay him up front. He seems trustworthy, but first you have to make sure he can produce a visa for you."

He laughed. "Don't worry, Reza. I'm a businessman myself. I know the rules."

Gary came back. I reached inside my pocket to get a pen. Gary noticed my signal.

"Okay. Where were we?" Gary sipped his coffee. "About the fee. Yes. I'm not going to charge you for this meeting, and as for the next one, should you decide to go forward, my consultation fee is a hundred fifty pounds. But since my office might not be ready by then, and I know it is inconvenient to meet in a restaurant, I will not charge you for that one, either. After that, should you want me to proceed, I will apply that fee to the total cost."

"That sounds fair," I stated.

"Yeah. I think that sounds good," Rasool said. "I would like to proceed and find out if I can get a visa."

Gary handed his business card to both of us, and Rasool exchanged his.

"I will call you to set up something in a week and let you know what documents to bring with you," Gary told Rasool. Then he turned to me. "You should also talk to your wife and give me a call, Reza."

Rasool seemed content. Something nagged at me, though. If he really wanted to immigrate to America, he could have found an immigration lawyer in London at any time during the years he lived in England. When we were alone again, my curiosity got the best of me and I asked him why he'd never tried to do this before.

Rasool's expression became wistful. "I did. I had a girlfriend. . . ."

He paused. "Liz was British-American and did not need a visa. She left for America and asked me to join her." He stopped and looked for his pack of cigarettes, lighting one before he spoke again. "I saw a lawyer who told me that it was very easy. If I would just marry my girlfriend or get engaged, I would not even need a lawyer. I could go to America in a matter of a few months. Just apply through the American consulate either as a spouse to a citizen or under an engagement visa."

"What happened?"

"I called Liz and told her the good news." He puffed on his cigarette, staring down at the ground. "She said she was sorry but she did not think we should see each other anymore." He crushed his cigarette under his shoes.

I felt a rush of empathy for him. "I am sorry, big guy. Really sorry."

We parted and I found myself hoping that everything worked out for him. That he would take the CIA up on their offer, do good work with them for a few years, and then find a safe home on American shores.

Meanwhile, my own passage was nearly complete. Somaya was exuberant when I told her we were on our way.

"Reza, I can't believe this. I am so happy!" she said, giving me a huge hug. Before I could drown myself in her arms, though, she pulled away.

"What's wrong?" I asked in surprise.

She sat on the couch and pulled her legs up against her chest. The sudden change in her mood left me feeling unsteady.

"I am just not sure about this." She bit her nails and took a moment before continuing. "You know how long I waited for you to come here, away from your little mysterious life." She offered me a look that said that she knew I had not told her everything. "But it's been more than a year since you've gotten here, and you're still the same man you were back in Iran. You are so attached to this revolution. I just don't know, Reza. I don't know what you see that I cannot see."

It was clear that she was fighting her emotions as she spoke. I wanted to help her with this, but I also knew that I needed to let her say what she needed to say.

"I cannot get my hopes up just because we are moving somewhere else," she continued. "What if you have more obligations and more work to do for the Guards once we are there? I don't know if going to America is a good idea anymore."

She dropped her head.

I sat next to her, wrapping an arm around her. "I know. I know I have not been the husband you've deserved. I know I've neglected you and our son. Just give me another chance. We'll start our dream life. I'll make up for all the years I was not there for you and Omid. My work with the Guards is over. Completely. I promise."

Somaya looked at me and wiped her eyes with the end of her sleeve. "How do I know this isn't just more talk, Reza. I've waited so long for you to change. I am just so frustrated."

"I know. And I know that I can't possibly say anything to convince you that I mean everything I say this time. But I promise you with all of my heart."

I don't know if Somaya believed me or if she just decided to go along with me because of her incredible loving nature, but she started planning our trip and preparing Omid for the new and exciting life we were about to lead.

With great trepidation, I called Amiri to let him know that I was leaving the Guards. Even as I waited for him to come to the phone, I wondered if he was going to try to convince me to stay—or do something even more persuasive. As it turned out, though, I had misplaced my fears, at least in this case. Amiri said that since Rahim was no longer my commander and since I had no pending engagements in London, leaving was up to me.

"Whenever you are back, call me," he said. "If there is something you can do, I'll let you know."

The ease with which he let me go stunned me. Of course, I did not tell him I was going to the United States, nor did I tell anybody else. I even asked Somaya to tell her parents that we were going to take a tour around Europe. We agreed that we would tell her parents our real plans once we were settled in the U.S.

We met with Gary at the American consulate. I introduced him to Somaya as Harriet Johnson's assistant. There was no waiting in line for us as we entered the consulate's private door and met the consul general himself.

"Why are they treating us so specially?" Somaya asked with disbelief in her voice.

"I paid Harriet Johnson a lot of money," I whispered in Farsi. "They'd better treat us well."

We signed the papers, and both Gary and the consul general wished us luck.

We were nearly on our way.

I wanted to say good-bye to Rasool. He'd become a real friend and I couldn't leave England without calling him to let him know I was going. Neither Gary nor he had said anything about the direction of their conversations, and I decided it would be best if I didn't ask. Of course, I couldn't tell him that I was going to live in America, and it surprised him to hear that I was taking my family for a trip around Europe.

"My wife is not taking any classes this semester, so we decided to travel around the continent for the rest of the summer before Omid's school starts in the fall," I lied.

"That's a good plan," he said.

"It is. I haven't been able to spend enough time with them since I arrived in England, especially my son. I was worried Baradar Amiri would not approve of my leave, but he was okay with it."

Rasool didn't say anything for a moment. When he spoke again, his voice was more conspiratorial. "Reza, I did what I said I would do for you. I know you are a family man, so I talked to Amiri and told him you are not the right guy for what we're trying to do here. I hope that's what you wanted. You should not get involved, Reza."

"I know. You're right. By the way, how, exactly, did you say this to Amiri?"

"I just told him that you were a coward!" He laughed boisterously.

I laughed along with him.

"By the way, my meeting with that lawyer, Gary Sullivan, was not bad. Thanks for finding that ad for me. There might be a chance for me to get a visa. But I need one more favor from you. Please do not mention it to anybody. It might not work out, and I don't want to lose my job here."

I congratulated him, and said I would keep his secret—a secret that, for my safety and the safety of my family, I needed to take to my grave.

My last meeting in London with Gary was a couple of nights before our flight. To my surprise Gary had a list with him.

"Okay, let me go over these!" He showed me a sheet with a breakdown of annual salaries. "Should you decide to work in the States at the agency, here are the numbers. The first year would be this amount . . . the second year this amount . . . here is the bonus for the first year: this figure . . . plus the housing expense . . . this one . . ."

We hadn't discussed any of this, and I wasn't prepared to do so now. *No more, please!* I thought. *I cannot do this to Somaya and Omid anymore; they deserve a life without lies!*

Mercifully, Gary ended the sales pitch. He handed me a card. "Here is my number in the States. Regardless of what you decide, I would love to hear from you. Keep me posted."

"I will," I said, though I really didn't want to think about this. As we prepared to leave for the States, I had begun to feel the fresh breeze of freedom wafting through the deepest layers of my being— a breeze that would blow away all traces of Wally and the life I knew I could no longer live. I was ready to let that breeze carry me all the way to my new home.

Somaya hid her face in my shoulder as she burst into tears.

"Oh, honey, it's going to be okay," I said, wrapping my arms around her.

"I know, Reza. I am just so proud of Omid. These are happy tears."

I knew what she was talking about; I had been blinking away my own happy tears. We'd just dropped my son off for his first year at UC Berkeley, and I knew he was going to excel there. The school's rigorous educational standards and the diversity of its culture were ideal for him. He deserved this. He'd become an impressive scholar and an even more impressive young man.

On that warm mid-August afternoon, Somaya and I walked around the campus after we said good-bye to our son. The layout of the university, the tall trees alongside the road, and the fresh sense of life in the air reminded me of how my grandparents' neighborhood had been when I was a child. The memory this stirred in me was both bittersweet and surprisingly welcome.

I remembered the day I said good-bye to Kazem and Naser before I left for USC. I recalled our vows to be friends forever and to take this oath to our graves. Kazem and Naser had maintained their part of that oath, though none of us could have imagined that they would be resting in their graves so soon after making this promise.

On the other hand, I had betrayed them both. How different would my life have been if my father hadn't insisted I go to college in America?

Somaya broke into my tangled thoughts. "Berkeley is just delightful. Do you think we should move here?" She took a deep breath of the sweet air. "It is so different from LA. It reminds me of the north of Tehran where Agha Joon lived. Does it remind you of that, too?"

I looked at her lovingly and moved her hair gently away from her forehead. That hair was streaked with gray now, which I thought made her look even more beautiful. Of course, I'd betrayed Somaya as well. We'd been married for more than twenty years and she had no idea how deceptive I'd been. I wished that God would give me the strength to confess to her and ask for her forgiveness.

"Yes, it does remind me of Agha Joon's neighborhood. People say LA is like Tehran. But I get even more of that vibe here." I put my arm around her shoulder as we continued our walk. "But I don't know if we should move here." I realized that Somaya was saying this only because she wanted to be closer to Omid. But LA had truly become our home. There, we were among hundreds of thousands of our people who had escaped the Islamic Revolution to seek freedom. This offered us a sense of closeness with our homeland we would not have had in Northern California. And for me it served as a necessary reminder of all those who hadn't gotten the chance to escape.

Soon, we were back on the road. It's about a five-hour drive on I-5 from the Bay Area to Los Angeles, most of which is flat and boring.

"Highway 101 is so much nicer," Somaya complained. We had taken the scenic 101 up from LA. Every time Somaya encountered a beautiful view—which was very often—she made me stop the car so she could take pictures with Omid alongside the road.

"But this road is faster," I said with a smile. "We are saving at least three hours. Plus the extra five hours for your pictures."

She scowled at me and decided to take a long nap so she didn't have to listen to my "not very funny jokes." Since she was sleeping,

I needed something else to keep me awake. I decided to play a Persian CD.

> *"Vatan parandeyeh par dar khoon*
> *Vatan shekofteh gole dar khoon*
> *Vatan falate shahid o shab*
> *Vatan pat a be sar khoon*
> *Vatan taraneye zendani*
> *Vatan ghasideyeh virani . . ."*

Dariush's words did more than help me stay alert. They sent me on a journey through my past, the memories of which eleven years in America had done nothing to diminish. *Vatan,* my homeland, was always on mind. And it was still as Dariush had captured it . . . "a wounded bird drowning in blood . . . a blooming flower covered in blood . . . a desert of martyrs . . . blood from head to toe . . . an imprisoned song . . . a ruined poem . . ."

Hearing these words and thinking about another Dariush brought pain to my heart. About two and a half years earlier, the Islamic government assassinated the founder and leader of the Nation of Iran Party, Dariush Forouhar, along with his wife, Parvaneh. The assailants entered their home, tied the husband and wife to chairs, faced them toward Mecca, and stabbed them to death. In what became known as the "chain murders of dissidents," MOIS agents stepped up their killing spree, murdering dozens of dissident intellectuals, journalists, poets, writers, and political activists.

At this time, Mohammad Khatami was the president of Iran. Running on a reform platform, he had received 70 percent of the vote in a huge turnout. He'd managed to raise hope among young and old that he could bring change to Iran's domestic and international policies after eight years of Rafsanjani, who not only did not deliver on the promise he'd made to the Bush administration to improve relations with America but had worked with other radicals to further suppress Iran's citizens while increasing assassinations and

terrorist activities abroad. Khatami was trying to accomplish the re-
forms he promised, but his opposition was overwhelming, led by the
Supreme Leader, Ali Khamenei, Ayatollah Ahmad Jannati, chairman
of the Guardian Council, and Ayatollah Mesbah Yazdi, director of
the Haghani School, a radical Shiite seminary in Qom. Using the
Revolutionary Guards to exert their will, they snuffed out any attempts at reform.

When the regime shut down *Salam,* a pro-reformist newspaper,
students organized a peaceful demonstration. But that night, paramilitary vigilantes stormed Tehran University and attacked students
in their dormitories, leaving many injured and dead. The next day,
thousands of students demonstrated in the streets of Tehran demanding reform. The protests spread throughout Iran and were so
intense that those of us outside of the country began to believe that
we could be witnessing the end to decades of thugocracy and merci-
less bloodshed by the mullahs. Certainly, when the rest of the world
saw what was going on, they would rush to support a nation whose
identity had been stolen two decades earlier.

But Guards and Basijis brutally crushed the demonstrations.
Once again, many gave their lives to speak out for what they believed. And once again, the rest of the world looked the other way.
All that was left was the hope that someday Iran would be free again,
a hope expressed in a later verse of the song "Vatan," a verse I now
sang aloud.

> *"Emruze ma emruze faryad*
> *Fardaye ma ruze bozorge miaad*
> *Begu keh dobare mikhanam*
> *Ba tamamiye yaranam*
> *Gol sorude shekastanra*
> *Begu, begu keh be khoon misorayam*
> *Dobare ba del o janam*
> *Harfe akhare rastan ra*
> *Begu be Iran, begu be Iran"*

"Today is the day to shout for justice
Tomorrow is the promised day
Tell them I will sing again
Tell them I sing with all my companions
The anthem of freedom
Tell them; tell them I sing in blood
I sing again with all my heart
I sing the last song of salvation
Tell it to Iran, tell it to Iran"

Somaya turned in her seat, opened her eyes, glanced at the road, and went back to sleep. I wiped my face and turned down the music. She seemed to be in an uncomfortable position and I placed my hand under her neck to try to straighten it. She sighed and settled into a new spot.

I took my eyes off the open road for a moment to study her. Our life was so much simpler now than it had been during my years as Wally and as a member of the Guards. Gone was the disappointment and discord that had marked that time. Somaya and I didn't argue now, and I no longer felt as though I was letting her down every time I went to work. She loved that the job I did now with a local software company had nothing to do with the Guards and "dirty bearded *pasdar*."

Most important, I no longer needed to lie to her. My final lie came shortly after we settled in LA. In September of 1990, I flew to Washington, D.C., to see Gary. It felt different to see him in the U.S. While our meetings in London had always been shadowed by risk, this felt more like a reunion with an old pal. We talked about our new lives and what was happening in the world. Iraq had just invaded Kuwait and Gary characterized Saddam as an audacious man with a destructive mind.

"We've been following his troop movements for a long time," Gary said. "It was clear that he was up to something. He had amassed a large number of his troops on the Kuwaiti border."

"The man is a lunatic," I said venomously. "He destroyed so many lives when he attacked Iran. If the U.S. knew he was amassing troops, why didn't they send him a warning?"

Gary shrugged. "Maybe he interpreted our silence as a green light."

The implications burned me, though I held my tongue. Had it been politically expedient for the U.S. to let this madman invade a neighboring country? Did they do so to give them an excuse for taking military action? Saddam and his army had become quite powerful with the help of the West. Now, perhaps, America felt it was time to undermine that military power as a message to all Arab regimes that without U.S. support they would fall. Millions of innocent people had suffered during the Iran–Iraq war. Had that been political maneuvering on the part of the U.S. as well?

"What do you say we go out for lunch tomorrow?" Gary said, changing the subject, though the thoughts lingered in my mind. "I can show you around afterward."

The next day, we drove through Washington and down into Virginia, with Gary showing me different neighborhoods. "What do you think?" he asked.

In truth, it was difficult for me to think about anything other than the offer Gary had made during lunch. With no preamble, Gary asked me to join the agency to assist in covert operations around the world, making contacts among Iranians of interest working for the Islamic government. Showing me these huge homes in the prestigious neighborhoods of Washington and Virginia was part of the sales pitch. Gary told me that all I needed to do was bring my family east and we could live in one of these spectacular homes and sign up Omid in one of the best private schools in America.

Certainly this would be an upgrade. Upon our arrival, Somaya and I had rented a small town house and furnished it sparingly. Somaya had planned to go back to college, but she'd started volunteering at Omid's school and had become a fixture there, telling me that being around children brought her levels of joy and serenity she'd never known before. I loved this, but volunteering offered no income and I had yet to land a job. We were eating into our savings (the money Somaya thought I'd inherited from my mom), and it would have been impossible not to find Gary's offer tempting.

Gary stopped the car at a nearby park. "Let's walk around here."

We got out and strolled. "Just think about it, Wally. I don't need an answer right away."

He kicked back a ball to a group of boys Omid's age. "Thanks, sir!" one of the boys shouted.

Gary waved at the boy and then returned to me. "There would be intensive training, you would have us behind you wherever you traveled, and your family would be safe. And you have to admit that the salary is very impressive."

The temptation grew stronger. *A huge house in this neighborhood? Omid playing with these well-mannered boys?*

"I will think about it, Gary." How could someone not *think* about something like this? But I had already made my decision and nothing would make me reconsider. The life Gary was offering—as appealing as it sounded and as much of an improvement as it would be over our financial situation—was not what I wanted. I had found my long-sought peace and tranquility in the arms of my wife and the smile of my son. I could not leave that behind again.

I wished I could do something to make a difference for my country. That desire would never leave me. But I had to admit something to myself: all my years of spying had not changed Iran for the better. The information I provided to America might have been useful, but it didn't accomplish what I had hoped. And I couldn't take any more chances with my life or with my family for this purpose.

During my short stay in D.C., Gary and I'd met a couple more times. He was still recruiting and I was still incapable of telling him that I was unequivocally through with the CIA. I'm not sure what was holding me back. Maybe some sense that losing my connection to the agency meant losing an essential part of myself. Maybe some sense that I'd come to rely on being both Reza *and* Wally. Maybe some sense that turning my back on the CIA was one final betrayal of my homeland.

I never did tell Gary that I was done. Shortly after I returned to LA, he called to tell me that he had to take the offer off the table. He said that things had changed at the agency and that they couldn't offer me a position. He gave me a new contact in LA to use if I needed something or had any helpful information to pass on.

I read between the lines. Gary knew what was going on in my head and he was making things easy for me. He'd given me what I needed from the agency at this point—a local connection in case something happened—and wasn't going to ask anything more of me.

My contact with the CIA lasted on a local level for several years after that, during which I met with several different agents and sometimes with the FBI to offer help on suspected Iranian activities within the U.S. In one of those meetings, my CIA contact asked me to find an Iranian who would testify that Iran had developed a nuclear bomb. To me, this was a clear indication that the administration of the first President Bush had not succeeded in making the headway with the regime they thought they were going to make. It would have been pointless for me to say, "I told you so."

Eventually, after shuffling through several other contacts, my connection to the agency died away naturally.

This left Somaya, Omid, and me to live our new lives in America. To protect our identities, we had changed our names upon arrival. We applied for citizenship shortly after we reached the five-year residency requirement. I remember crying the day we took the Oath of Allegiance, both for the blessing America had bestowed upon us and for the heartache that had brought us here. Through that oath, we vowed to support and defend the constitution and laws of the United States of America. And once more I wished that my adopted country would step in and spread its democracy, freedom, and human rights throughout the world, and especially to my homeland.

When we returned from our trip to Berkeley, Somaya spent a

great deal of time in Omid's room trying to contend with the fact that her only child was now heading off on his own. Her mother had died a few years earlier after a bout with breast cancer and she tried to convince her father to leave London to live with us. He kept saying that he would, but he always found a reason not to do so. Finally, Somaya decided to go to England to bring him back with her. However, this trip would not happen.

The day before Somaya planned to fly to London, we were going through our usual morning routine. I was dressing for work and Somaya put on the television. Suddenly, I heard her screaming my name hysterically. I ran to the family room, where she sat on the floor, the remote in one hand and her mouth covered with the other.

"What is it?" I asked, worried about what could possibly have her this upset. Before she could say a word, though, I found the answer on the screen, which was showing a commercial jet crashing into one of the Twin Towers.

"Oh my God," Somaya screamed. "That was the second building!"

We sat, shocked and confused, in front of the television for untold hours. Eventually, Somaya went to the phone to tell her father that she wouldn't be visiting him any time soon.

I knew what bin Laden was thinking when he ordered these acts of terrorism on American soil. He believed that he could cripple the country with fear. He had completely miscalculated America's resolve—anyone with the tiniest understanding of the U.S. would have known that they would recover from this—but he had dealt a devastating blow. And I had to believe that this happened because the government had not been more decisive in dealing with his prior attacks on America's interests and entities. This lack of a response had encouraged him.

The pattern was clear to me. Being soft on bin Laden emboldened him to commit a heinous act. Leaving the Taliban unchecked allowed them to enslave their own people. Trying to appease the mullahs allowed a thugocracy to extend its reach. Did the message finally get through as the towers fell? Radical Islamists had no regard for our values of human rights and democracy. When the West, the defender of such values, sidestepped those principles for vague political purposes, it left its citizens vulnerable.

For a short period, it seemed that everyone understood this. The world was in complete solidarity with America, Afghanistan was freed from the Taliban madmen, and bin Laden and Al Qaeda were on the run. I believed it was only a matter of time before this force created a united front against the mullahs—the terror masters of the world—and once more empowered the people of Iran.

But instead there was the invasion of Iraq and a divided world again. Though I was glad to see the fall of Saddam, I did not want to see innocent Iraqis suffer. I worried that America would not do everything they needed to do to help Iraq become a fully democratic country. I worried that they didn't fully understand the mullahs' plans for Iraq. For decades there had been close collaboration between the two Shiite hotbeds, Qom in Iran and Najaf in Iraq. During the Iran–Iraq war, they had formed the Badr brigades from Iraqi recruits and had helped create the Supreme Council for Islamic Revolution in Iraq, now one of the largest and most powerful political parties in that country. The clerics in Iran had been methodically setting the stage for an Islamic government in Iraq that mirrored the one in Iran.

America had gone into Iraq to bring those people democracy. But the only true avenue to lasting peace in the Middle East was to help bring about a free and democratic Iran.

Would I live to see that day?

OMID, HOPE

2005

GOD FINALLY GAVE me the strength to do what I should have done many years before. This hardly seemed like a blessing at the time, and I would have done anything to change the circumstances, but I was convinced he was sending me a message and that I had to come clean, at last and completely, to Somaya.

She'd been diagnosed with breast cancer. My wife of twenty-five years, so young and so beautiful, was fighting for her life. She'd been through a highly invasive operation and was in the midst of four debilitating cycles of chemotherapy with the prospect of thirty-three days of radiation still in front of her, and she was struggling mightily to regain her strength, even though doctors couldn't be certain at that point if they'd gotten everything.

Omid flew home as soon as he heard, deciding to delay the second semester of his senior year to be with his mother. Somaya didn't want him to do this, but he insisted. He even shaved his head to show solidarity with his mother after the chemo had stolen hers.

I sat by her bed every night before she fell asleep. She was nauseous and weak, and she'd lost so much weight.

"Where is Omid?" she asked one night.

"He is in his room, honey. Do you want me to get him?" I kissed her hand. "Do you know what Omid told me the other night? He told me how proud he is that his mother is so strong. He also said he has plans to move back to LA after graduation. Kelly is moving here with him. He wants to propose right after he is done with school." I squeezed her hand gently. "Isn't that great?"

Omid had told me nothing of the sort, but I thought I needed to break my commitment against lying to my wife to bring her some light now. Somaya was staring at the ceiling, but I saw a dim smile.

"If they marry and have a child," I said, "we will be grandparents soon. Have you thought about that?" She turned her head to me slowly. "You'll be a grandma—a fine, young, and beautiful one. We will have a 'little Omid' in our life again."

I saw a tiny glow in her half-opened eyes and she mumbled Omid's name. The Farsi word for "hope." Then she rubbed her wet eyes. "I am glad we named him that. He is my hope. My only *omid*." She sighed.

Before I sent our son in, I told him that, to give Somaya a little boost, I lied to her about his pending engagement to his girlfriend of two years.

Omid looked at me in disbelief. "That's not a lie, Dad! I was going to let you and Mom know that I planned to propose to her, but I did not know if it was the right time to say anything."

I smiled at him. "I think it is the perfect time, Son. Go in and talk to her about it."

Omid came out of Somaya's room a short while later, rushing past me in the hope that I wouldn't notice his tears. He'd seen what we'd both been seeing for months now—that his mother seemed to be disappearing in front of us. The doctors had been optimistic, but what if they were wrong? What if I was rapidly running out of time to tell her what I needed to say and what she deserved to know?

I made up my mind in that moment. I was going to do it now. Hesitantly, I opened the door.

"Why aren't you coming in?" Somaya said weakly when she saw me reluctant to enter the room. "I am still awake. Could you get me a glass of milk? I am a little hungry."

I did so gladly. She hadn't touched any food that day. A glass of milk would bring her some strength. I arranged her pillows, and she sat on the bed sipping her food.

"All of a sudden I feel so much better. I am so glad Omid is here." She stirred the drink with the straw I'd placed in it. "He told me that after my radiation is over, he wants to introduce us to Kelly's parents." She smiled and her eyes reflected the hope that her son, true to his name, always brought her.

"Somaya *jon,* you are an angel," I said with a broken voice. I hesitated one last moment, then I added, "And . . . and I am so evil."

She released the straw between her lips and her eyes widened. What did she think I was about to tell her?

"I know I should have confessed this to you long ago. But I need your forgiveness, Somaya. Please tell me you will forgive me."

Somaya seemed to grow paler, if that was possible. I castigated myself for adding to her suffering. I should have been soothing her, not causing her more torment.

"Reza, what are you talking about?" she asked weakly.

I moved closer to her and held her hand in both of mine. "I was a *jasoos.* . . . "

She shook her head and looked at me in total confusion. Her half-open eyes had lost the glow that Omid had brought to her a few minutes ago. "You were what? . . . A spy?" She handed me the unfinished glass of milk, which had started shaking in her hand.

"I betrayed you; I betrayed my son, my parents, and grandparents. I betrayed my friends and my country. I am ashamed of what I have done to you."

Somaya stayed quiet while I told her my life story. I told her about how Naser's death erupted like a volcano deep inside me. I told her how Roya's letter propelled me to become a betrayer to fight for all of the others like her. I told her how I contacted the CIA, how I invented stories about what I was doing in London, and how I'd played so many shameful and dangerous games with her. Rather than challenging the regime directly, I'd taken a coward's route.

With this last admission, I sobbed. Somaya hadn't said a word through all of this. Now she pulled my head to her chest and started petting my hair. "Hush, Reza. Hush." I couldn't believe that I had put her in a position where she needed to comfort me when she was in so much need of comfort. This shamed me further.

"I betrayed you," I said through my tears. "I lied to you and I deceived you."

"Reza, don't. Don't do that to yourself. You are ripping your soul. You did nothing wrong."

I sat up to face her. "But Somaya *jon*, I am a *jasoos,* a traitor! How could you ever forgive me?"

She pulled the blanket all the way to her neck and drew her body in. "All I know, Reza . . ." She was so weak that she was having trouble speaking. She took several long seconds before she continued. "You should not be ashamed of what you did for your country."

This brought another sob from my heart. "Somaya *jon,* I love you so much. But I need to know if you can forgive me for all I have done to you."

It was past midnight, and she looked incredibly tired. But still she found the strength to reach out to me. "Reza, I understand why you lied. It's good to know that I did not waste my life living with a man who was a supporter of a brutal regime. Now I know why you behaved the way you did." Her voice was fading, but she struggled to stay awake. "I wanted so badly for all those years to believe that you were not one of them, and now I know. I know you wanted to protect our son and me. Of course I forgive you. But promise me something. Don't give up. Tell the world what you witnessed and what these criminals have done to us."

A tear ran across her face. "You are not a coward, Reza. You are not," she whispered before she closed her eyes.

Omid had been very close with his grandfather when he lived in England. Unfortunately, once we moved to America, their only contact was over the phone or on the rare vacation visit to London. We were finally able to convince Moheb Khan to move to Los Angeles, though, and Omid spent as much time with him as he could when he was home from college. They became even closer during the 2008 presidential election, which was interesting because they supported different candidates. Omid loved Barack Obama, while Moheb Khan found the policies of the Republican Party more to his liking and therefore backed John McCain.

"Omid *jon,* Senator McCain is who we need now," Moheb Khan said decisively during one of their many debates on the subject. "He can get rid of the mullahs in Iran. And if he solves that problem, he will bring peace to the entire Middle East." He had seen Lebanon, his homeland, devastated in the 2006 Israel–Hezbollah war, and he believed this resulted directly from the mullahs arming Hezbollah and promoting the destruction of Israel.

"Grandpa, Obama is a breath of fresh air. After years of war and radical foreign policy, we need to show the world that we are a compassionate people. That's the only way we'll regain respect and authority. We need a united world to fight the religious fanatics. Obama can provide the hope to achieve that."

At this point, my father-in-law would shake his head. "Those words are nothing but fancy talk. *Change. Hope.* We need a powerful and experienced leader. This Ahmadinejad is not the kind of human to negotiate with. He is demented."

Omid would grow more animated in his response. "*Hope* is not just a fancy word. Hope can bring the whole world together. The Iranians inside the country *need* hope. And they definitely need change."

I stayed on the sidelines for most of these conversations. I had my opinions, but I didn't want to impose them on my son or his grand-father because I found their debate so stirring, and I didn't want to tilt the discussion in either direction. It still amazed me how people who loved each other in America could disagree so vociferously without fear of consequence. It brought me back to the Fridays of my childhood with Agha Joon and Davood. I found exchanges of this sort inspiring, and whenever I heard them I prayed that people in Iran would be free to engage in them again before too long.

"'Hope' *is* a strong word, Moheb Khan," I said, allowing myself to butt in only this much. "Certainly we can all attest to that."

Somaya knew more than anybody else in that room how powerful that word was. With the hope she had, she overcame the battle of her life and had been cancer-free for three years. As this debate continued, she sat next to Kelly and put her hand on her daughter-in-law's stomach to see if she could feel her grandchild moving. With her health, the nearness of her family now that Omid and Kelly were renting a place close to our home, and her son's baby on the way, Somaya was the very manifestation of hope.

Moheb Khan and Omid kept trading opinions throughout the election season. At the same time, I shared my thoughts with the rest of the world by writing articles in various media outlets in which I spoke about the relationship between the American election and the mullahs' aspirations for an Islamic conquest of the world. Of course, I used a pseudonym—one separate from the names we'd taken when we came to America—to protect my identity. After I confessed to Somaya, we agreed that it would be safest to keep this secret between the two of us for the rest of our lives. But, as I had promised her, I was telling the world what I'd witnessed. The simple fact was that the West had a tremendous influence on the policies of Iran—despite what the mullahs might say—and I knew the next American president would have a chance to give the young people of my homeland their first real glimpse of freedom. Regardless of which candidate won, I prayed that he would not repeat the mistakes his predecessors had made of trying to appease the regime. When Barack Obama won the election on the same day that our grandson, Arya, was born, I saw this as a very positive sign.

Still, as much as our own household radiated optimism, Iran continued to face dark times. Mahmoud Ahmadinejad, the current president of Iran, was a closed-minded radical Islamist. He'd been vaulted into power by the same clerics who'd so completely undermined former president Khatami in his attempts to bring reform: the Supreme Leader, Ali Khamenei, Ayatollah Mesbah Yazdi, and Ayatollah Jannati, the true believers of *Mahdaviat* who awaited the coming of Mahdi, the twelfth Shiite Imam, who would rule the world before the end times. Before becoming the president, Ahmadinejad, then mayor of Tehran, had secretly instructed the city council to build a road especially for Mahdi that led to the mosque of Jamkaran. Once he became president, Ahmadinejad allocated millions of dollars to enhance the mosque for the reappearance of Mahdi from the adjacent well where the president and other zealots believe the twelfth Imam is in hiding.

Like others who think as he does, Ahmadinejad believes that many of the signs of Mahdi's return have emerged. Known as hadiths, these signs include the invasion of Afghanistan, the bloodshed in Iraq, and the global economic meltdown. According to prophecy, the hadiths will grow increasingly furious as Mahdi's return comes closer, including "persecution and injustice" engulfing the earth, "chaos and famine," and "many wars." The hadiths predict that "many will be killed and the rest will suffer hunger and lawlessness." People like Ahmadinejad so completely believed that these conditions would hasten the return of the twelfth Imam that they were willing to foment universal war, chaos, and famine to bring it about.

After the 9/11 attacks and the fall of the Taliban, I decided that I needed to activate a handful of sources within Iran. The world seemed to hold the Islamic government blameless in the attacks, but I knew that the mullahs were likely to have had a hand in any act of terror directed toward America. My sources told me that the Guards were harboring Al Qaeda members and that Ahmad Vahidi had close contact with bin Laden's organization. Back when I was working for the CIA, I'd reported on Vahidi, then chief intelligence officer of the Guards, who was involved in the U.S. Marine barracks bombing as well as many other terrorist acts, including the bombing of a Jewish community center in Buenos Aires in 1994 that earned him an arrest warrant from an Argentinian judge and a red-alert listing on Interpol. By 2008, he was deputy defense minister (and he is now defense minister), overseeing Iran's ballistic missile and nuclear programs with only one goal in mind: to obtain the bomb. My sources also told me that the Guards were running multiple covert operations for their nuclear bomb project and that one was set in a secret underground facility west of the province of Mazandaran, a mountainous region in the north of Iran. This latest revelation was something of a tipping point for me when combined with what I'd learned on my own—I had become more vigilant about my surroundings and more aware of radical Islamist activity in the U.S. I realized that I needed to share what I had learned. Since I no longer had a handler, I called the CIA headquarters in Virginia to arrange a meeting with a local agent.

I had high hopes that the Obama administration would be tougher on the Islamic government of Iran, especially given what they knew about the regime's nuclear activities. However, his first overture to the mullahs disappointed me. He sent greetings for the Persian New Year in which he urged better relations between America and Iran. He then repeated this in letters to Ayatollah Khamenei. To me, this was a sad case of not learning from history. Once again American politicians refused to see that the mullahs were not men of reason, and that their animosity toward America was rooted in the interpretation of a prophecy that called for the annihilation of the West and all non-Muslims. I knew the regime would see Obama's entreaties as a sign of weakness, and that this would embolden them to take radical steps.

While I continued to hear from my contacts within Iran, I strove to stay focused on my family. The summer of 2009 was an idyllic time in our household. Somaya and I had fallen in love with our grandson. "Oh! He looks exactly like Omid," Somaya would say every time she held Arya. Our home brightened with the presence of a new baby, and though we never discussed my sickbed confession again, I think the baby helped heal any lingering wounds this confession might have caused. As summer began, Somaya told me that she would not go back to work the next fall. She wanted to stay home, where she could spend more time with her grandson when Omid and Kelly were at work. With Arya around, she would not miss the children at the elementary school.

I wish Iran could have experienced some of our joy that summer. Instead, it continued to serve as a source of heartbreak for all of us. Worldwide headlines blared the news that the people of my homeland were in the streets of Tehran protesting peacefully for the freedoms they felt the regime had stolen from them yet again. A presidential election very different from the Obama-McCain election had just taken place between Ahmadinejad and reformer Mir Hossein Mousavi. On the eve of the election, all signs pointed to a landslide victory by Mousavi. Interior ministry officials informed him that he was going to win and Ali Larijani, the speaker of the parliament, congratulated him. Then Guards commanders entered his headquarters to inform him that Ahmadinejad would be pronounced the winner the next day. They told Mousavi that he should not object to this as it was in the best interests of the Islamic Republic and that this outcome had the approval of the Supreme Leader.

As a result, Ahmadinejad "won" a second term, and the people of Iran simply couldn't take it any longer. I found it inspiring to see young people loudly broadcasting their desire for change. In the crowd scenes beamed back to America, I saw Nasers, Royas, Soheils, and Parvanehs. I saw the protesters as the tenders of Agha Joon's garden full of flowers, a new generation spreading their seeds in its soil, nurturing freedom, and helping it to blossom in my lost country once again. They were strong and united and ready to rid themselves of the pain my generation had brought them. Even without the support of the West, they were going to bring about change. They were escalating a movement that had begun only moments after

Khomeini betrayed Iran by lying to us about his intentions. He was responsible for the deaths of hundreds of thousands and the killing had continued in the two decades since he died. But no one could kill the spirit of this movement.

The protests drew the attention of the world in unprecedented ways. Iran was the focus of headlines for weeks, and world leaders denounced the results of the election and the regime's brutal response to the protests. With the eyes of the world on them, the mullahs and the thugs who took orders from them fought mercilessly to hold on to the power that had never been their right, using extreme force to deny that their time was over. In their minds, Mahdi was coming and the blood they shed now was yet another hadith. When a Basiji shot young Neda Agha-Soltan dead as she stood on the periphery of a protest, Neda became the international symbol of the fight for freedom and the regime's utter disregard for life. The government threw all foreign journalists out of the country and suppressed the media, but they couldn't prevent the video of the dying Neda from reaching every corner of the world.

As I complete the writing of this book, the regime seems to have pushed back another attempt at reform. In late September 2009, Ahmadinejad spoke defiantly to the UN, and days later Iran tested long-range missiles. In addition, one covert nuclear facility was exposed, though it was not the facility I had information on. This means that there are others that have not yet been revealed. The American response so far has been to seek a world coalition to enact the toughest sanctions yet in an effort to force the Islamic government to participate equitably in the world community. The sanctions would target Iran's oil income among other things and they would be devastating—if there is a true coalition. Unfortunately, the world has not united to uphold sanctions against Iran in the past, so there's little reason to believe it will do so this time.

While the regime is standing tough, I truly believe their iron rule over Iran is coming to an end. The Iranian people have announced to the entire world that they want the liberties that are their birthright. They are not going to accept anything less.

Twenty-eight years ago, I began a quest to free my people. My efforts took us only so far. But now an irresistible movement is forming. Iran *will* be free again. And when that time comes, in spite of the heartache I endured and the shame I felt at needing to resort to betrayal, I will rejoice.

ACKNOWLEDGMENTS

When my wife suggested that I had to tell the world my story, for a long moment I glanced back on almost three decades of my life. I was not sure anybody would want to know how someone could betray his own country, his family, and his best friends. But my wife taught me that by telling my story, the world would understand the pain of a nation, not just an individual. I thank you, Somaya, for your kindness and support, and for the trust I did not deserve.

During this journey of more than three years, I was so lucky to have a literary manager who believed in me. Peter Miller never doubted my story, and his encouragement gave me strength throughout this project. Peter, you are a true lion!

I made so many friends throughout this journey; the friends whom, for safety reasons, I never had the chance to meet in person, friends who had never insisted on knowing my true identity. They just believed in my story, and their help made this book possible. My thanks to Mary Strobel, to whom I am indebted genuinely for her care and guidance and incredible work of more than a year day and night editing and re-editing; Darrend King Brown, who opened my eyes in so many ways with his to-the-point critiques; Joe Quirk, for his enthusiasm, unbelievable talent, and great work; Tamim Ansary, for his insightful comments and critiques; and John Strobel, for his unmistakable line editing.

I am so thankful of my dear friend Shirley for her kindness, support, and trust. Thanks so much for all you've done for me and for reading the manuscript and believing in me. I will never forget your fondness.

Special thanks to Washington, D.C., attorney Mark Zaid, who helped me navigate through all sorts of unimaginable hurdles that stood in the way of the publication of this book. Without his efforts, many pages might have been nothing more than black lines.

I also would like to take this opportunity to thank the great Iranian singer Dariush and Mr. Iraj Jannatie-Ataie, the legendary songwriter, for all the beautiful and caring songs they've performed for Iran and the Iranians, especially the heartfelt song "Vatan."

Finally, I have to admit that this book would have not been published without the help of Lou Aronica. His hard work, talent, critique, comments, and fine editing make this story flow like a river. He raised my confidence, and his involvement was an honor. Lou, I thank you for all the hard work and for making this possible.

Needless to say, I am indebted to everyone at Threshold Editions, and to Patrick Price, for his hard work, great review, and recommendations, and particularly to Anthony Ziccardi, for his faith in my story and for believing that my voice should be heard!